THE SCOTT AND LAURIE OKI SERIES

IN ASIAN AMERICAN STUDIES

THIS BOOK IS PUBLISHED WITH THE ASSISTANCE
OF A GRANT FROM THE SCOTT AND LAURIE OKI
ENDOWED FUND FOR THE PUBLICATION OF ASIAN
AMERICAN STUDIES, ESTABLISHED THROUGH THE
GENEROSITY OF SCOTT AND LAURIE OKI.

University of Washington Press
P.O. Box 50096, Seattle, WA 98145, U.S.A.
www.washington.edu/uwpress

Unless otherwise noted, all photos courtesy
of Ken and Alice Takemoto. *Title page:* Ken and Alice
Takemoto, wedding photo, 1951, Washington, D.C.;
facing page: Howard M. Urabe, courtesy of Elaine Tamura.

Library of Congress Cataloging-in-Publication Data
can be found at the back of this book.

The paper used in this publication is acid-free and 90
percent recycled from at least 50 percent post-consumer
waste. It meets the minimum requirements
of American National Standard for Information
Sciences—Permanence of Paper for Printed Library
Materials, ANSI Z39.48-1984.

*Judgment without Trial: Japanese American
Imprisonment during World War II*
by Tetsuden Kashima

*Shopping at Giant Foods: Chinese American
Supermarkets in Northern California*
by Alfred Yee

*Altered Lives, Enduring Community:
Japanese Americans Remember Their
World War II Incarceration*
by Stephen S. Fugita
and Marilyn Fernandez

*Eat Everything Before You Die: A Chinaman
in the Counterculture* by Jeffery Paul Chan

*Asian American Literature:
Form, Confrontation, and Transformation*
edited by Zhou Xiaojing and Samina Najmi

*Nisei Memories: My Parents Talk about
the War Years* by Paul Howard Takemoto

Nisei Memories

My Parents Talk
about the War Years

Paul Howard Takemoto

UNIVERSITY OF WASHINGTON

Seattle and London

To the memory of Howard Urabe

Foreword

World War II Japanese American experiences are now fairly well known because of exposure in Hollywood films, documentaries, novels, histories, and museum exhibitions. And yet there appear to be innovative treatments and unusual stories emerging at every turn. Paul Takemoto's interviews with his mother and father are illustrative. Quite by accident, Takemoto was able to persuade his parents to talk at length and in depth about events they had long since assumed should rest, forgotten, in the past.

While the last three decades have provided examples of Nisei finally able to work through and discuss the fantastic experience of being perceived as demonized threats to national security, Takemoto's interviews are unusually engaging. The elements of discovery and revelation that grow in the course of these interviews help us to understand the nature of the traumas that were inflicted on Nisei (second-generation Japanese Americans) during World War II. Alice Takemoto's experiences on the mainland in Arkansas were very different from Ken Takemoto's experiences in Hawai'i in the fabled 442nd Regimental Combat Team.

Perhaps equally important now, this book takes the reader through the half century of uncertainty and trauma that transpire before the family can confront issues central to its existence. How many American families with Arab / Middle Eastern / Muslim / Sikh affiliations will go through experiences similar to Ken and Alice Takemoto's as racial profiling continues? What happens if terrorist attacks continue? While we work to contain the damage wreaked by misguided concerns for national security, it will be important for families to talk with one another and with families in other communities, both during the challenging times and for decades to come.

FRANKLIN ODO, Director
Smithsonian Asian Pacific American Program

Acknowledgments

Few things of emotional value in this world are accomplished alone, and this book is no exception. It would not have been possible, of course, without my parents opening their hearts in the first place, and for that I am grateful. Beyond that, it was a family effort, with relatives from the Takemoto and Imamoto sides offering their memories, love, and support. Among those who read and passed along a dog-eared copy of the manuscript were Grace and Grant Noda, Marion Sakurai, Lily and Karen Matsuoka, Tanya Yan, Kathy Miura, Steve and Natalie Sakurai, Haruto Takemoto, Lanky and Minnie Yoneshige, and Kay Shigekuni—as well as Elaine Tamura, Howard Urabe's sister, who by wonderful coincidence happens to be my Uncle Haruto's friend and neighbor in Kapaa, and is now considered part of the family.

Help came even from those who are no longer with us, such as my maternal grandfather, Zenichi Imamoto, who may have driven my grandmother crazy by being a pack rat, but without his having saved every letter written to him by his children, we would not have a written archive of his family's wartime experience. The debt to all of my grandparents, needless to say, goes far beyond this book: we owe everything to them.

Getting this book published would not have been possible without Aiko Yoshinaga-Herzig, a Nisei and former inmate at Jerome who, though she is too humble to say so, is a leader in the Japanese American community. She was among the first outside the family to read the manuscript, returning nine-and-a-half pages of praise, much-needed corrections, and suggestions for further research. When seeking accuracy and context, I turned to her more than to anyone else. Thanks, too, to her husband, Jack—we wish the two of you were still living on the East Coast.

Aiko introduced me to Dr. Franklin Odo, director of the Asian Pacific American Program at the Smithsonian Institution, and to Dr. Art Hansen, director of the Center for Oral and Public History at California State University, Fullerton, both of whom are at the forefront of the study of Japanese American history and took time from busy schedules to read a manuscript from a complete stranger. This book would not have been published without their support, and their kind words—among the highlights of this entire experience—helped, as my mother put it, "to make a little more of the pain go away."

Finally, Aiko introduced me to Naomi Pascal, editor-at-large at the University of Washington Press, who, along with her colleagues, including managing editor Marilyn Trueblood, editor Kerrie Maynes, and acquisitions assistant Beth Fuget, accepted and shepherded the book through the editing and publishing process. My parents and I are deeply grateful to the University of Washington Press, which, despite existing compelling Japanese American oral histories already compiled by Dr. Hansen and the Center for Oral and Public History, the Japanese American National Museum, and the Go For Broke Educational Foundation, among others, generously agreed to publish this one.

It is difficult to describe the value of people who work for university presses, universities, museums, and nonprofit organizations like those mentioned above, except to recall the phrase "Those who forget the past are condemned to repeat it," and to understand that they are devoting their lives to teaching others about the past so it is *not* forgotten.

Thanks, too, to others who read the manuscript or provided help and guidance, including Eleanor On, Allyson Nakamoto, Greg Robinson, Russell Bearden, and Tetsuden Kashima. Katherine Matsuki, one of the nicest people I have ever known, shared her original issues of the *Santa Anita Pacemaker*. And thank you, Elaine, for the picture of your brother.

Special thanks to my sister Ruth, Kevin McInroy, and Kara and Rosemarie Mangialardi for their love and friendship.

I am grateful to my family, to my wife, Lisa, and to our children, Ben and Molly, for their love and encouragement. Ben and Molly, in particular, must be singled out; this project was done in large part with them in mind, and would not have been completed without them. They accompanied me to my parents' house for the interviews and served throughout the process as research and editorial assistants. They are wise, wonderful people.

Lastly, and most importantly, I wish to thank all the people who are remembered in this book, whose lives make up the memories my parents have shared with us.

Nisei Memories

Prologue

Middle names are often unusual, and mine—Howard—is no exception. A funny name, never explained, the object of frequent, good-natured ridicule while I was growing up—much of it from myself. No relatives were so named, and my parents never spoke of anyone named Howard—it had been attached to me, it seemed, purely by whim.

In 1983, when I was twenty-six, I went with my father and sister to Hawaii, where my father had been born and raised. The trip, as I recall, was a bit awkward—a family vacation minus one of its members (my mother chose to stay home in Maryland), my twenty-eight-year-old sister Ruth and I a little too old for that sort of thing. There were minor arguments over where to have dinner; an aborted attempt to watch the sun rise over the lip of a volcano; and a pointlessly long ride in the rental car over a winding, two-lane road on Maui, jagged cliffs plunging to the ocean on one side and mountains rising on the other, during which my father and I fell asleep and my sister, unable to enjoy the view or turn around, drove, increasingly angry, all the way to the end. She woke us up to tell us she wasn't driving back.

On Kauai we stayed with relatives and spent our days driving idly around the island, from Waimea Canyon on one side to Hanalei (Bali Ha'i in the movie *South Pacific*) on the other. At the approximate midpoint, my father's hometown of Kapaa, we stared at a shack, complete with corrugated tin roof, where he and eight siblings had been raised. The shack was obscured by thick, tropical foliage, save for the roof, and in the yard stood an ancient Coca-Cola freezer—"Ice Cold" it proclaimed through rust—and a single breadfruit tree. Other people lived there now.

And one afternoon, venturing off the main road that encircles three-quarters of the island (the rest is inaccessible by car) we came upon an isolated cemetery beautifully positioned on a slope between the ocean and the volcanic mountains that occupy the island's center. The cemetery was surrounded on all sides by fields of sugarcane; a steady ocean breeze blew the cane toward the mountains.

We got out of the car and split up, walking among the graves. My sister and I began to make our separate ways toward the far corners of the cemetery, though at some point—the same point—we realized our father had come to a stop and was gazing down at one grave in particular. There was nothing unusual about his aspect, but something compelled us to go back and see what he was looking at.

It was a grave like any other, marked by a simple concrete slab angled slightly toward the front and surrounded, as many of them were, by empty Mason jars that had once contained flowers. Red volcanic dirt stained the surface of the tombstone, on which, etched in centered lines beneath an encircled cross, was the following:

HOWARD M URABE
HAWAII
SGT 442 INF
WORLD WAR II
MARCH 16 1923   JULY 4 1944

"That's why your middle name is Howard," my father said.

He is a complicated man, not prone to sentiment. That he fought in World War II (against the Germans in Italy) was a subject about which he rarely spoke, and never in detail. Still, that he would not say anything about the person for whom I was partly named—not even to stop the good-natured ridicule—was stunning, though not nearly so much as the fact that, had we not happened upon the cemetery in the first place, he might never have said anything at all.

Howard Urabe, as it turned out, was a childhood friend; he and my father had grown up together in Kapaa, were students at the University of Hawaii when the Japanese bombed Pearl Harbor, and, after spending a year of labor to prove their loyalty to the United States (initially Japanese Americans were not allowed to volunteer), signed up for the army. They went to basic training in Hattiesburg, Mississippi, as part of the newly formed 442nd Regimental Combat Team, and were subsequently shipped to Italy, my father in March of 1944 as a replacement for the 100th Battalion (prewar–Japanese American draftees already in combat), and Howard Urabe three months later with the remainder of the 442nd. He was killed a few weeks after his arrival.

My father's silence about the war is not uncommon (I've heard the same thing said of other combat veterans from this and other wars) and perhaps reflects the gulf that exists between those who have fought in a war (or, for that matter, experienced any kind of trauma) and those who have not. How to bridge it? Well, awkwardly, if you're lucky, but all too often not at all. Five years after that trip, not another word having been said (or asked) about Howard Urabe, I sat with my father and infant son in a brightly lit shopping mall eatery and, while spoon-feeding the baby, listened to my father describe, apropos of nothing, being trapped in an Italian farmhouse, surrounded by Germans, with four others, one of whom had been fatally wounded. This man suffered without complaint for hours, my father said, asking only for water, but at the end abruptly sat up, announced, "I'm going to pretend that I'm dead," laughed, and died.

Twelve years after that, on the evening of November 9, 2000, following the dedication that afternoon of the National Japanese American Memorial in Washington, D.C.—a memorial inconceivable to those it honors during the time of the events that gave rise to it—I sat in another brightly lit eating place and this time listened to my father describe, apropos of everything, some of his friends who had been killed in the war, and whose names are inscribed on a wall of the memorial, one being Howard Urabe. On a whim I asked if he would talk about these men into a tape recorder, and, not given the chance to say no, he said yes. The next day, before either of us could change our minds, I bought a cheap recorder and took it over to my parents' house.

My mother's wartime experience—she is from California, and was sent to an "assembly center" at the Santa Anita racetrack before going to a "relocation" camp in Jerome, Arkansas—was something I wanted to record as well, but knew I would have to start with my father. She has always spoken openly and without bitterness about what happened to her (though this would be the first time we discussed it in detail), but with him the window of opportunity, small to begin with, was already closing. Having had a night to think about it, he was reluctant to talk, doing so, tersely, only under gentle prodding. But soon enough—much sooner than I expected—he became caught up in the memories, and the words (most of them) came with surprising ease.

Not that the process itself was easy. At the outset, thinking (as much for my sake as for his) that a cloak of objectivity might make things less awkward, I offered the absurd suggestion that he pretend I was not his son. And sixteen years as a (mediocre) trade reporter notwithstanding, I was dismayed, time and again, by the poor quality of my interviews: questions were asked too quickly, prompting answers that, during the transcription, were found to have been cut short; or were not asked at all; or were asked but never answered, and never pursued. This required calling him up or going back to their house with the recorder and asking questions that, no longer in context, now seemed embarrassingly bald. ("How did he die?" "What were your emotions?") On one occasion a long, painful description of going, after his return from the war, to see the families of friends who had been killed, starting with Howard Urabe's, had not been recorded at all—pressing the "play" button revealed, to my horror, only the quietly mocking sound of unwinding tape. I immediately bought a new, more expensive recorder, but it was a week before I could bring myself to use it, and a couple of months before I was able to summon the nerve to ask him to tell me again. But beyond our initial exchange, he answered this and every other question with unfailing patience, and in the end filled eight ninety-minute tapes. After that I interviewed my mother.

Our conversations, conducted mostly in the dining room of their home in Kensington, Maryland, found his memory, the years of silence notwithstanding, to be much sharper than hers. This might be a function of age— on December 7, 1941, my father was twenty-one, my mother fifteen—but more likely reflects the fact that, while he has relived his wartime experiences "over and over in [his] mind," she blocked many of hers from memory ("They were too traumatic"). Or it might simply be that, as he put it, smiling, "I have a better memory than mom." Regardless, I was fortunate to be able to fill in some of her memory gaps with information gleaned from correspondence—her father saved every letter written to him by his children ("Marion's were the best," she said)—and documents, including those she obtained via a Freedom of Information Act request filed at the National Archives in 1990.

There was no plan beyond getting their memories on tape and paper— certainly no plan to turn them into a book ("If there was," my father said,

"I never would have talked")—and even then I wasn't sure what I was doing. I eliminated my questions entirely from the first transcript, wanting only their words, but lost in the blocky, monolithic narratives—one for my father, one for my mother—was the necessary interplay between questions and answers, questions they might not have asked themselves, answers they did not always know how to give. So the questions were (painstakingly) restored, and the monoliths dismantled by being woven together. With regard to the latter, the memories are arranged as they were given, in chronological order, but do not necessarily coincide—1942, for example, was a particularly eventful year for my mother, during which her parents were arrested and she was sent to Santa Anita and Jerome, but for my father was a relatively uneventful year during which he built iceboxes for troops training in the fields around Schofield Barracks on Oahu. By the end of the war, though, their memories catch up to each other.

Still wanting their voices to come through as simply and clearly as possible, I kept my intrusions to a minimum, adding parenthetical explanations or corrections (bracketed within documents) only when necessary. (One note: "Thinks" means they were remembering something, while "pauses" means they were hesitant to put what was remembered into words.) And, still hiding behind the cloak of objectivity, I refer to them by their names, Ken and Alice, rather than "Mom" and "Dad." (My father's birth name was Kaname Takemoto; he had it legally changed to Kenneth Kaname Takemoto in 1950, explaining, "No one could pronounce my name." My mother's birth name was Alice Setsuko Imamoto, which was unusual, since most of their generation received Japanese names. "Father gave all of us English names," she said. "I guess he figured we'd be staying here.") The resulting form owes an obvious debt to other oral histories I have read and admired, including those by Studs Terkel, Lawrence Ritter, and Haruki Murakami, and if this oral history is successful it is for the same reason that any oral history is successful: the honesty of the people being interviewed. Simply put, oral histories do not work if the truth is not being told (unless the reader is informed otherwise), or if, less egregiously, those being interviewed insist on portraying themselves in the best possible light. In this case, my parents proved incapable of portraying themselves in anything but the light of what actually occurred.

The project, from start to finish, took three years to complete, though it would have been completed much sooner had I been more consistent in my work habits. It is difficult to revisit ground painful to those you love—

to see your father, who never cries, become so emotional he has trouble speaking, and your mother struggle to remember what was blocked from memory—and I would have to steel myself for it, which I couldn't always do, sometimes staying away for weeks at a time. But I would always return, and upon my return would become so absorbed in the work I couldn't concentrate on anything else. Still, the lapses proved costly—my maternal grandmother, who would have been one of the first to see the manuscript, died nine months before it was completed. And, needless to say, none of this speaks to the years during which the subject was not broached at all.

That my father served his country at the same time that my mother was imprisoned by it is a contradiction not nearly as unusual as it might seem: my parents can count at least a dozen other Japanese American couples who share the same contradiction, and there are certain to be (or to have been) many others among the 120,313 Japanese Americans who were forcibly relocated and the 28,000 who served in the armed forces during the war. My point being that my parents' history is, regrettably, not unique, a fact my mother made clear as she looked out at all the Japanese Americans who had come to the dedication of the memorial, thousands of them, some from as far away as California and Hawaii, so many the adjacent street had been blocked off in order to accommodate everyone. "Each one of these people," she said, "has a story."

This is theirs.

Chapter One

[To Ken.] Okay, my main concern is that you'll be worried about talking to me. I don't want you to water anything down just because I'm your son. My advice would be to focus on the memories as best you can—maybe even pretend that I'm not your son. Does that sound like a good idea?

KEN

[*Puzzled.*] All right.

Why don't we start with your parents? There's a lot that I don't know about them.
    [*Points to Alice.*] Well, I think you should begin with her. Talk about her family.

I don't even know their full names. Your father's first name was Yutaro?
    That's right. Yutaro. [*Spells it.*] Yutaro Takemoto.

What was his middle name?
    No middle name. Japanese don't have middle names.

They don't?
    No. Just first and last.

And grandma's first name was Sumi. What was her maiden name?
    Hironaka.

I never knew that.
    Sumi Hironaka.

Where were they from?

They were both from Yamaguchi. My father was born and raised in the city of Yanai. I don't know where my mother was born, but it was in the same prefecture. But why don't we start by talking about mom's family?

Do you know the circumstances under which they left Japan? Why they came to this country?

So we're going to start out talking about my family?

It doesn't matter.

[*Long pause.*] Okay. Alright. Well, my father came over [to Hawaii] with his father when he was a young boy. I don't know how old he was. [Passport records indicate he arrived in 1895, when he was nine years old.] But when his father—my grandfather—went back to Japan, my father didn't go with him. He wanted to stay in Hawaii with relatives. So that's what he did. As far as I know, they lived in the town of Koloa [on Kauai]. Near Poipu Beach? That's where he lived.

Why did he want to stay?

I don't know. I never asked him.

Which relatives did he stay with?

[*Shakes his head.*] I don't know anything about them. But I do know that he learned some English, which came in handy, because he got a job as an interpreter on a [sugar] plantation. Management didn't speak Japanese, and the workers didn't speak English, so he served as an interpreter between management and the workers.

How did you communicate with him?

I spoke English with him. He used to carry on a lot of conversations with whites.

How did he come to marry grandma?

Well, back then all marriages were arranged, so when he decided to get married, it was arranged by his family in Japan. According to custom, once the prospective bride agreed to marriage, she left her family and stayed with her future husband's family until he sent money [for passage]. So that's what happened. He was in Hawaii, she was in Japan, and she moved out of her house and stayed with my father's family.

But the money didn't arrive. She waited over half a year. Finally she decided she'd had enough and went back to her family. My grandfather went and got her. He took her by train to Kobe, which was quite a ways from where they were living, and bought passage for her on a ship going to Hawaii. So that's how she got to Hawaii. That was in 1908. She was eighteen.

How old was grandpa?

He was four years older than she was, so he would have been twenty-two. And when she arrived in Hawaii—this was something she told me—she asked him, "Why didn't you send the money? I was waiting." He said, "I couldn't. I lost my job. I got fired." [*Laughs.*]

Why?

[*Shrugs.*] I don't know. She didn't tell me.

What was he like? I always heard he was a hellion.

ALICE

[*To Ken.*] He was just like you. Looked just like you.

KEN

Well, he drank a lot, but he wasn't a rambunctious man. I was afraid to ask him for things. When I wanted money to buy candy, I'd ask my mother. If she refused, I'd pester her for the longest time—just for a nickel or a dime.

She arrived in Honolulu?

Yes. The immigration station was there. All immigrants had to have someone waiting for them. If it was for marriage, the future husband had to be there. Frequently a whole group went through the marriage ceremony at the same time. Right there.

They'd never met before?

No. All they had were pictures of each other. My father met my mother in Honolulu, took her by boat back to Kauai, and they started their life together.

What was his level of education?

He might have gone through grammar school, but that was about it.

Did he plan on returning to Japan?

My guess is that he hoped to make enough money to go back someday.

What about grandma?

No, I don't think so. Kay [sister] might know, because she used to talk to her about those things. [Kay was one of nine siblings—three boys and six girls; two more—female twins named for the Japanese words for "dew" and "frost," since neither lasts long—died shortly after birth.]

But one thing my mother did tell me was that she was lonely. Very homesick. She would go down to the beach and sit there, looking out at the ocean. Thinking about how far away Japan was. And then she'd cry. She'd just sit there and cry.

How did grandpa make a living after he lost his job on the plantation?

He started a laundry. See, in those days everybody had hats, and one of the things my father did was press hats. He had a steam iron and wooden forms. As a kid, I remember seeing all these wooden forms in the shape of hats.

But at some point he decided to become a photographer—I guess he wanted a better life. He served as an apprentice to a photographer, and while he was doing that, he learned everything he could about the business. He used to come home with pieces of paper on which he'd written the names of different chemicals used in solutions to process negatives. He'd ask Sam [oldest brother], "What is this? How do you say it?" Eventually he became confident enough to start his own business. By that time, he and my mother were living in Kapaa.

[James] Michener mentions a photographer in Kapaa [in the novel *Hawaii*], and when I read it I thought it might be my father. In those days, each town had a photographer, and he was the photographer for Kapaa. [On page 260, a character walks "out to the main highway and on into Kapaa, where the ostracized Hashimoto had a photography shop and an agency for ships traveling to Japan."[1] However, Ken's father did not have a travel agency, and it would be difficult to determine who, if anyone, the

---

1. James Michener, *Hawaii* (The Ballantine Publishing Group, New York, 1959).

character was based upon; when asked if his father was ostracized, Ken laughed and said, "No."] He took all the school pictures, the graduating grammar school classes. There were also individual pictures, and he'd print the names of the students underneath their pictures. Isn't that interesting? So he'd learned how to print.

[*Thinks.*] He was all for being in business for yourself. He was very opposed to the idea of working for someone else. You were your own boss. I'd go with him on jobs to take pictures—I had to help set things up—and while he was driving, he'd preach to me about being my own boss.

Did he encourage you to go to college?

No. The concept of going to college was unknown to him.

The person who encouraged me to go to college was Haruto [second oldest brother]. He himself had started to go [to the University of Hawaii]—one of his teachers arranged for him to stay with a family and work for them as a houseboy—but he came home after a week. I don't think the conditions were very pleasant. Working as a houseboy and trying to go to school.

[*Smiles.*] Haruto and I used to take baths together. Japanese-style baths. It's called *furo*. We had a small building separate from the house that held the bathtub. You'd build a fire underneath the tub to heat the water. My father used to buy truckloads of wood, and I'd have to chop it up for firewood. In the late afternoon, it was my job to build the fire. You'd scrub and rinse outside the tub—you didn't want to dirty the water for everyone else—and then you'd sit in it. It was very relaxing.

During those moments he'd talk to me. He'd tell me, "When you finish high school, you should go to college."

What would've happened without that encouragement?

I wouldn't have gone to college. And he was the one who supported me. My father couldn't afford it—we had a big family, a lot of little kids growing up. During my first year in college [before the war], Haruto paid all my expenses. He paid for my tuition, my housing. In those days it cost about thirty dollars a month to stay in the dormitory. To save that kind of money—it must have been quite a struggle for him. So he was a big influence on me. I should write to him and tell him these things, because I never did. I owe him a lot.

Most of my father's business was with Filipinos. There·were a lot of Filipino immigrants. These were single men working on the plantations—

they'd have their pictures taken and sent back to their families in the Philippine Islands. My father must have been somewhat of an imaginative photographer, because he had a cowboy suit—as a kid I remember seeing this suit made out of leather, with all the fringes hanging down—two holsters, and two toy guns. I used to take out the guns and play with them. He had a cowboy hat, too. So these Filipino laborers would pose as cowboys with the suit and the hat and the guns. Print after print of Filipino cowboys. [*Laughs.*]

No women?
No women. All single men.

What did they do on the plantation?
Hard labor. Cut cane. Loaded the cane onto trains.
Anyway, that's what he did for the rest of his life. He also had Sam learn photography. Sam went to photography school in Indiana.

Why Indiana?
I don't know.

Where in Indiana?
Fort Wayne.

That's not why Wayne [Sam's son] is named Wayne, is it?
Yes. That's why Wayne is named Wayne. [*Laughs.*]

Were you poor?
I don't think we were poor. We ate very well compared to other families.

You once told me that you didn't have birthday parties.
No, we never had birthday parties, but Japanese don't have birthday parties—New Year's Day is everybody's birthday. We didn't celebrate Christmas, either. But I remember decorating boiled eggs for Easter.

[To Alice.] Now, your father's name was Zenichi.

ALICE

James Zenichi Imamoto.

14

But James was not his given name.

No. He gave that name to himself. It became his legal name.

And grandma's name is Yoshi. [The lone surviving grandparent—103 years old at the time of the interview; she died on February 28, 2003, at the age of 105].

Yoshi Iwamasa.

When did grandpa come over?

Father came over in 1907, when he was eighteen years old [he was born on September 8, 1889]. He was also from Yamaguchi. After his arrival, he worked as what was called a schoolboy. Schoolboys lived in someone's home rent-free, and in return they did the dishes, scrubbed the floors, whatever needed to be done.

Why did he leave Japan?

He didn't want to fight in the war. At that time, Japan was expanding into Manchuria and Korea. Mother's brother—my uncle—was a soldier in both places.

Did he survive?

Yes. He died two years ago—two months shy of 105.

Father never spoke much about his childhood. I don't know how old he was when his parents died, but he was sort of an orphan. He never talked about them. He always talked about mother's family—he boasted about her family. So mother said that when she agreed to marry him, she went to his sister's home. He had two sisters—I have a picture of them somewhere— and mother said they were very cultured, very learned. Flower arranging, the tea ceremony. That sort of thing. She lived with them for nine months or so.

Was she a picture bride as well?

Yes. And father turned down a lot of pictures. [*Laughs.*] He was picky— he was good-looking. She was about the tenth one. Her mother didn't want her to leave, because one daughter had already gone to Korea, so she sent the ugliest picture. But he picked her anyway. I heard that some people wanted their daughters picked so badly they'd send someone else's good-looking picture.

Most of the people in her town—Yagi—raised silkworms. Mother hated silkworms. She said all the houses had these little worms in them. She agreed to marry father because she figured that if she married someone from Yagi she'd be raising silkworms. I went there [in 1981] and stayed in the house where she lived. It had earth floors in the kitchen and an old cast-iron bathtub.

Was it filled with little worms?
[*Smiles.*] No.

When did grandma come over?
I have it here somewhere. [*Produces immigration questionnaire answered by her mother prior to becoming a U.S. citizen in 1953.* The Walter-McCarran Immigration and Naturalization Act of 1952 abolished the prohibition against Japanese nationals becoming U.S. citizens. *Reads.*] "I came to the U.S. as a picture bride in 1918. People nowadays are surprised about picture brides, but at that time marriages were generally arranged by the parents. My father, who was a representative of a county [in Japan], recommended Mr. Imamoto because his letter to him was very sincere. He didn't drink." [*Laughs.*]

What was a "representative of a county"?
He was like the mayor of this little burg.
[*Pauses.*] There was a problem with money in the village. It was not my grandfather's fault, but because he was in charge, he took responsibility and he took his life.

What?
He jumped in front of a train. I never knew that. Grace [sister, oldest of four siblings, all girls] told me about it years after the fact—after you kids were born. I never discussed it with mother, and she never said anything about it.
Grace learned about this from our cousins when she went to Japan [in 1949]. He came from samurai stock, and they said he first tried to kill himself with a sword—the Japanese call it *seppuku*. Ritual suicide.

When did this happen?
Before the war. Mother was about thirty. I was just a little girl.

So you're telling me that my great-grandfather committed suicide?

Yes. I thought you knew that.

No, I didn't. I think that's something I would have remembered. [Laughs.]

[*Not smiling.*] It was a great tragedy in mother's life. He was a very well-respected man. It's hard for us to understand—that you would take your own life for something that was not your fault. But things were different then. He took responsibility for the whole village.

In 1979, when mother was eighty-one, she returned to Japan. That was her first and only time back. The Buddhists held a Hohji ceremony—a ceremony for the dead. It was the twenty-fifth anniversary of her mother's death and the fiftieth anniversary of her father's. She said she just cried and cried and cried.

Where did grandpa arrive?

San Francisco. But by the time mother arrived, he was living in Berkeley.

What did he do for a living?

He had a job as a secretary at the Nihonjin-kai in San Francisco. The Nihonjin-kai was a Japanese association. It was like a YMCA—a community center for all the single Japanese men. He did paperwork.

When mother arrived, he was there to meet her, along with a minister—Reverend Terazawa—and the minister's wife. They went to the minister's home and got married.

Grace was born a year later. I have a picture of Grace as a baby at Christmastime with a beautiful tree.

Lily and Marion [her sisters] were also born in Berkeley, but at some point the family moved to Alameda, south of Berkeley. Then they moved to Garden Grove [near Los Angeles]. I was born in Garden Grove on November 28, 1926.

What were grandpa and grandma's first impressions of each other?

[*Laughs.*] Oh, they didn't talk about those things. It was too personal. They didn't even call each other by their first names.

What did they call each other?

"Papa" and "Mama." That was the custom with Issei [first-generation Japanese Americans—from *ichi*, the Japanese word for "one"; Nisei is derived from *ni*, Japanese for "two," and so forth. Japanese Americans consider the first generation to be the first to arrive in the United States].

KEN

My father used to say *kore*. That means "this." [*Laughs.*] Isn't that odd? *Kore.* Terry's [Kobayashi, family friend] mother used to say "Hello" to Terry's father. "Hello, Hello." They owned a store, and the white customers thought his name was Harlow. One day he wasn't there, and they all asked, "Where's Harlow?" [*Laughs.*]

ALICE

He also used to call her "Oka-san," which is a polite form of "Mother." If you put "O" in front of it, it makes it sound a little more polite. You could just say "Ka-san." Mother used to call him "Oto-san," the polite form of "Father."

Mrs. Nakajima [family friend] used to call her husband "Chot-to." That means "wait a minute." [*Smiles.*]

KEN

[*Leaves room, returns with papers.*] Okay, here it is. "We were married on March 1908." These are notes my father took when he was studying for his citizenship [in 1959]. Look at the things he had to learn. The Puritans, the Continental Congress. The Declaration of Independence. It's amazing— he was in his seventies. Here's a list of the thirteen original states.

"She born on December 28, 1890." [*Laughs.*] She born.

[*Reads from citizenship questionnaire.*] "If the law requires it, are you willing to bear arms for the United States?" "Yes." My sister [Minnie] wrote in the margin, "He was willing to bear arms for the United States at seventy-five years of age." [*Laughs.*]

Some of these questions are funny. "Have you ever been a habitual drunkard?" "No." "Have you ever derived income principally from illegal gambling activities?" "Have you ever been a polygamist?" "Have you ever been a prostitute?" [*Laughs.*]

[*To Alice.*] *So you were living in Garden Grove when the war started?*

No, by that point we had moved again. We were living in Norwalk.

Norwalk was the center of dairy farming country in Los Angeles County. The middle of nowhere. Flat, ugly, smelly. You rolled up your windows when you went through Norwalk.

There was absolutely no culture in Norwalk. I don't even know what the town of Norwalk was like—if there *was* a town.

Why did you live there?

Father got a job as the principal of the Japanese school in Norwalk. The principal lived in a house that belonged to the school—so we lived rent-free. It was a fairly big house. Old. There were termites. [*Laughs.*] Now it's a freeway. You know where Lily lives in Orange? Well, if you go from her house to Los Angeles, you go right through Norwalk on a freeway.

Before that he'd been teaching at a Japanese school on Terminal Island. Terminal Island is a man-made island between San Pedro and Long Beach. Only Japanese people lived there. They were all fishermen—that was the sole industry. Everyone who lived there spoke Japanese—even the kids— and father felt that was not a good place for us to live.

Why not?

Oh, it was a ghetto. Strictly a ghetto. There was nothing there—I don't know how those people even did their groceries.

So he commuted from Garden Grove, which meant he had to drive at least an hour each way. It was a hardship for him. Garden Grove was a nice community—it was a small place, everybody knew each other—but in Norwalk he could live right where he taught.

What was taught in a Japanese school?

The language, basically.

Why?

So children could communicate with their parents. And to preserve the culture, I suppose.

[*Pauses.*] The schools used books that were published in Japan. That's what got my parents in trouble—the FBI felt that those books were tools of propaganda. But I don't remember any kind of propaganda. And as mother pointed out, none of those books were published here.

Learning the [Japanese] language is difficult. It's not just the vocabulary. You have to learn how to write it. It's not ABCs—you have to learn the characters.

KEN

We went to Japanese school every day. For one hour after [regular] school. I think we had Japanese school even on Saturday.

ALICE

It's amazing how little you learned.

KEN

I was just plain dumb. [*Laughs.*]

Most of the time I skipped class and played baseball. When it was time to go home, I went home. My father was the treasurer of the church, so he knew the priest, and the priest finally told him to take me out of school— he said my father was wasting his money.

Did most Nisei kids go to Japanese school?

ALICE

Most, if not all. Every Japanese community had a Japanese school.

Father was one of the few Issei who spoke English. He'd gone to Berkeley High School, and also to the University of California for a year. So he spoke English quite well. He studied all kinds of things. Grace said he studied architecture, German.

He taught the older ones and mother taught the younger ones. He also drove the school bus. It was a pretty large school—about 100 students in all. Some of the other places he taught were just one-room schoolhouses with maybe twenty kids. So this one was big. I remember seeing pictures— they'd have all the kids lined up. Parents, too. Big crowd.

Did he make a good living? Were you poor?

[*Emphatic.*] Never poor. [According to War Relocation Authority documents, her father's salary in 1941 was $105 per month, or $1,260 per year; according to the U.S. Census Bureau, the average salary in 1940—no figure was available for 1941—was $1,300.] We all had music lessons. Mother would sew for us. So we always had pretty clothes. I played [piano] concerts, and mother made all my dresses. They had these little ruffles. Do you know what a hemstitcher is? There was a hemstitcher in town, and mother would take the ruffles to her to get them finished.

How did you get started playing the piano?

Well, Grace was taking piano lessons from a lady named Helen Johnston in Anaheim, which is a short distance from Garden Grove. Grace was ten and I was three. One day when Grace was practicing, I was sleeping in another room with a cold, and I was telling mother that Grace should be playing B-flat instead of B-natural. I'd been going to her lessons, so I knew the names of the notes. Mother thought that was rather unusual, so she took me to Miss Johnston. As it turned out, I have perfect pitch. I thought everybody had perfect pitch.

Miss Johnston wanted to teach me. At three. She didn't charge me. So that's how I got started.

When did you start playing concerts?

When I was six.

How did that come about?

I don't know. You'd have to ask mother or Grace. But I played in practically every church in southern California.

What church did you go to?

The Garden Grove Baptist Church. The way it worked was that the Japanese minister would have his service on Saturday night, when the Caucasian people weren't using it. That's when the Japanese people would use the church.

Why did you go to a Baptist church?

Because the Japanese minister was given space in the Baptist church.

In the little town of Garden Grove you could walk to several churches. There was a Baptist church, a Methodist church, and a Foursquare Gospel church. Aimee Semple McPherson? That was her church.

The Baptist church opened its doors to us.

Were your concerts for Japanese people?

No. Mostly Caucasians. And not just Baptist churches. Every kind of church. They'd call me. Father kept a scrapbook, so I have a collection of clippings from when I played.

How many concerts did you give?

There was one month when I played thirty-two concerts. I was eight. I remember that distinctly. Father would accept all the appointments, and I would play. With no difficulty, he thought. Sometimes as part of a program, and sometimes just by myself.

I was so little I couldn't reach the pedals. So father invented an extension for one of the pedals—there are pictures somewhere—and before each concert he'd get under the piano and screw on the pedal extension. I also wore a [leg] brace that went up to my hip, so my leg stuck out like that [*sticks leg straight out*]. He'd have to put a stool there for my foot.

[*Pauses.*] As a kid, you know, certain things embarrass you. And that's what embarrassed me. The pedal extension and the stool. Father having to screw on the extension and set up the stool.

What was wrong with your leg?

My kneecap went out of place when I was about two years old.

Why?

I don't know. But it was out like that [*places hand on outer portion of left knee*] from the time I was two until I was six, and then they operated on it. I had another operation when I was eight. I wore a brace until I was ten. I have only a partial kneecap.

It was one of those braces—there was no flexibility in the knee. It was perfectly straight. The brace had a hinge at the ankle, so there was some flexibility there. But the rest of it was straight. I took it off at night, when my leg was wrapped in a splint and bandaged up to my hip.

[*Thinks.*] That was how many years ago? Sixty-eight? Things have changed, the way they do therapy.

Were you paid for the concerts?

No. Never.

What were they like?

You'd wind me up and I'd play. I had a whole repertoire that I'd memorized. Chopin. Paderewski. Mozart.

Were they complicated pieces?

Oh, yes. I still have the music downstairs.

[*Thinks.*] There was a tournament of pianists. You'd play a program by memory in front of a judge who sat behind a screen. The judge had a list of the pieces you were going to play, and he'd grade you. I used to play twenty-two pieces at age eight. When somebody asked me to play, I'd play.

Was it fun?

[*Laughs.*] No. It wasn't fun. That's not normal. At the time, I just did it. There was really no pressure. Father and mother never said, "Do it." I would just do it. But I used to bite all my nails until they bled, so there must have been *some* tension. [*Laughs.*]

I think the fact that I was so little and had this handicap made it so there was always a story.

PIANO PRODIGY ACCLAIMED
Little Crippled Girl Plays Old Masters From
Memory as Invention Aids Pedaling

GARDEN GROVE, March 13—Her spirit undampened by the ravages of an illness which crippled one limb, 8-year-old Alice Setsuka Imamoto, Japanese musical genius, demonstrated here today how she can play from memory an entire program of compositions from the old masters.

She rests her crippled limb, encased in a steel brace, on a stool especially designed by her father. She is too small to reach the pedals of the piano and this obstacle is overcome by the father's invention of a steel appliance.

She recently attained a place on the honor roll of the National Piano Playing Tournament of America and was awarded a gold seal certificate.

When but 18 months of age she could sing through the entire song "Jesus Loves Me." At the age of 3 she played her first hymn on the piano. Her musical career started in earnest when she commenced to study piano under Miss Johnson [Johnston] of Anaheim.[2]

2. From the *Los Angeles Times,* March 14, 1935, underneath a photo with a caption reading, "Setsuka [Setsuko] Imamoto, 8-year-old crippled Japanese girl of Garden Grove is acclaimed a musical genius. She is rapidly winning new honors."

KEN

[*To Alice.*] We were at a dinner party in Hawaii in 1972 and someone asked, "Whatever happened to that crippled Japanese prodigy?" Do you remember that? It was at the Yasunobus'. He was the chairman of the department of biochemistry. There was another couple there—the husband was a professor at the University of Hawaii, I think in the history department. It was his wife who asked.

ALICE

[*Nods.*] I said, "That was me." She was so embarrassed. I don't think she said another word the rest of the night.

[To Alice.] So you were living in Norwalk when the war started. How old were you?
  Fifteen.

Did you have any sense of the increasing hostilities between the United States and Japan?
  Oh, absolutely. It was scary. Even as a young kid, you could feel the atmosphere.

Do you remember how you heard about it?
  Heard about what?

Pearl Harbor.
  [*Pauses.*] No.

You don't?
  No. It was such a state of—.
  All I remember of that day is that we didn't go anywhere. All I remember is fear.

Chapter Two

How old were you when the Japanese attacked Pearl Harbor?

KEN

Twenty-one. I was a sophomore at the University of Hawaii.

What do you remember about that day?

Well, it was Sunday morning, of course. Seven o'clock or so. Most of the guys were sleeping late. But somebody said Pearl Harbor was being bombed, so we all ran out into the yard and looked in that direction. We could see black smoke coming up. The governor came on the radio and announced that Pearl Harbor was being bombed, and shortly after that he declared martial law, which meant civilian authority was taken away. Everything was placed under military jurisdiction. I don't remember doing much for the rest of the day. Listened to the radio. Got very little news.

That night everything was blacked out. No streetlights, city lights, nothing. Everything was dark.

Where were you living?

In a dormitory called Students' House. There were about twenty-five of us.

Japanese Americans?

Mostly. A few Chinese and one Korean.

What was everyone's reaction?

Shock. Wondering what was going to happen to us.

Did you think, "Uh oh, these are Japanese, now we're in trouble"?

Yes, I did. And there *was* trouble.

I remember some of the things that were written in the papers. One guy—a white man—said all Japanese should be placed in concentration camps and deported from the islands. But they couldn't do that, because we comprised over a third of the population. The workforce needed us—otherwise everything would have collapsed. So, unlike the mainland, we were left alone. [In 1941, Hawaii had 157,000 residents with Japanese blood, comprising 37 percent of the islands' population of 424,000³; of those with Japanese blood, 1,875,⁴ or 1 percent, were sent to mainland camps. By comparison, nearly all mainland residents with Japanese blood—120,313⁵—were forcibly removed to camps; they comprised less than 1 percent of the U.S. population of 133,402,471.] But there was this hatred. [His sister Minnie remembers that their father was taken in for questioning in the days following Pearl Harbor. "They never told our mother where he was going or when he was coming back," she said. "She didn't sleep all night. They brought him back the next afternoon."]

Japanese Americans were no longer allowed to work at Pearl Harbor. Chinese could. At other military installations they had to wear a special badge with a black border, so it was immediately apparent what they were.

[*Thinks.*] In those days students at what were called land-grant colleges, like the University of Hawaii, had to have military training. Reserve Officers' Training Corps. So that's what we did, first thing in the morning, five days a week. Marching, things like that. I had already completed my ROTC requirement, but those who had not were called up to the National Guard [officially the Hawaii Territorial Guard]. But after a month or so, when things had quieted down and it became clear that the Japanese were not going to invade Hawaii, they discharged all the Nisei. Implying, of course, that they weren't to be trusted with guns and ammunition, guarding important installations. Strictly on the basis of nation-

3. Allan Bosworth, *America's Concentration Camps* (N.p.: W.W. Norton & Co., 1967), 121.

4. *Personal Justice Denied,* report by the Commission on Wartime Relocation and the Internment of Civilians (established by Congress in 1980).

5. U.S. Department of the Interior, *The Evacuated People: A Quantitative Description* (Washington, DC, Government Printing Office, 1946).

ality. They were needed while the threat was there, but when the threat was gone they weren't needed anymore. We were all reclassified as 4–C. You know what 4–F means? That you're physically unfit for duty? Well, 4–C means you're an enemy alien.

All of this came as a shock. I had never encountered racial prejudice before. But now there was an immediate stigma to being Japanese.

Not long after that someone passed around a petition. A Chinese man by the name of Hung Wai Ching had been talking to a bunch of kids at the university, telling us we should do something positive. He said we should all sign a petition and send it to the army, offering our services for whatever purpose we were needed. So we did. It was sent to the commanding general of the U.S. forces in Hawaii, a General [Delos] Emmons.

Hung Wai Ching is ninety-five now. I saw him at the Medal of Honor ceremony. [Twenty-two Asian American veterans, including twenty Japanese Americans, received Congressional Medals of Honor for valor during World War II in a White House ceremony on June 21, 2000.] He's an amazing man. It was his idea to petition the army for work, to prove our loyalty, and the army accepted us. We spent the next year at Schofield Barracks.

You stopped your schoolwork?

We stopped everything. It was like we were in the service. We lived in barracks and worked all week. On Saturday we took the bus back to town. We were still at Students' House—that was our home in Honolulu. On Monday we took the bus back to Schofield Barracks.

What did you wear?

Civilian clothes. We were called the Varsity Victory Volunteers, because we were all university boys. The Triple V. We built roads, ran barbed wire along the beaches. Whatever they needed. Some of the bigger guys worked in the quarries, breaking up rocks. We worked a regular eight-hour day. We ate army food.

What did you do?

I was in a group assigned to making iceboxes. There were a lot of troops training in the fields, and we made portable iceboxes to keep their food cold. We did that day after day, making the same thing over and over. Iceboxes. [*Shakes his head.*] It was so boring.

How many guys were in the Triple V?

About 170. We were divided into gangs. A dozen or so guys made up a gang, and each gang was under one person. Sus [Yamamoto, late family friend] was in charge of one of the gangs.

There were also five or six guys who weren't from the university, who didn't fit in at all. They looked like bums. Kept to themselves. Finally I asked someone, "Hey, who are those guys?" It turned out that Hung Wai Ching worked with the YMCA, so he knew a whole range of people in the city, and he had taken them out of the worst section of Honolulu. He thought if they came under the influence of university kids they might change. They stuck it out, but I don't know what happened to them after the Triple V was disbanded. None of them volunteered for the Army.

Did you have any interaction with the regular troops?

Yes. We had athletic competitions—the white troops against us. We played baseball and softball. Fast-pitch softball. I pitched—I remember pitching several games. We also had two football teams. One hundred and thirty-five pounds [*laughs*] and unlimited. And tennis. My partner and I ended up in the doubles finals, but we lost.

Did they accept you?

Sure.

Do you remember any instances of prejudice?

No.

Why not, do you suppose?

I don't know. But we didn't encounter any unpleasantness.

How long did the Triple V last?

Almost a year. It started in February of '42 and ended in January of '43. It was disbanded because the army—based in large part on the work we did—finally allowed us to volunteer.

Here's a funny thing about that. Someone told me there would be so many volunteers it would be very difficult to get in. I was told there would be about 10,000 volunteers, but the army was only going to take 1,500 to 2,000, and if I wanted to get in I should write a letter to the draft board requesting that I be included. So I did. I wrote a letter and mailed it to the draft board. Of course they took me. [*Laughs.*]

I was inducted in early March. So I had about a month off before induction.

What did you do?

A bunch of us went to Hilo [Hawaii]. That's where Lefty [Kuniyoshi, lifelong friend] was from. He said, "Why don't you guys come home with me? Spend a few days there before we go into the army." So we flew to Hilo, four or five of us, and stayed with his family.

[*Thinks.*] Now, I always knew I had relatives in Hilo, but I'd never met them. One afternoon I was standing in front of a drugstore in downtown Hilo when a man came out and called to me. He didn't call me by my name, though—he called me by a different name. He said, "Waichi? Are you Waichi?" I said no. He said, "What's your name?" I said, "Kaname." "What's your last name?" "Takemoto." "You're from Kauai?" I said yes. He said, "I'm related to you." It turned out that he was my [first] cousin. I'd never met him before, but he thought I looked familiar. [*Laughs.*]

Who was Waichi Takemoto?

I have no idea, but he must have been related to me. [Military records list a Waichi Takemoto as one of thirty-three Takemotos who served with the 100th or 442nd.]

My cousin was so glad to meet me. He insisted that I stay at his house. So I went and had dinner with his family and stayed for the night. His son, who just graduated from high school, had volunteered, too. He became a very decorated soldier. Norman Ikari [family friend] was in the same company, and he said my cousin's son was fearless. He ended up getting the Distinguished Service Cross.

What's his name?

Tsuneo. Tsuneo Takemoto. He was one of those considered for the Medal of Honor [in 2000], but he didn't get one. He almost didn't get the DSC, either. The papers recommending him for the DSC were being carried by a company clerk, and the clerk was killed in battle. They couldn't recover his body for a couple of days—it was out in the open—and it was only when they were going through his possessions that they found the citation for my relative's DSC. If they hadn't recovered those papers, he never would have received it.

What did he do?
He destroyed several German machine gun nests. Attacked them by himself.

Whatever happened to him?
He lives in Hilo.

ALICE

We met him.

What's he like?

KEN

He's a quiet person.

ALICE

You forgot this, but when we went to Hilo [in 1954, her first trip to Hawaii], we went by that same drugstore, and you didn't want to go in. We needed directions, and you made me go in. The father came out and saw you.

Why didn't you want to go in?

ALICE

Who knows?

KEN

He would have insisted that we stay at his house again.

ALICE

But we *did* go to his house. He was a little annoyed that you didn't want to see him.

Did a lot of your friends volunteer for the army?

KEN

Yes.

[*Pauses.*] There was a big argument over that. Back at Students' House. One night a bunch of us were in someone's room, and two of the guys got into an argument. One of them said that everybody had to volunteer. No exceptions. Any eligible Japanese American had to volunteer in order to prove his loyalty. He said we *had* to do it. The other guy said no, it was an individual matter. According to him it was up to the individual to determine whether he wanted to go into the army or not.

It was not said, but it was known, that this could be a life-or-death decision. You could get killed or maimed. It was no trivial matter to volunteer for combat duty. And that was his argument. That it was up to the individual.

Do you remember who they were?

[*Firmly.*] Yes. The guy who was a fervent ultra-patriot was Kats Tomita. His Japanese name was Katsumasa, but everybody called him Kats. The other guy's name was David Miura. He was the one who said it was up to the individual.

The argument got so heated they were ready to go out into the yard and have it out. Have a fight. We all jumped in and stopped it.

But the surprising thing was that Miura, for whom I have great respect, volunteered. He wasn't arguing because he was not going to volunteer— it was the principle of the thing. When I found out he was volunteering, I was really surprised.

Did the other guy volunteer?

Yes. Both of them did.

[*Pauses.*] This David Miura. He got very badly wounded. Severely wounded. [*Voice thickens.*] They said he almost died. He had machine gun bullets across his chest. He was bleeding to death, but somebody picked him up and saved him. He was in a hospital in Italy for a long time. I was already home and discharged and he was *still* in a hospital. When the ship brought him home, we all went down to see him, and he was immediately transported to a hospital on the island. He was there for a long time.

31

Where did you come down on that argument?
I didn't take sides. I just listened.

Did you know that you were going to volunteer?
Yes.

Why?
[*Pauses.*] There was a sense of wanting to prove our loyalty. And the only way to do that was to go into combat.

Did you like both of them?
Yes, I did.

What happened to the other guy?
Kats? [*Smiles.*] He was safe. He was a cook, so they made him a cook. He never did any actual fighting. Now, it wasn't by choice that he became a cook—that's what he was assigned to do. He'd been a cook in the Triple V, so they knew he could cook for large groups of people.

Was he a good cook?
He was a very good cook. He used to cook for us at Students' House.

What happened to them after the war?
Kats became a social worker. He died about five years ago. David Miura became a dentist. He's a dentist in Long Beach.

How many volunteered?
Of the twenty-five guys in Students' House, nine volunteered.

Who were they?
Well, in addition to those two and myself, there was Lefty Kuniyoshi and Howard Urabe. Masaichi Sagawa. [*Spells Masaichi.*] Like Fusaichi Pegasus? The racehorse? [*Laughs.*] He became a dentist, too. There were two from Maui. One was a guy named Don Shimazu and the other was a guy named Yoshimasu. I don't remember his Japanese name because we called him by his nickname: Camel. Everybody had a nickname back then. His was Camel, for the cigarettes? That makes me think of another guy with a funny nickname: Cannonball. His real name was Kawate, but we called

him Cannonball because he was built like a cannonball. Stocky, muscular guy. He was from Kauai, too.

I should also say that there were two other guys from Students' House, who had been drafted the year before, when I was a freshman. They were already in the army, and ended up in the 100th.

What was the 100th? I've seen it written as the 100th Infantry Battalion/442nd Regimental Combat Team.

The 100th was made up of Nisei who were already in the army when Pearl Harbor was attacked. They were prewar draftees, starting from about 1939. So they were older than us. Most of them were from Hawaii. But after Pearl Harbor the army didn't know what to do with them. They didn't trust them. I was told that some had their weapons taken away and weren't allowed to leave the base. If they wanted to go to the toilet, they had to call a guard and a guard would take them.

Some were even discharged. That's what happened to Joe Ichiuji [family friend]. He was a prewar draftee from California, but after Pearl Harbor the army sent him home. When they relocated mainland Japanese Americans he was sent to a relocation camp, and when they asked for volunteers [for the 442nd], he volunteered. I said, "Joe, they kicked you out of the army, put you in a relocation camp, and when they asked for volunteers you went back in?" [*Laughs.*]

Eventually, though, they pulled all of those guys out of their regular units—if they hadn't been discharged—and shipped them off to train as one group—now called the 100th—[at Camp McCoy] in Wisconsin. The army still wasn't sure what to do with them, but by the time we got to Camp Shelby [in Hattiesburg, Mississippi] they had finished their training, and came down South for maneuvers. We saw some of them before they were shipped overseas.

Do you remember the two who were drafted when you were a freshman?

Yes. One had the same last name. Joe Takemoto. He was from Kona [Hawaii]. The other was a guy named Gary Hisaoka. He was killed. He won the Silver Star.

What did he do?

There was a major with the 100th named Jack Johnson. He was from Hawaii. Big guy. Captain of the University of Hawaii football team. He was wounded out in the open—the Germans were firing, and they couldn't get to him. So Gary Hisaoka jumped out of his trench, ran over to the major, and carried him back. Big guy, but he got him back. They gave him the Silver Star for that. The major died, though. This happened in France, and he was buried there. I saw a documentary where some of the 100th Infantry guys put flowers on his grave and sang "Aloha 'Oe." It was a very moving ceremony.

How was Gary Hisaoka killed?
I don't know, but it wasn't in that action. It was in a later battle.

What happened to the nine guys who volunteered?
[*Long pause.*] Well, Howard Urabe was killed. The ones who were seriously wounded were myself and David Miura. Others had less serious wounds, like Lefty.

[*Thinks.*] Lefty was my best friend. We're *still* friends. Very nice guy. I don't know a single person who disliked him. He's one of those unusual guys with no enemies. When you mention him, everybody says what a nice guy he is.

[*Shakes his head.*] He went through the whole war without getting wounded. That means he went from just north of Rome [in June 1944] all the way up to Pisa, got shipped to France, fought in southern France for four or five months, and was shipped back to Italy for the last battles before the war ended [V-E Day was May 8, 1945]. That's almost an entire year of combat. To survive—it's amazing. He was one of the rare ones.

But he had a lot of close calls. He said the closest was when he was about three or four feet behind this guy—the Germans had put booby traps all around, and this guy set one off. Big explosion. The other guy got killed, but Lefty wasn't touched.

The battle of the Lost Battalion? He was in that. This was in southern France, near a town called Bruyères. [*Spells it.*] In France the 442nd was attached to the 36th Division—the Texas division—and the Lost Battalion was part of the 36th. They'd gone too far out, and the Germans cut them off. Now they couldn't draw back. They were surrounded, and getting slowly decimated by artillery. The 36th tried several times to rescue them, but couldn't. So they sent in the 442nd. Some people think the general—his name was [Major General John] Dahlquist—did that because he thought

Japanese Americans were expendable. You know, send them. But they got them out.

[*Angry.*] This Dahlquist. After the battle was over he asked the 442nd—the whole regiment—to gather in formation for review. Only about a third were present. He scolded the colonel in charge—Colonel [Virgil] Miller—thinking he had sent the others out on passes. The colonel told him that was all that was left.

Colonel Miller was said to have run into Dahlquist after the war on several occasions, but he never talked to him. Never acknowledged him.

Anyway, of the 200 guys in Lefty's company only 17 were left. All the others had been killed or wounded. Seventeen guys out of 200, and he was one of the 17. After the battle he was told that he was being put in for a field commission to be a lieutenant, but he turned it down. He thought, "Gee, if I become an officer, I can't fool around with my friends anymore." [*Laughs.*] He didn't want that, so he said no.

He was a platoon sergeant. He wasn't in my company, but I knew a guy who was transferred into his company. This guy had a funny nickname, too: Bragger. Like a braggart? In basic training Bragger once picked on a friend of mine, but in combat he was so scared he begged Lefty to let him stay close to him. In other words, he wanted Lefty to take care of him. So Lefty said, "Bragger, you can stay close to me, but from now on you're going to dig my foxhole." Bragger said, "Okay, sure." [*Laughs.*]

Lefty was an unlikely platoon sergeant. Such a gentle guy. You wouldn't think of him as a rough, tough guy.

We met as freshmen at the University of Hawaii. That was over sixty years ago. Nineteen thirty-nine. And we're still friends.

[*Leaves, returns with an eight-by-ten, black-and-white photograph of sixty-one Japanese Americans in uniform in a restaurant in Hattiesburg, Mississippi.* Two-thirds of the soldiers sit on wooden chairs at long tables set for dinner; the remaining third stands along the back. A handwritten caption reads, "Reunion, Varsity Victory Volunteers, Camp Shelby, Miss. 1943."] This is skipping ahead a little, but when we were in basic training somebody organized a dinner for the Triple V guys, so we all got together and had dinner.

Are you in this picture?

I'm in this picture. [*Looks intently. Points.*] This guy got killed. Dan Betsui. He and I were good friends. Howard is in here somewhere. Here's Lefty.

35

This guy got killed, too—Bobby Murata. He was a boxer. This guy was a football player. [*To Alice.*] He was the guy we tried to see in Salt Lake City [after the war]. Wallace Doi? He was in the same hospital with me in Rome. Lost his leg. Grenade. Jenhatsu Chinen was killed. Hiromitsu Tomita. Tomita was what they called a runner—he ran messages between headquarters and the troops. He had just come back to headquarters with a message and was standing in the doorway when a German shell landed right on the building. Killed him.

This guy and I, we came back together. He was wounded and considered disabled, too. Melvin Nagasako. Fun guy. In 1992 they had the fiftieth reunion of the Triple V in Honolulu, and I went back for that. I asked about Nagasako. They said he had drowned. He was fishing on the rocks somewhere and was swept into the ocean.

[*Shakes his head.*] Some of these guys—I don't even know their names anymore. But I remember their faces. The faces I remember.

Chapter Three

What was your life like after December 7?

ALICE

Well, I went to a very good high school. Excelsior. The day after the war broke out, the principal called an assembly. This would have been on Monday. It was a big school—maybe 1,500 kids—and he called everybody together to say, "The enemy is not here. The enemy is not the Japanese students here." He set the tone for the school.

Do you remember his name?
[*Proudly.*] Yes. His name was Burnight—Ralph Burnight.

How many students were Japanese American?
I would say about seventy-five. Maybe more. I have the annual downstairs.

Do you remember feeling any prejudice against you?
No. None. I never felt anything like that in school. And I never heard of any instances involving anyone else.

Do you think that was because of what the principal had said?
I think it was definitely because of what he had said.
[*Thinks.*] I was very active in school. I played the organ for every assembly. Seven or eight pieces while the whole school was marching in. I was a junior but this started back when I was a freshman. They bought an electric organ knowing I would play it. And I never took [organ] lessons—I had to learn how to play it myself. The pedals and all that. So I played the

organ for the assemblies and the piano for school plays. One year we performed the *Mikado* and one year we performed *The Pirates of Penzance*. Those were musicals, and I was the orchestra. I played everything.

My existence was going to school and coming home—there was nothing more to it than that. We didn't have activities on weekends, except that I went to church. I went to church on Saturday night, Sunday morning, and Sunday night. I played at the Clearwater Baptist Church on Saturday night and Sunday morning, and I played at the Norwalk Quaker Church on Sunday night.

Saturday nights we had songfests with youth groups. [*Smiles.*] Everybody sang in those days. Not hymns. Fun songs, like "I've Been Working on the Railroad." That was our recreation.

Was there a feeling that something bad was going to happen?

Yes. It was terrible. You had the feeling that we were being grouped together [with the Japanese]. That we were viewed as one and the same. And then mother and father were arrested.

EXECUTIVE ORDER 9066

NOW, THEREFORE, by virtue of the authority vested in me as President of the United States, and Commander-in-Chief of the Army and Navy, I hereby authorize and direct the Secretary of War, and the Military Commanders whom he may from time to time designate, whenever he or any designated Commander deems such action necessary or desirable, to prescribe military areas in such places and of such extent as he or the appropriate Military Commander may determine, from which any or all persons may be excluded, and with respect to which, the right of any person to enter, remain in, or leave shall be subject to whatever restrictions the Secretary of War or the appropriate Military Commander may impose in his discretion. . . .

[signed] Franklin D. Roosevelt
The White House
February 19, 1942[6]

6. Maisie and Richard Conrat, Executive Order 9066 (Los Angeles: Anderson, Ritchie and Simon, 1972).

When was that?

March 13, 1942. That was the date when ministers and schoolteachers were taken.

Were they the first?

No. Businessmen were first, some on December 7. But March 13, boy. That was it. Friday the 13th.

What do you remember about that day?

Well, father wasn't home, so mother was taken first. He was in another town—Santa Ana—trying to settle citizenship for a [Japanese] family that lived in Norwalk. I think he was at the Santa Ana courthouse. So they [the FBI] took mother. She said they surrounded the house first.

I was called home from school. What I had forgotten—see, I forgot these things—was that Mr. Burnight came home with me. He took me home.

[*Thinks.*] He was a wonderful man. An extraordinary man. You know, after the war, when father and mother moved here to Washington, he came every year to see them. By that point he was the superintendent of schools in southern California. Every year they would have a convention in Atlantic City, and every year he would stop by Washington just to see them. He took a bus and walked down Tilden Street. And if that didn't boost their feelings.

Did you know that mother and father went to the Burnight's fiftieth wedding anniversary? This was in the sixties, after mother and father had retired to Berkeley. They flew down for the celebration. The Burnights still lived in the same place—either Bellflower or Artesia, which is near Norwalk. He was a real friend. So, certain things I *do* remember.

Do you remember the FBI taking grandma away?

No. I don't remember them taking mother or father away. I don't remember either one of them getting into a car. I was too upset. Blocked it all out. I remember the FBI being there, though.

What did they do?

We had a little table radio, and they kept fussing with that. [*Imitates someone turning the knobs.*] They seized some books as evidence, which were later used at their hearings. Teaching materials. Craft books. It was all so innocuous.

Re: YOSHI IMAMOTO   File No. 146–13–2–12–2411

The charge against this subject is that she was a teacher in the Japanese Language School. The Federal Bureau of Investigation report reflects that subject was apprehended as being a teacher in a Japanese Language School at Norwalk, California. A search of her premises at or near the time of her apprehension resulted in the seizure of a number of articles, to-wit: 6 religious pamphlets published in Japan, one high school textbook of physical education published in Japan, 1 book on information of Los Angeles published in Japan, 3 exercise books published in Japan, 1 book of the Daughters of the American Revolution published in the United States, 1 Japanese grammar published in Japan, 2 homework books published in Japan[,] and others. It appears from the report that she has been a teacher in the Japanese language school for about 5 years. She reads no foreign language newspapers and belongs to no associations. Her husband[,] however, is Secretary of the Japanese Farmers Association of Norwalk, California.

After that I always had a fear of the FBI. A terrible fear. For years and years. Until we met Mal [Heggie, a friend and former neighbor in Kensington who was an FBI agent]. I never told him that, though.

So mother was taken, and the FBI waited for father to come home so they could take him, too. I was the only one there, because Marion was at Fullerton Junior College, which was about ten miles away, and Grace and Lily were up north. Grace was going to the University of California [Berkeley], and Lily was in nursing school in Oakland. Grace was a senior—this would have been her last semester. She didn't get her degree until later. She wasn't able to take her finals, so she didn't get her degree.

Grace was twenty-two, Lily was twenty-one, Marion was eighteen and I was fifteen.

Was there any advanced notice?

No. Mother and father weren't prepared at all. If you knew you were going to be taken, you would prepare, get your things in order. But they didn't know, so they had done nothing.

Did they let her bring anything?

She took her toothbrush, toothpaste, and a Bible.

On what grounds was she arrested?

Well, I'm *still* trying to find that out. I filed a Freedom of Information Act request with the National Archives and obtained some documents, but they don't say why she was arrested. I also wrote to the FBI, but didn't get anything from them. You saw those FBI papers, didn't you? All blacked out. One of them said there was no evidence that mother and father had ever been arrested.

She was one of only 44 women who were arrested. About 4,200 men were arrested, but only 44 women. Of those, 11 were arrested on earlier dates. Mother was arrested with the remaining 33. Of the 33—and they came from all over the West Coast, Oregon, Washington, California—father knew five of them, including mother. He'd taught with them at one school or another.

What happened to her after her arrest?

She was taken to the Norwalk jail and kept there for a couple of hours. Five Issei men we knew were already there. She wasn't allowed to use the bathroom without someone guarding her. Then they took her in a paddy wagon to a jail in Los Angeles. She stayed overnight with three other women—all Issei—in a regular cell. Grace said they refused to eat, in protest of their arrest. After that she was sent to Terminal Island, the same place where father had taught, where there was another jail, a federal prison. She was there for three months. During that time one of the women committed suicide.

THIS CASE ORIGINATED AT LOS ANGELES FILE NO. 100–12003

REPORT MADE AT:	Los Angeles
DATE WHEN MADE:	3/28/42
PERIOD:	3/10, 12, 13/42
REPORT MADE BY:	Edmund D. Mason
TITLE:	YOSHIKO IMAMOTO, with alias Yoshi Imamoto
CHARACTER OF CASE:	Internal Security—J, Alien Enemy Control

SYNOPSIS OF FACTS:

U.S. Attorney LEO SILVERSTEIN authorized emergency apprehension of female subject on March 10, 1942. Subject apprehended March 13, 1942, by Bureau Agent. Booked Los Angeles County Jail, en route to Immigration and Naturalization Service. Subject is a teacher at Norwalk Japanese School, Norwalk, California.

REFERENCE:

Report of Special Agent EDMUND D. MASON, Los Angeles, March 28, 1942, entitled "Japanese Language Schools."

DETAILS:

Assistant United States Attorney LEO SILVERSTEIN authorized emergency apprehension of Subject on March 10, 1942. Subject was apprehended on March 13, 1942, by Special Agent DON OWENS, JR. She was placed in the Los Angeles County Jail, booked en route to the Immigration and Naturalization Service.

The United States Attorney is requesting a Presidential warrant for the Subject, and has ordered her held for hearing before the Alien Enemy Hearing Board.

At Terminal Island they slept in one long room. Mother said there was a bed, a small place to put your belongings, and then another bed. These were Issei women who were very private, very modest. They didn't want to dress in front of everybody else. So someone turned out the lights, and all hell broke loose. Mother said bells started clanging, the matrons rushed in. After that they weren't allowed to turn off the lights, even at night. The matrons watched them at all times, even when they went to the bathroom.

When was grandpa arrested?

Later that same day, after he got home from Santa Ana.

He was also taken to the Norwalk jail, and then to the LA jail, but he didn't see mother. He didn't know she was there, and she didn't know he was there.

But from LA he didn't go to Terminal Island. He went to a place called Tujunga. It's up in the mountains—I think near Hollywood. [Tujunga is about 12 miles north of Hollywood, in the foothills of the San Gabriel Mountains.]

Was that another jail?

No. See, there were so many men, they couldn't put them in jail. I'm not sure what it was—it might have been a conference center, something like that. They lived in dormitories. So for that part of it, at least, mother's experience was more difficult than father's. She was in jail. He would go to jail later.

Did you know where they were?

No. We didn't know where they were for about a week. Once we found out that mother was at Terminal Island and father was at Tujunga, which is in the opposite direction, we were busy visiting them, taking things to them.

Why didn't you know?

No one told us. I don't remember how we found out, but the police and the FBI didn't tell us, that's for sure. It was probably from someone whose parents were also taken. And, because of the curfew, we had to go to the police station to get permission to see them.

What was the curfew?

From six in the morning until eight at night we [people of Japanese ancestry] weren't allowed to travel more than five miles in any direction. From eight at night until six in the morning we weren't allowed leave our homes at all.

How did you get to Terminal Island and Tujunga?

A man named Mike Wada drove us to Terminal Island. Both of his parents were taken—Mrs. Wada was with mother, and Reverend Wada was with father. Reverend Wada was the minister of a Japanese church in Garden Grove. We knew the whole family.

Mike Wada lived in Pomona, which was not that close to us, and he would pick us up in Norwalk and take us to Terminal Island. That meant he had to go from here to here to here. [*Draws three imaginary points in the air, forming a big triangle.*] I don't know who drove us to Tujunga.

[*Pauses.*] I remember talking to father through a fence. We were outside. I don't remember anything else about that place, what it looked like, nothing. But I remember that. Talking to him through a fence.

Dear Father,

How are you? I hope you are just fine. We are all at home and we miss you and mother very much.

Please keep in good health. When we saw you, we noticed that you have certainly got brown on the face. Do you play baseball father? I hope you have lots of fun. Say hello to Mr. Shizuoka, Wada, Tamura, Fujimoto, Ikezaki, Itaya, etc.

Another one of your daughters,
Alice

Chapter Four

It was during that month [before induction] that I also went home with
Howard Urabe so we could tell our fathers we were volunteering.

What was grandpa's reaction?

[*Pauses.*] Well, I've often wondered what my reaction would have been
under similar circumstances. What I would have done if you had told me
that you were volunteering. I think I would have stopped you, because I
wouldn't have wanted you to get killed. Yet even before the war started,
when I was still in high school and it was evident that there was this con-
flict between Japan and the United States, my father used to tell me, "If
the United States and Japan ever go to war, and somebody asks you, 'Who
would you fight for?' your answer must always be, 'The United States.'
You're an American, and you're going to fight for the United States." He
always used to tell me that.

So when I arrived home, the first thing he said was, "You're going to
volunteer, aren't you?" Before I could even open my mouth. I said, "Yes."
There was no further discussion.

What did grandma say?

She didn't say anything. None of my brothers and sisters said anything.
Nobody tried to dissuade me from volunteering.

[*Thinks.*] But I don't know what my father really thought. I don't know
how he really felt as a father whose son was going into combat. Later, of
course, the reports started coming in. Every day. The number killed. Who
was killed. Which family. And a lot were from Kauai. 442nd guys, 100th

Infantry guys. There were a lot of [funeral] services. I don't know how he felt about that.

[*Pauses.*] But do you know what Howard's father said? What he said when Howard told him he was volunteering? He said, "This will be the end of you."

That's what he said?
[*Nods.*] "This will be the end of you."

What was it like leaving Kauai? Knowing it would be a long time before you ever got back? That you might not come back?
Well, Haruto drove us to the airport. At the time it was very difficult to get passage. There were only a couple of flights a day, and a lot of people were trying to get back and forth.

What did you talk about?
There was no conversation. But as we were driving out of Kapaa—and maybe it was because of what his father had said—Howard turned around in his seat and was looking at the town through the back window. It was early morning, still kind of dark, and he said, "This might be the last time I see this place."

What was he like?
Howard? [*Smiles.*] Well, one of the things I remember was that when we were still in grammar school—this was about the sixth grade—we got into a gang fight. We had a fight in front of the Roxy Theater.

You and Howard?
There was a bunch of us. He had three of his friends, I had three of my friends, and somehow we got into a fight. We were trading blows, four against four, going at it. I was the biggest in my group, so I was fighting the biggest in their group. Howard was not the biggest, so he was fighting someone else. We went at it until a man came along and broke it up. He told us to stop, so we stopped.

Who started it?
I have no idea.

And you became friends after that?

[*Laughs.*] Yes. I had nothing against him. I did have bad feelings against the guy I was fighting. We used to play a lot of football, and once after I was tackled with the ball he came charging in and kneed me. I was so angry that on the next play, just as he was about to tackle someone else, I ran up and punched him in the eye. Just smacked him right in the eye. He was totally unprepared. Talk about a sneak attack.

Do you remember his name?

Yes. Yoshida. Soichi Yoshida. We were at Japanese school. This took place during recess, and when class resumed, he wasn't there. I went outside and found him behind the school, crying. I didn't know what to do. I felt bad, because his eye was all swollen. It was completely shut. I used to go past his house on the way to school, but I never walked in front of his house again. I didn't want to see his parents. His eye—it was black-and-blue for a whole week. I really whacked him.

After the war he opened a little store, and I went to see him. We had a nice talk. Boy. [*Shakes his head.*] I wonder if he remembered me punching him. I'm sure he did.

Howard never mentioned our gang fight, so maybe he didn't remember it. Or maybe he didn't want to talk about it. [*Laughs.*]

What was he like? He was a nice guy. He was smart, too. And after that we became good friends.

What happened after you returned to Honolulu?

I had to go to the draft board and take a physical. Unfortunately, I passed. [*Laughs.*] We raised our right hands and swore allegiance to the United States. Then they took us by trucks to Schofield Barracks.

At Schofield Barracks we were given the standard army intelligence test. [*Laughs.*] I can't imagine conditions being any worse for taking a test. We were in a huge tent, sitting on benches, with boards for tables. They handed out the papers, we went to work, and when they called time, we turned our papers in. That was it.

I didn't think anything of it, but later, in basic training, I was suddenly transferred out of my original squad. It turned out that my new squad leader had seen the test scores, and he wanted me to be his assistant because he said I had the highest score in the whole company.

What was your score?

One-forty.

Out of how much?

I don't know. [*Laughs.*]

But, you know, this guy turned out to be someone I didn't like as squad leader.

Why not?

Well, one day when we were out on maneuvers, the captain came around to check on us and our squad was completely out of line. He raised hell. He yelled for the squad leader. "Who's the squad leader here?" I waited for him to step up, but he was nowhere to be found. He'd disappeared. So I had to say that I was the acting squad leader. The captain chewed me out, and after that he had no use for me. He took down my name and never promoted me. I was supposed to be made corporal—everybody else made corporal, but I never did.

How long were you at Schofield Barracks?

About a week. We were issued uniforms and equipment. Given shots and whatnot.

[*Thinks.*] One day they took us by train to Honolulu. We had to march from the train station all the way to Iolani Palace—the old palace, from when Hawaii was a monarchy? They had a formal ceremony for us because we were going to be shipped out. It was ridiculous, when you think about it—here it was wartime, but there was no secrecy. There were speeches. I think the governor spoke, a man by the name of Stainback—Ingram Stainback. Isn't it strange that I remember that? And a Hawaiian singer, a woman, sang a Hawaiian song. It was called, "To You, Sweetheart, Aloha." A lot of girlfriends and mothers and fathers were there. All crying.

Was anyone from your family there?

No. They were back on Kauai.

When we left for good, at the end of the week, the same thing happened. Again we went by train to Honolulu—the train station was about two miles from the docks—and again we had to march a long way, this time all the way to the docks. We were loaded down—our stuff was in big duffel bags. I remember how tired we were. People were lining the streets. There was nothing secret about it. It was kind of ridiculous, advertising the shipment of a whole boatload of guys.

What were your emotions?

My emotions? I don't know. I never thought about the danger of not coming back, though. I never thought I might not be coming back.

Why not?

[*Smiles.*] Oh, young and foolish. Maybe in the back of my mind I thought they would form this outfit and we would train, but they'd never send us into combat. I didn't think, gee, someday somebody's going to be shooting at us. Killing us. There was also the thought that maybe, by the time we finished training, the war would be over. That we wouldn't have to fight. [*Laughs.*]

It's kind of strange when you think about it, but I never heard anybody talk about that stuff.

Where did you go from Honolulu?

San Francisco. We were on a ship called the *Lurline*. [*Spells it.*] It was a passenger cruise ship that had been converted to a troop transport.

[*Thinks.*] Leaving by ship is so different than leaving by airplane. When you leave by airplane you leave, that's it. But when you leave by ship, it takes a while to get away from the dock. People are waving. They used to have these rolls of ribbon paper, and they'd throw it to someone on deck and hold on until it broke off.

How long did the trip take?

About six days.

What do you remember about it?

Only that there was a lot of gambling. Dice. Craps. And that from a distance, as we were approaching the Golden Gate Bridge, I thought we were going to ram into it. It looked that low. I was surprised, when we sailed underneath, by how much clearance there was.

We landed in San Francisco and took a ferry across to Oakland. From there we boarded trains to go to Mississippi.

Did you know you were going to Mississippi?

No. We had no idea where we were going.

What was the train like?

Very uncomfortable. No beds. We were in coach seats, so we had to sleep sitting up. When we went through towns, the blinds were drawn—our movements were supposed to be secret. We were on that train for days.

I didn't know we were going to Mississippi until we arrived.

Chapter Five

What happened after your parents were arrested?

ALICE

Well, it left Marion and I alone. Marion was going to Fullerton, as I said, but she lived at home.

The Japanese Americans who lived on Terminal Island? There were about 2,000 of them, all fishermen. They had been told to evacuate their homes within forty-eight hours, so they had to find places to live, and a lot of them lived in Japanese schoolhouses. The Quakers [actually the American Friends Service Committee, a Quaker organization] helped them. About sixty of them lived in our schoolhouse. Right next door to us. Some of them were high-school students, so they went to high school with us. We'd go down in the morning and catch the bus together. I didn't know them, but I think Marion and I felt like we weren't quite alone because they lived right next door.

I don't know what they slept on or anything. How they cooked. What they ate. Can you believe that? Sixty people. They were evacuated with us, too.

Marion and I were alone for two weeks. They wanted to send a matron to stay with us, but we refused. After two weeks, Grace and Lily came home.

Why didn't they come home right away?

They wanted to, but we told them to stay [in school] as long as they could. We didn't want their school interrupted. But when we found out there was going to be a curfew, they had to come home, because otherwise they would have been stuck up north.

4/10/42
Dear Father,

Thank you for your letters. I am sorry that I did not write sooner. Things happened so rapidly that I am always behind schedule.

I was deeply sad when they took mother and you and to leave poor Marion and Alice home alone. They were indeed brave girls. Now we are home together so do not worry about us. Everyone is so nice to us that we do not know how to ever thank them all. . . .

Today is Friday and one month for mother and you away from home. Lily and I came home to not be met by you & it was indeed very sad & a lonely feeling. The house seemed so empty. At every dinner time, we speak of how much we wish that you were home with us. . . .

Mother had her hearing Friday [inaccurate: according to Justice Department documents the hearing was held on April 17] so we are anxiously waiting her return to us. Rev. Nicholson wrote to us and said he would be in Santa Fe to witness your hearing too. I pray that you can return to us too. . . .

Since lights go out at 10 PM I better close this letter as it is nearly 10 already. Take care of yourself, as we are doing fine here.

Your daughter,
Grace

Why did they have a hearing for grandma?

[*Shrugs.*] She was arrested, so they gave her a hearing. She was arrested in March and had her hearing in April. She was released in June. By that time we were already at Santa Anita [racetrack that served as an "assembly center" while permanent camps were being built].

Who conducted the hearing?

I thought it was the army, but it was actually something called the Alien Enemy Hearing Board. It was part of the Department of Justice.

Was it a hearing or a trial?

It amounted to the same thing. Either way, she had no one to defend her.

DEPARTMENT OF JUSTICE
ALIEN ENEMY HEARING BOARD
Southern District of California
In the Matter of the Detention of
YOSHI IMAMOTO
NOTICE OF HEARING

To: YOSHI IMAMOTO
(Alien Enemy)

You are hereby notified that the above matter will be brought on for hearing before this Board at Room 600 in the Federal Bldg. at 312 N. Spring St. Los Angeles, California on the 17th day of April, 1942, at 9 o'clock in the forenoon or as soon thereafter as the matter can be reached.
Dated: Los Angeles, California, April 14, 1942

Wm. Fleet Palmer
United States Attorney
Southern District of California

NOTE: In the said hearing a relative, friend, or other adviser of yours may be present, but such person will not be permitted to act for you in the capacity of attorney.

(Copy to the Immigration and Naturalization Service, Federal Bureau of Investigation, the Hearing Board, and the Attorney General.)

[*Thinks.*] I didn't know this at the time, but my sisters got people to write letters vouching for mother and father. For their loyalty. These people did so willingly. They were longtime friends.

Excelsior Union High School
Ralph F. Burnight, District Superintendent
Norwalk, California
March 30, 1942

United States District Attorney
Federal Building
Los Angeles, Calif

Attention of Mr. John M. Gault
Asst. U.S. District Attorney

Dear Sir:

I have known Mr. and Mrs. Imamoto for a number of years. Because Mr. Imamoto has been in charge of the Japanese Language School in Norwalk and also because they have had children in our school who have taken an active part in the musical activities of the school[,] I have come to know them better than I have most of the other Japanese in our district. Both Mr. and Mrs. Imamoto are very earnest Christians, being members of the Hynes Japanese Baptist Church. As such they have not been in sympathy with the beliefs of the Shintoists concerning ancestor worship or the worship of the Emperor of Japan. I think that one of the best ways of knowing what has been taught the children in the language school is the attitude these same children have shown when they have come to the regular public schools. With very few exceptions, the children from the Norwalk Japanese School have been most cooperative and by their chance remarks and their discussions have given every indication that they feel a strong loyalty to the United States. The few exceptions to this have been rather noticeable and we at school have attributed this to home influence rather than to the teaching they have received at the Japanese school.

On many occasions I have heard both Mr. and Mrs. Imamoto make statements indicating their loyalty to the United States and their adherence to the ideals of the United States and to Christianity. They have stated on a number of occasions, and their actions have indicated the sincerity of their beliefs, that they wished to make loyal American citizens out of the Japanese children who come under their influence. I have never heard one word from either of them which could be interpreted as being disloyal. Neither have I heard the slightest rumor which would indicate that such an attitude had been expressed either by word or action at any other time.

I am willing to personally vouch for either of them.

Sincerely,
[signed] Ralph F. Burnight
District Superintendent

D. S. Myer
War Relocation Authority

Dear Sir:

We have known Mrs. Yoshiko Imamoto for many years. She is a very fine Christian woman well thought of in our community and an unusually good mother. She sews very nicely and often sewed for the needy in our town [and] also knitted for the Red Cross. I'm sure she could be trusted anywhere.

Sincerely yours,
Mrs. J. G. Allen

That took a lot of courage, don't you think? To stand up for grandma and grandpa when everyone else was against them?

[*Puzzled.*] But there was no reason why they wouldn't. They were our friends. They were [part of our] church. It would have been terrible if they didn't.

Who were the Allens?

They were advisors at the Baptist church in Garden Grove—we'd kept in touch with them after we moved to Norwalk.

What were advisors?

It was sort of like—you had an ethnic group. And then you had these white couples. They were the advisors. They were always at our services.

Other people helped, too. Rev. Nicholson—Rev. Herbert Nicholson—was a witness at mother's hearing. He also served as the interpreter. He was a Quaker—he'd been a missionary in Japan, so he spoke Japanese. Apparently, they were really hard on her, and afterward he told them that mother was a fine Christian woman and they had no business treating her like that. He wrote a book about his experiences, and in it he talks about her hearing:

The Department of Justice man was very large and rather rough of speech. He had a Japanese textbook, which Mrs. Imamoto said she used. He turned to a page that had a Japanese soldier and rising sun flag on it and asked if she taught that page. She said that she replaced the flag with the stars and stripes and taught loyalty to America. When he asked which way she would shoot if standing between the Japanese army and that of the USA, she said she was a Christian and would not shoot either way.[7]

What was the result of the hearing?
She was paroled.

MEMORANDUM FOR CHIEF OF REVIEWING SECTION
ALIEN ENEMY CONTROL UNIT
May 14, 1942
YOSHIDO [YOSHIKO] (YOSHI) IMAMOTO   142–13–2–12–2411
765 Gridley Road
[So. Dist. Calif.]
Norwalk, California

BOARD'S RECOMMENDATION: Parole.

CHARGE: A teacher in a Japanese language school.

STATEMENT: The F.B.I. report reflects subject was apprehended March 13, 1942, as being a teacher in a Japanese language school at Norwalk, California. A search of subject's premises at or near the time of her apprehension resulted in the seizure of a number of articles, to-wit: 6 religious pamphlets published in Japan, 1 book on information of Los Angeles published in Japan, one high school text book of physical education published in Japan, 3 exercise books published in Japan, 1 book of the Daughters of the American Revolution published in the United States, 1 Japanese grammar published in Japan, 2 homework books published in Japan[,] and others. It appears in the report that she has been a teacher in a Japanese school at Norwalk about 5 years.

The questionnaire discloses that she was born in Japan, was 45 years old, and married. She attended the grammar and preparatory schools and a sewing school in Japan. She speaks Japanese and English, entered the United States legally as an immigrant for permanent residence and states that her purpose in coming principally was to get married and make her home in the United States. She is registered as an alien under the Act of 1940. She claims to be skilled as a dressmaker and seamstress and is a housewife in her own home. Her husband was born in Japan and entered the United States in 1909. He is also a teacher in a Japanese school. They have four daughters whose ages are 22, 21, 18, and 15, all born and educated in the United States, having attended American schools in California. Her parents are living in Japan, her father being 87 years of age [inaccurate: he committed suicide fifteen

---

7. Rev. Herbert V. Nicholson, *Treasure in Earthen Vessels* (Whittier, CA: Penn Lithographics, Inc., 1974), 67.

years earlier] and her mother 75. Two brothers and two sisters are living there; her brothers, she states, are physically unable to serve in the Japanese army. She reads no foreign language newspapers and belongs to no associations. Her husband, however, is Secretary of the Japanese Farmers Association of Norwalk, California.

Subject testified before the Hearing Board and seemed to have made a favorable impression. She testified that she did not teach pupils loyalty to Japan nor the Japanese flag, that she is a Christian and belongs to the Friends (Quaker) Church, that she had both the Japanese and American flags in her school but never had ceremonies with reference to the Japanese flag though every Saturday they would raise the American flag and salute it and bow to it. Her children are all girls and they never have been registered with the Japanese consul. She felt sorry for the people of China and did not want Japan to win over China but does not hope that Japan will conquer China but she hopes for peace. She has never been back to Japan since her first arrival and she is with the United States. Her feelings are the same as her children's. She hopes the United States wins. She lives in this country and, therefore, with her children, she is always for this country. America is her country. She thinks more of the United States.

Rev. H. V. Nicholson was a witness for the alien and stated that he was a missionary to Japan for 25 years and is connected with the Friends (Quaker) Church. Speaking of the books used in the Japanese schools he said the books that were gotten out last year were absolutely impossible. No language school in this country is using them. The Editorial Committee felt it was necessary to get out another book and they had them ready last September. They were run off in a mimeograph machine because they couldn't use the other ones. It was impossible to use the other ones in this country. Quite a few of the schools dropped these Japanese books because they were absurd. He found a number of small schools where they used no books at all but taught just conversation; that the purpose of these schools was to teach the pupils enough Japanese so they could understand the folks at home; that this particular school was very loyal to America and feels that the alien and her whole family are 100% loyal Americans.

The following is an excerpt from the report and recommendation of the Hearing Board: "It appears from the evidence adduced at the hearing the subject Yoshido Imamoto is a Christian (Quaker) and has taught loyalty to the United States although in a Japanese language school; that she hopes for a United States victory over Japan; that all of her children are American citizens; the Rev. H. V. Nicholson, a missionary of the Quaker religion testified in her behalf and vouched for her complete loyalty to the United States.

CONCLUSION AND RECOMMENDATION: In view of the subject's conduct since being in this country and of the fact that she had educated her children in American schools and has not registered them with the Japanese consulate for dual citizenship and has stated so clearly and firmly that she prefers the United States to Japan and hopes that it will win over Japan, and in view of the testimony of Rev. Nicholson before the Hearing Board[,] I conclude that the subject is eligible for release except for the fact that her parole would probably afford a protection for her against the persuasion of other Japanese. I, therefore, recommend that she be paroled.

(unsigned)

In the Matter of:

YOSHI IMAMOTO,
Alien Enemy D.J.
File No. 146–13–2–12–2411

ORDER

WHEREAS,   Yoshi Imamoto, of Norwalk, California,
a subject of Japan, over the age of fourteen years, is within the United States and not a naturalized citizen thereof and has heretofore been apprehended as being potentially dangerous to the public peace and safety of the United States; and,

WHEREAS, the Alien Enemy Hearing Board has recommended that said alien enemy be paroled; NOW, THEREFORE, upon consideration of the evidence before me,

IT IS ORDERED that said alien enemy be paroled in the custody of a suitable United States citizen, not related to the alien, to be selected by the Hearing Board for the Southern District of California upon consultation with a representative of the Immigration and Naturalization Service; that the parole be conditioned upon the alien enemy's reporting his [her] activities to his sponsor twice a month and to the District Parole Officer once a month; and that the said parole be further conditioned upon the execution of and compliance with the sponsor's and parolee's agreements provided by the Immigration and Naturalization Service.

May 18, 1942
Certified a true copy:
Certified a true copy:

(signed) Francis Biddle
ATTORNEY GENERAL
(signed) S. A. Diana
Chief, Alien Parole Section

Did you know she had been paroled?

No. Not right away.

There was no rhyme or reason to it. Mike Wada's mother had her hearing at about the same time, but instead of being released, she was sent to a prison in Seagoville, Texas. She was there for several years. She was so sweet—not a mean bone in her body. Just a wonderful lady, and they sent her to prison.

When was grandpa's hearing?

Well, he had two. The first was also in April [April 21, 1942, according to an FBI report].

Was it held by the Alien Enemy Hearing Board?

Yes. Also in Los Angeles. Neither was open to the public. After the first one, he was sent from Tujunga to a prison in Santa Fe.

So whatever it was that he was charged with, he was found guilty.

Yes. He was declared a prisoner of war.

According to an FBI document, the Alien Enemy Hearing Board was made up of three people, and all three agreed that he should be paroled. But the attorney general overruled them and ordered that he be sent to prison.

MEMORANDUM TO CHIEF OF REVIEW SECTION
ALIEN ENEMY CONTROL UNIT

JAMES ZEMICHI [ZENICHI] IMAMOTO   146–13–2–12–1580
765 No. Gridley Road   S.D. CAL
Norwalk, California

HEARING BOARD RECOMMENDATION: Parole.

CHARGE: Dangerous alien enemy.

STATEMENT: Subject was apprehended March 13, 1942, upon information that he was a teacher in a Japanese language school which schools are indirectly controlled by the Japanese Government through text books approved in Japan, designed to instill patriotism and loyalty to the Emperor, the schools being regarded as a possible source for the dissemination of Japanese propaganda. To an agent of the F. B. I., subject admitted that he is secretary of the Japanese language school, teaches on Saturday and that he subscribed and reads the Rafu Shimpo and the Japanese Daily News, both Japanese language papers.

Subject is 53 years old and married. His school education consists of 8 years in the grammar school in Japan, 1 year in the intermediate school in Berkeley, California[,] and 2 years at the University of California. He speaks, reads and understands the Japanese and English languages. He states that he entered the United States in 1907 to study, from Kobe[,] Japan, but that he is not in possession of a passport or traveling documents of any kind. He is registered under the Act of 1940 as an alien, but is not registered under the Selective Service and training Act. He states that his occupation is that of secretary for the Japanese Farmers Association and a teacher for the Japanese school of Norwalk, California, and receives a salary of $105.00 a month and that he formerly taught at the Garden Grove Japanese School.

It appears that subject has about $410.00 in a savings account in a California bank and about 1500 yen on deposit in the Yokohama Specie Bank in Japan. He has a house in Japan which he inherited from his father. His wife was born in Japan. She entered the United States in 1918. They have four children, all girls, and born in the United States. Upon birth, the subject registered all of his children with the Japanese Consul in Los Angeles thus giving them a dual citizenship. However, at the request of his children, he recently instituted cancellation proceedings inasmuch as the children did not desire the Japanese citizenship which their father had gained for them. The oldest daughter[,] who was a senior at the University of California this year, [is] training to teach; the second daughter is studying to be a nurse[;] the third was in Fullerton Junior College. The youngest was in the Excelsior Union High. All four of his children are members of the Baptist Church while subject's wife is a member of the Christian Church and he himself is a member of the Presbyterian Church. Subject and his family have lived in this country continuously since his arrival in 1907. According to his testimony, the subject taught the Japanese language school only on Saturdays and he only taught the Japanese language and not Japanese customs.

In his testimony before the Hearing Board, the subject stated that in the event of an invasion and the obeying a command of the Emperor, he naturally would have to obey, presumably because he is a subject of that country. He said, however, he would like to go back to Japan sometime to visit but he preferred to live in this country. He preferred the American democratic form of Government to the Japanese Government, but he stated he did not know much about the latter, but he was positive he would prefer to live under the democratic form of Government rather than under the Japanese Emperor.

In its summary and recommendation the Board stated:

"In spite of subject's connection as a teacher in a Japanese language school and secretary of the Japanese Farmers Association, the Board believes there is sufficient countervailing circumstances brought out in his interview to justify a parole. We believe subject to be honest and sincere. He is a teacher type and not a military type in any way, and in addition appeared to be a Christian in his attitude."

FEDERAL BUREAU OF INVESTIGATION

DATE: Jan. 28, 1943   FILE NO. 100–12002

TITLE: JAMES ZENICHI IMAMOTO, alias Zenichi Imamoto.

CHARACTER OF CASE: INTERNAL SECURITY—ALIEN ENEMY CONTROL.

DETAILS: On December 15, 1942, the Alien Enemy Hearing Board reviewed the letters in support of subject's application for re-hearing as well as the original basis for the subject's internment. In the original hearing of the subject held April 21, 1942, the Alien Enemy Hearing Board had unanimously recommended that the subject be paroled. However, the Attorney General had subsequently ordered the internment of the subject. The Alien Enemy Hearing Board again unanimously recommended that the subject be paroled and united with his family at a war relocation camp.

The Board was composed of the following individuals: LYNN G. PETER-SON, Chairman, HARRY A. WISHARD, and GARDNER TURRILL. Assistant United States Attorney ATTILIO DI GIROLAMO and the writer (Special Agent W. J. O'Connor) also attended the re-hearing of the subject.

That's what really bowled me over—that these people unanimously thought he should be paroled, but the attorney general overruled them. I didn't realize this had happened until I got those papers and was looking through them.

Was this the attorney general for California?

No. For the entire country. His name was Biddle [Francis, 58th attorney general, 1941–1945].

What did grandpa mean when he said he would "naturally have to obey" the emperor?

I think his point of view was that Japan was his mother country and America was his adopted country. America would not allow him to become a citizen, but he was not going to do anything to harm either country. I thought he had a lot of integrity to take this position.

Was he able to appeal?

No. It was similar to what's happening now with the Patriot Law. Those people were arrested with no chance of having a lawyer. Not that father could have afforded one.

Honourable Francis D. Biddle
Attorney General of the States
Washington, D.C.

Excellency:

Under the most tragic circumstance, I was terribly nervous at the Parole Board Hearing which I had April 21, 1942, at Alien Detention Station, Santa Fe, New Mexico. It was soon after I heard from my family that my wife, Yoshiko Imamoto was detained in the Immigration and Naturalization Service, San Pedro, California, leaving our daughters, Marion Imamoto 18 years old and Alice Imamoto 15 years old without parental care. The other two daughters were not at home, the eldest of whom was a student of the University of California, and the other was studying at the County Hospital, Orange County. [Inaccurate: Lily was at a nursing school in Oakland.]

Thirty five years ago, I migrated to this country in order to live democratic way of life. I never went back to Japan since then, and now America is my mother country. While I am an adopted resident, I do not know any country well enough to love but this country, United States of America. I proud myself to be an American who have four American daughters who are born in this country. I proud of my daughters, every one of them, Grace, Lily, Marion, and Alice. They were born in this country and educated in the American way, highly talented in music. Especially Alice, the youngest one[,] played piano and was honoured by Paderewski to be a born genius. I am really thankful to the country whose culture gave birth to her talent. Moreover, they are Christians serving as young people's leaders in the Church to which I belonged more than thirty years. They are always asking me why [a] Christian spirited and highly Americanized father can be interned for [the] duration of war.

I cannot see myself any reason to be interned. If it is only because I am [a] Japanese national, I should like to inform it to my daughters, who are Americans not only by birth but ideological[l]y. They may think that I am an un-American, being interned. I am an American, I believe, and yet I am interned—it cannot be. Let me tell them the reason. Otherwise, my daughters may be taken away into suspicion and cinicism [sic]. They should not lose their faith in Christ and America. I pray that they remain to be Christian and American all through their lives.

I should like to ask your authority in the above reasons to re-open the hearing on my case in the earliest opportunity.
Respectfully Yours,

(signed) Zenichi Imamoto, 30–A
U.S. Immig. and Natur. Service
Santa Fe, New Mexico

Okay, I have to ask. What did grandpa mean when he said you were honored by Paderewski to be a born genius?

[*Laughs.*]

Who was Paderewski?

He was a concert pianist. One of the greats. He was also the premier of Poland. Ignace Paderewski.

Why did grandpa say that?

I don't know.

Did you meet Paderewski?

I played for him.

What do you mean?

[*Reluctant.*] Well, in those days people traveled by train—there were no planes—and he had a private railroad car. He'd go from city to city playing concerts. He had a piano tuner, a cook, a valet, and a poker player, all traveling with him.

A poker player?

[*Laughs.*] He played poker, so he had a poker player. I imagine the piano tuner and the cook played poker, too.

He performed in Washington, New York, the Chicago Exhibition. I went to his car—it was parked in a rail yard in Los Angeles—and played for him. I was about eight. We knew some people in common—grandpa knew a Japanese man who knew these people who were friends of Paderewski. That's how it was arranged.

What was he like?

Well, in his pictures he looked so fierce, but he was very nice. He asked me to play on his piano. He wrote a nice thing in my autograph book. What else could he say? [*Laughs.*]

Anyway, father was in Santa Fe for four months, from April to August of '42. After that he was sent to another prison in New Mexico. Lordsburg.

He was in Lordsburg for six months. He had his second hearing in January of '43 and was allowed to return to us in February. He was in prison for a total of eleven months. By that time we were in Jerome [Arkansas].

So, whatever happened at the second hearing, he was allowed to leave prison.
  Whatever.

Was he still considered a prisoner of war?
  No, he was considered a parolee.

  Did you know that when he came to Washington [after the war] he was still considered a parolee? He and mother had to report to the Immigration and Naturalization Service twice a month and to a district parole officer once a month. They had to do that for at least two years, even though the war was over.

  [*Pauses.*] So that's how it went. Mother and father were arrested on March 13. After that Marion and I were alone for two weeks. After Grace and Lily came home, the four of us were together for two more weeks. Then we had to leave.

Chapter Six

What was your first impression of Mississippi?

KEN

That it was cold and ugly. Mississippi is dull—scrub pines and maple trees. Oak. It's not green, like Maryland.

Much of it is vague. I remember that they had trucks ready to take us to the camp, and that the camp itself was outside of town, maybe five miles away, but I have no recollection of anyone telling us where to go. I don't know how they assigned us to different companies, for example   and there were about 3,000 of us arriving at the same time.

The camp itself was very bleak. No grass. Just sandy soil. They put us in barracks, a twelve-man squad to each barrack. The barracks had cracks in the walls, so the wind came right through. There was a potbellied stove in which we burned coal, but it didn't heat the whole cabin. And because there was no grass, they had to build ramps so we wouldn't be tramping through the mud when it rained.

Is that how many were in the 442nd? Three thousand?

No. The regiment was eventually filled up with mainland Nisei who came from the camps. There were about 3,000 from Hawaii and 1,500 from the mainland, so the total was 4,500 or so.

Did you know the unit was going to be made up entirely of Japanese Americans?

Yes, but we didn't know it would be called the 442nd until we arrived at Camp Shelby. That was so we could let our families know how to get in touch with us.

We were divided into three battalions—First, Second, and Third. Each battalion had four companies, each company had four platoons, and each platoon had three twelve-man squads.

I was in the First Battalion, Company A, Third Platoon. Within the Third Platoon I was originally in the Third Squad, but, as I said, I was transferred to the First Squad.

Why was it called a regimental combat team?

Because we were supposed to be used as a force independent of other divisions. See, a regular regiment is made up of three infantry battalions. But we had our own artillery [the 522nd Field Artillery Battalion], our own engineers [the 232nd Combat Engineer Company]—they built bridges and roads and whatnot—and our own antitank company. We also had what was called a cannon company—big guns. So we were essentially a built-up infantry regiment.

As it turned out, though, we were always attached to another division. Initially, in Italy, it was the Iowa Division—the 34th "Red Bull" Division.

Guys from Iowa?

[*Nods.*] Their patch was a red bull, so we all wore patches with a red bull.

What were the other divisions?

In France it was the 36th—the Texas Division with the Lost Battalion—and back in Italy, toward the end of the war, it was the 92nd. That was the all-black division.

Why were you attached to other divisions?

Battles are typically fought by divisions, which are roughly 20,000 men. We were only a regiment of 5,000, so they had to put us somewhere. It's all determined higher up, usually based on need.

Getting back to the regiment being filled up with mainland Nisei—I've heard you talk about fights between Japanese Americans from Hawaii and those from the mainland. What was that all about?

[*Thinks.*] For some reason, the only people who were made noncommissioned officers—the corporals and sergeants—were mainland Nisei. Not mainland Nisei from the camps, but Nisei who, like those in the 100th, had been drafted before the war. This created a lot of hard feelings, because

66

they were given all the authority. They became the leaders, and we had no chance to compete for those positions. I didn't like many of them. I thought they were arrogant.

Is that how it started?

That's how it started, but there was more to it than that, because the Nisei who came [later] from the camps didn't get those positions either—they were privates like us—and still there were fights. It was a cultural problem. There was a lot of misunderstanding. And the mainland guys were badly outnumbered.

What do you mean by a cultural problem?

Well, I don't know how it is with young people today [in Hawaii], but in my day the only people who spoke good English were the whites, and they were the bosses. They had everything, and we had nothing. The mainland Nisei, of course, spoke good English, so when the Hawaii-born Nisei heard them talk it brought up bad feelings. The expression was, "Don't act *haolefied*." [*Haole* is the Hawaiian word for "Caucasian."] That's my assessment, anyway.

How bad was it?

It was pretty bad. And I think in general the Hawaiian boys tended to be cowardly about it. They'd have three guys, for example, beating up one guy. The one guy had no chance. This happened to one of our cook's helpers. When food was brought out to us in the fields, there was only so much for the whole company. Guys would be very hungry, and they'd say, "Put more on." But this guy wouldn't do that, because he had to make sure there was enough for everyone. So, because of that, one night—and this was how cowardly they were—three of them waited for him in the dark when he went to the bathroom, and as he was walking back to his barracks they jumped him. They beat him up so badly he ended up in the hospital. Three against one. [*Shakes his head.*] Some guys even went to other companies to beat people up. Someone in another company would tell them about some mainland guy they didn't like, so they'd go over there and beat up a guy they didn't even know.

It got so bad the battalion commander made four or five companies assemble in a big field. A stand had been set up, and he was up on that stand. He gave us hell for getting in so many fights. Not only among ourselves, but with white soldiers.

White troops were there?

White troops were training in the same area.

On one occasion—I didn't go—there was a dance in which white soldiers were mixed in with Nisei soldiers. A fight broke out. But the Nisei soldiers outnumbered the white soldiers by a large margin, and pretty soon the Nisei soldiers were beating up every white soldier there. I heard that some of the white soldiers were so desperate they were trying to climb the walls to get to the windows, but they'd get dragged back down and beaten up.

It's been said—even [Sen. Daniel] Inouye [D-Hawaii] said it—that the fighting stopped after some of the Hawaii boys went to one of the relocation camps in Arkansas, either Jerome or Rohwer.

ALICE

It was Jerome.

KEN

It was said that when the Hawaii boys saw how the mainland Japanese Americans were behind barbed wire with guards—armed guards—surrounding them, they began to think differently about them and the fighting stopped. But I don't think that's accurate. I didn't even know that some of the guys went to one of the camps. No one in my company went. And there were fights after that anyway.

I became friends with a guy who was originally from Hawaii—born in Honolulu—but he was going to school at Berkeley when the war broke out, so he was relocated, and he volunteered from one of the relocation camps. His name was Takei. Butch Takei—his real name was Robert, but we called him Butch. He came to the 442nd with a whole group of mainland Nisei, and because of that some of the Hawaiian boys thought he was a mainlander. One of them started picking on him. This guy Bragger? The guy in Lefty's squad who wanted to stay close to Lefty? He was the one picking on my friend. But unknown to Bragger, Butch was a boxer, and it got to a point where he wasn't going to put up with it anymore. He got a set of boxing gloves, threw a pair at Bragger and said, "Put these on. We're gonna go a few rounds." Bragger chickened out. [*Laughs.*]

68

A lot of these guys were fighters. One night our platoon went out to dinner in Hattiesburg. Thirty-six guys. We chartered a bus to bring us there and take us back. After dinner we boarded the bus and were waiting for one guy, and when he came on the bus he was crying. But crying in *anger*. We asked him what had happened, and he said he'd been peeing against the wall of the building and somebody came up and punched him. He'd been a featherweight boxing champion in Hawaii—his name was Oshiro, Henry Oshiro—and he was crying because he didn't get a chance to get back at the guy. [*Laughs.*] That's why he was crying. The guy punched him and took off.

When I came to Washington after the war—this was in '47—I arrived by train at Union Station and got in a cab. The cab driver had the patch of the 34th Division—the Iowa Division—on his windshield, so I asked if he'd been in the 34th. He said yes and turned around. He asked if I was in the 442nd and when I said yes he immediately told me about a friend of his who'd gone to Rome on a pass and got into a fight with a guy from the 442nd. He said three or four other guys from the 442nd jumped in and beat up his friend so badly he came back to camp with a battered face.

So even after they were overseas they were getting in fights?
They got in fights all the time.

Who organized the trip to the camps?
I don't know, but my guess is that just a small percentage of the men went. That's why I don't believe it made a big difference.

[To Alice.] Do you remember them coming to the camp?

ALICE

Vaguely. I was not into dating or anything like that. I was only fifteen—I might have turned sixteen by then. But the person who was responsible for that—to have this USO [United Service Organization]—was a woman named Mary—what was Mary's maiden name? Nakahara. She was also the advisor for our girls' club. We had a little club for teenagers.

What did they have for the soldiers?
Dances. We had barracks that were used as recreation halls.

How many soldiers went?
I think a few busloads.

KEN

I wish I had gone. I'd like to have seen a camp.

ALICE

It was probably no different from the army camps.

Don't you find it strange that both of you ended up in camps in the deep south? At the same time?
[*No reply from either.*]

KEN

Mom, how far is Hattiesburg from Jerome?

ALICE

You could look it up on a map.

[To Ken.] *Did you know that the rest of the regiment would be filled up with Nisei from the camps?*

KEN

No. Nobody said anything to us about that. And when they arrived, that was the first I heard of Japanese Americans being put in relocation camps. That was the very first time. There was one guy who joined our squad— I remember asking him where he was from. He said, "Poston." I said, "Poston? Is that in California?" Because everybody came from California. And he said, "No, it's in Arizona." I said, "You grew up in Poston, Arizona?" He said, "No, I didn't grow up in Arizona. I grew up in California." I asked him what he was doing in Poston, Arizona, and that's when he told me he had been in a relocation camp. That was the first I heard about it.

What did you think?
I wondered why they would volunteer to join the 442nd after they had been put into camps. All their rights as citizens taken away. Without trial. There was a sense of outrage in me. I admired them for being able to overlook that.

I'm reading a book about these guys who were drafted from Heart Mountain and a few other camps and refused to be inducted.[8] This was later in the war, when the 100th and the 442nd were suffering heavy casualties and needed replacements. The army wanted to maintain an all-Nisei regiment, and the only source was the Nisei in camps. They asked for volunteers, but there weren't enough, so they started drafting them. And these guys—there were about 300 of them—refused. On the grounds that they were locked up. Behind barbed wire. I give them a lot of credit for standing up for their rights. What they said was, "If you release our families and give us back our rights as citizens, we'll go." Of course the government wouldn't do that, so they refused to report. They had to stand trial as draft-dodgers and were sent to prison. Some of them were pretty young, and were later drafted and served in the Korean War.

They were all given presidential pardons [by Harry Truman] in 1947. Because it was wrong, what happened to them.

What did the guy from Poston have to say about coming from a relocation camp?
Not much. I didn't know him that well. So I didn't know what the conditions were like. I had no idea.

Do you remember his name?
That's another curious thing—that I remember his name. Henry Izumizaki. Isn't that an unusual name? [*Spells it.*] When I was going through the list of the dead [*holds up list handed out at the dedication ceremony for the National Japanese American Memorial*], I wanted to know how many men from my company in Camp Shelby had been killed, and I saw his name. Henry Izumizaki.

You didn't know until a few days ago that he had been killed?
No. I never saw him after I left the company to join the 100th.
[*Looks again at name on list.*] Henry S. Izumizaki. He was a quiet guy.

Did any of the mainland guys talk about the camps?
No.

8. Eric L. Muller, *Free to Die for Their Country* (Chicago: University of Chicago Press, 2001).

Why not?

[*Pauses.*] I don't know. It's like you, mom. When you got out of camp and went to school, I bet you didn't talk about camp life to your friends.

ALICE

Not for fifty years.

KEN

Nobody did. People didn't talk about it. I bet many of the friends you made in college didn't even realize you came from a camp.

ALICE

No.

Did you ever talk about your experiences with each other?

ALICE

No.

KEN

Never.

Why not?

ALICE

I guess I don't particularly like to live in the past.

KEN

It's just not something we ever did. Sit down and talk about it.
[*Thinks.*] I should mention this, too. When the 442nd was formed, anybody with a Japanese name or having Japanese blood was automatically sent to the 442nd. Regardless of their background. So in our squad at Camp Shelby we had two guys who were half-Japanese and half-white. I got to know both of them. They didn't look Japanese. One was named Kobayashi, but he'd dropped the "i," so it was Kobayash.

Where was he from?

New York. They were both from New York.

The other guy's name was French. Duclos. [*Pronounces with a silent "s."*] The guys called him Duclose. They didn't know any better. During mail call, you'd hear all these Japanese names: "Yamasaki!" "Sato!" "Miyazaki!" [*Pauses.*] "Duclose!" [*Laughs.*]

Kobayash, especially, was very sad. He would just lie on his bunk. He made no friends. He was completely out of place. Here were all these guys from Hawaii speaking pidgin, and he couldn't understand a word we were saying. I didn't know it, but both of them were trying to get transferred out. They shouldn't have been sent to us in the first place. Just because they had Japanese blood didn't mean they should have been in the 442nd. So eventually they were shipped out. I heard one of the guys talking to them, asking why they were transferring out. I didn't hear the explanation, but I heard this guy say, "I think you're making a big mistake." I don't know why he said that. I didn't blame them for wanting to get out.

[*Smiles.*] Did you know I tried to get out of training? Henry Nakasone, my good friend—he and I were sick of it. This was toward the end of our time in Hattiesburg. They were recruiting Nisei to go to a language school in Minnesota [Camp Savage] to be used as interpreters [in the Pacific], and we tried to sign up. [The Military Intelligence Service—MIS—was comprised of Nisei who served as interpreters with other American units, as well as units from England, Australia, New Zealand, and China. Their duties included interrogating prisoners of war, trying to persuade Japanese soldiers to surrender, and translating captured documents.9] Some of the guys had already been accepted. I never thought this was a way out for me. [*Laughs.*] But Henry said, "Why don't we apply?" I told him, "Henry, I don't know any Japanese. I could never go to language school." He said, "Oh, c'mon. Take the test with me." So I did. He went in first, was interviewed, and came out in a matter of minutes.

Did he speak Japanese?

Yes. He was very good. So now it was my turn. I went in, and there was this Nisei sergeant sitting behind a desk. He had three books. He said, "Read this." He gave me the hardest book first. I opened it up. I couldn't read a single word. [*Laughs.*] I said, "No, this is too hard for me," and gave it back. He said, "Try this one. This one is easier." So I opened the second book. It had easy Japanese characters mixed in with hard ones, but

9. *Go For Broke Education Foundation* Web site (www.goforbroke.org).

I said, "No, that's too hard for me, too." So he gave me the third book, which had the simplest Japanese—beginner's Japanese. I looked at it and said, "I know some of that!" [*Laughs.*] Finally I said, "Look. No point in kidding you. I don't know much Japanese. Even though I went to Japanese school, I don't know much. But I'd *like* to go to language school. I'm a good learner." He told me they'd look up my records to see how I scored, and if they thought I'd do well they would take me.

Well, they took me! They took Henry *and* me! So now we were waiting for our orders to ship out of the infantry and go to Minnesota. Every time we were digging foxholes Henry would say, "These could be the last fox- holes we dig in Mississippi!"

We kept waiting and waiting. Two weeks went by. Our orders were to be posted on a board, so we kept looking at that board. Nothing. Then one day we saw our names. We were on the list to go to Italy as replace- ments for the 100th. [*Laughs.*]

Why didn't they let you go to language school?

Oh, I think the captain found out we were trying to get out of the infan- try and put us on the list to go fight the Germans. [*Laughs.*] Within two weeks we were shipped out.

Chapter Seven

How did you find out you were going to have to leave?

ALICE

Rumors. The first were that we were going to Manzanar, in Northern California, and that we would need high-topped boots. So all four of us bought high-topped boots—leather boots that laced up to here. [*Touches leg below knee.*] Isn't that crazy? Some of the rumors turned out to be true, such as the one that said we would be allowed to take only what we could carry. But we certainly didn't need those boots.

Why Manzanar?

I don't know. I think because it was already open. [Lieutenant General John L. DeWitt, commanding general of the army's Western Defense Command, ordered in March of 1942 the establishment of two "reception centers," one at Manzanar in the Owens Valley of California and the other in Arizona near the California border, south of Parker Dam;[10] both became what were called "relocation centers"—Parker Center was renamed the Colorado River Relocation Center, though it was commonly referred to by its post office address, Poston.] But, in any event, we didn't go there.

We were among the early ones to be evacuated. Our family number, which was given to us when we arrived at Santa Anita, was 2183. That means that out of 120,000 [Japanese Americans forcibly relocated], our family was in the low 2,000s.

How were you notified? I've seen photographs of signs that were attached to telephone poles.

10. Page Smith, *Democracy on Trial* (New York: Simon and Schuster, 1995), 146.

WESTERN DEFENSE COMMAND AND FOURTH ARMY
WARTIME CIVIL CONTROL ADMINISTRATION
Presidio of San Francisco, California
April 1, 1942

INSTRUCTIONS
TO ALL PERSONS
OF JAPANESE ANCESTRY
Living in the Following Area:

All that portion of the City and County of San Francisco, State of California, lying generally west of the north-south line established by Junipero Serra Boulevard, Worchester Avenue, and Nineteenth Avenue, and lying generally north of the east-west line established by California Street, to the intersection of Market Street, and thence on Market Street to San Francisco Bay.

All Japanese persons, both alien and non-alien, will be evacuated from the above designated area by 12:00 o'clock noon Tuesday, April 7, 1942.

No Japanese person will be permitted to enter or leave the above described area after 8:00 A.M., Thursday, April 2, 1942, without obtaining special permission from the Provost Marshal at the Civil Control Station located at:

1701 Van Ness Avenue
San Francisco, California

The Civil Control Station is equipped to assist the Japanese population affected by this evacuation in the following ways:

1. Give advice and instructions on the evacuation.
2. Provide services with respect to the management, leasing, sale, storage or other disposition of most kinds of property including: real estate, business and professional equipment, buildings, household goods, boats, automobiles, livestock, etc.
3. Provide temporary residence elsewhere for all Japanese in family groups.
4. Transport persons and a limited amount of clothing and equipment to their new residence, as specified below.

The following Instructions Must Be Observed:

1. A responsible member of each family, preferably the head of the family, or the person in whose name most of the property is held, and each individual living alone, will report to the Civil Control Station to receive further instructions. This must be done between 8:00 A.M. and 5:00 P.M., Thursday, April 2, 1942, or between 8:00 A.M. and 5:00 P.M., Friday, April 3, 1942. . . .[11]

11. Allan Bosworth, *America's Concentration Camps* (New York: W.W. Norton & Co., 1967).

[*Nods.*] Signs were posted everywhere. Telephone poles. Storefronts. Libraries. There was no official notice to each family, so they had to make sure every Japanese American saw it.

What happened after that?

We had to clear out our house. Get rid of our things.

April 7, 1942

Dear Papa,

Thank you so much for the letter. We are very busy packing more books, throwing away our junks and getting things ready for storage. I have been busy sewing slacks and clothes for camp. Each of us have hiking boots now and eye goggles. I am glad that you like the robe we sent you.

This may be bad news but we can not take our cars so we thought the best thing to do is to let Miss Johnston use it and keep it for us. Those people who take their cars have to let the government store it and leave it on a hill or out in the open. If you think we should sell it please let us know.

Everyone who lived on the coast up to Artesia Street had to leave by Sunday night. The Nakagawa's live on this side of Artesia Street so they did not have to leave. We heard rumors that we have to leave this week or early part of next week. This side north of Artesia Street, Atlantic Street up to the Orange County line is next and so that includes Norwalk, Bellflower, Downey, Compton and Whittier. We are getting ready as quick as possible.

Mr. Burnight is helping us as much as possible. He will keep the cello for us, his friends will keep the stove, refrigerator and piano. Mrs. Yates is keeping our chinaware, silverware and mother's good tea set. Jerry [the family dog] is going to Mrs. Yates['s] friend who goes to Excelsior. It's going to be lonesome without Jerry. We can tell that Jerry misses you very much.

Last Thursday, the F.B.I. came to Norwalk and took Mr. Nawa, Fujita, Asawa, Kimoto, Kameyama, and Mr. Endow. Now they are all in Tuhunga. They took Mr. Ishikawa but much to our disgust he was released after a 5 hour questioning and now he thinks he's so good. I don't think that's fair to the rest of the people. He's so selfish and cruel. Mother says that Mr. Shizuoka is still in Tuhunga. It's so hard to go see her now because we have to get a traveling permit and getting across to the island. Those men were taken because their daughters or sons took Kendo, but I don't see why they didn't take Ishikawa. He's trying to run all Norwalk.

The Fujimoto family moved to Parlier near Fresno and Masato and Esao are going sometime this week. The Yamaga's, Hiraoka's and many from Norwalk have gone to Colorado.

We had our Easter service one week early because everyone was moving and only a few are left now. Mrs. Ogawa and Louise were baptized and also James Sasano and Masato Fujimoto.

We have to go where the rest go so probably we won't be sent to Owens Valley. The last group went to Santa Anita where the race track is near Pasadena. I heard that the Orange County people will be sent to the reception [assembly] center in Pomona fairgrounds. The people from Washington and north are being sent to Manzanar so probably we won't be sent there. I heard that it is very sandy and windy there all the time.

I can't buy a typewriter case since they do not make any more for that size so what should we do? I never got the paper for the car you were supposed to sign.

Mr. Ishikawa probably told the Terminal Island people to go with the Norwalk group so they are still here. I wonder if it's wise to get an American to stay in at this house to watch the things and if we can't do you want us to board up the windows? I am going to get Mr. Sieverson's affidavit tomorrow morning and we'll get one from Mr. Burnight and Nicolson's as soon as possible.

How is the climate there? Sorry I couldn't write in Japanese, but I just finished writing to mother and it takes so much time. Take care of yourself. We are all just fine. Mr. Nakamoto sold that radio so we don't have it anymore.

Your daughter,
Marion

Mr. Burnight took care of our musical instruments. He brought a truck and loaded up the piano and the cello and the violins. Can you imagine? He stored them at the Quaker church in Norwalk, and when we were at Santa Anita he came to see us and brought some of the instruments with him. He used to visit us.

What did he bring?

The violin—two violins. And when we went to Jerome—because we couldn't take them with us—he came back and got them. He took care of them and gave them back to us after the war. You know the little one that Molly [granddaughter] was playing? That's one of them.

But other things, like mother's good tea set? We didn't get that back. That went to my high school music teacher. She was my teacher for *The Pirates of Penzance* and *The Mikado*. The *HMS Pinafore*. Wilda Yates. Isn't it funny that I remember her name? We gave it to her to keep for us, but we never got it back.

Did you ever see her again?

Yes. We went to see her in the summer of '45—Grace was living in Whittier, which is near Norwalk, and I was visiting Grace from school [Oberlin College, Ohio]. It was difficult to get there, because we didn't have a car. We had to take a bus with a couple of transfers. And I remember seeing the tea set in her house.

Did you ask for it?

No.

Why not?

[*Pauses.*] I don't know. You know, we were very shy. Coming out of camp—we were scared.

What did you do with your other belongings?

I don't remember. All I remember is that there was so little time. There was absolutely no time. Lily remembers throwing things out of a second-story window. And that we had a bonfire.

Also, we lived out in the country. We didn't have the know-how on how to get rid of things. Where to take them, and so forth. Second-hand merchants would come in and buy entire households for twenty-five dollars. Some people drove their cars to Santa Anita, where there was some kind of mass selling. We didn't know about that.

[*Pauses.*] But for me the hardest thing was giving away our dog, Jerry. He was a little toy fox terrier. That was the hardest thing. To part with him. I don't even remember who got him.

April 13, 1942
Dear Daddy,

How are you? We are all fine except me because we just gave Jerry away to the nice girl in Bellflower who is going to take care of him. I was so sad that I came home and cried myself sick. Jerry was so close to us and one of the family that I didn't want to give him away.

We are all packed and ready to go so please do not worry about anything. We go tomorrow at 12 o'clock and leave Downey at 10 o'clock. Mr. Litsey is so kind to come after us and take us there. We have such a load that it's really tough to leave things behind. The Terminal Island people left this morning with [the] Ishikawas, so that's why we didn't want to go today. Tomorrow

Nawas, Nakagawas, Asawas, Endows, Chikamis and many of the Clearwater Church group also Harper Kazuo Sakaue and his family are going.

Last Wednesday we went to see mama in San Pedro and she was so glad to see Lily and Grace that we wanted to go again today but we could not get a travel permit. It seems hopeless for mother to get out yet, since the men are going to get a hearing first.

Mr. Sieverson, Delmet, Wilson, Burnight, Donovan, Nicholson, Litsey, [and] Sakaue have written affadavits for you and they have been notorized. Mr. Burnight took them to L.A. to Mr. Gault, a district attorney or lawyer who is flying to Santa Fe to the hearing so he has them. I'm waiting for the time when we can all get together[,] even if it has to be in a camp.

We are going to let Miss Johnston keep our typewriter, car, books and some clothes. We stored some books in a locked room at Fujimoto's. Mr. Allen took some books also. Today at 5 o'clock our piano, stove and refrigerator went on a truck to Mr. Burnight's friends. Mr. & Mrs. Yates are so good to us and come over to visit us quite often. Mr. Burnight is doing all he can to release mother first and also is concerned very much about you. We never found out if the good slippers we bought for you reached you.

Tonight we were invited to Dr. Bruff's home for dinner and they are such nice people. Every one of our friends are so good to us. Masato really helped us pack books and took us to see Mama a lot. Hiroshi Furutani comes over and helped us carry loads of boxes filled with junks up to our junk room and really was a great help to us.

[Tuesday] We are leaving today and it is sprinkling. I will write to you as soon as I reach Santa Anita.

Love,
Marion

The night before we left, we got phone calls all through the night. "Dirty Japs. Get out of town." That kind of thing. Grace finally called the operator and said we were going to leave our phone off the hook. It was really scary.

So that was the climate.

Chapter Eight

Who were your friends in basic training?

KEN

My friends? Henry Nakasone was one. He was in the squad I was transferred into. Nobuo Kajiwara was in that squad, too. George Yamasaki? Yammy? He was in it. We all became good friends. But I never made corporal. [*Laughs.*]

Do you remember all the men in that squad?

I can name seven or eight, but that's about it. I can picture the others, but I can't remember their names. I wasn't close friends with them.

Did they make it through the war?

No. Two were killed. One was a guy I didn't know very well. Nakano. Tsutomu Nakano. His name is on the wall, too.

What do you remember about him?

Only that he was very quiet. Didn't say much.

How was he killed?

I don't know. I didn't find out he was killed until a couple of days ago, too. I saw his name when I was going down the list.

The other was Nobuo Kajiwara. He was from the mainland. He and Henry and I—the three of us became close friends. We trained together and were shipped overseas together. And, initially, when we landed at Anzio, we were still together. But Henry and I, along with two others, were picked to become medics, and Kajiwara wasn't with us at the time. So he wasn't picked, and he later got killed. I heard about it through someone else.

[*Pauses.*] I felt very bad about that. I thought if he had stayed with us he might have lived.

Why?

Because the four of us survived. We made it through the war.

How was he killed?

He was attacking a German position. The story I heard was that he was about to lob a grenade. He had pulled the pin—you know, a grenade has a safety pin attached to it, and once you pull the pin you have to hold the handle down so it won't go off. If you release it, you have three seconds to get rid of it. You count "one, two, three," and throw it. So he had pulled the pin, but before he could get rid of it, he was shot. His hand released the grip, and the grenade exploded. His own grenade. Blasted him.

[*Pauses.*] The story I heard was that he didn't die right away—he was in such pain that he ran around screaming until he collapsed and died. So it was a horrible death.

Where did this happen?

Somewhere above Rome. I don't know where, exactly. Once we got separated, I never saw him again.

He was from the mainland?

He was from Oakland. I knew he had a sister, because he used to talk to me about her. I also knew he had a girlfriend, and that just before we went overseas, he became engaged. He never told me her name, though. But not too long ago, on a trip to visit the Sakurais [family of Alice's sister Marion, in Concord, California], I told Tomio [Marion's late husband] to ask around and see if there was anyone who knew the Kajiwara family. I wanted to get in touch with them and talk to them about their son. Well, on our last visit before Tomio died [in 1996], he told me he had found someone who knew Kajiwara's sister, and he gave me her phone number. She was living in a place called San Leandro. So I called her. We talked for quite a while. She said they brought his body back to California, and he was buried in a veteran's cemetery in San Francisco. She even gave me his grave number. So maybe someday I'll visit the grave.

Did she know who you were?

She didn't indicate that she knew about me. But she did say that Henry Nakasone had gotten in touch with her, because somebody who was a friend of Nobuo's had made a painting of him from a picture, and Henry wanted to give it to her. So he gave her the painting.

[*Thinks.*] She asked me about something he had sent to her. He'd gone on pass to Rome with some of his friends—this was after we'd taken the city—and bought something for her. She described it to me and wanted to know if I knew anything about it. She didn't know what it was—in a letter he had said he would explain it to her when he got home.

What was it?

[*Shrugs helplessly.*] I don't know. I couldn't picture it, so I couldn't help her.

I made a rubbing of his name from the [National Japanese American] Memorial. I wanted to send it to her, but I don't have her address anymore. Maybe Marion has it.

One other thing. When I was talking to her, I said I knew Nobuo had a girlfriend, and that he was engaged to her. I asked whatever became of her. She said that she had gotten married, but the marriage didn't work out, so she got divorced. After that, I guess his sister lost touch with her.

What was he like?

Nobuo? [*Smiles.*] He was the most unlikely infantryman you ever saw. Very short and very squat. I'd say he was only about five-two. Maybe five-three. When we marched, we had our rifles in a sling and carried them over our shoulders. But he was so short the butt almost dragged along the ground. [*Laughs.*] It's hard to imagine someone like that fighting, being in a war.

He was a pleasant guy. A nice guy. I liked him. He never had a bad word to say about anybody. Never complained. Never complained about anything.

What else can you tell me about basic training?

That we were always hungry. [*Laughs.*] They fed us breakfast at three o'clock in the morning, and at that time they'd also give us a sandwich for lunch. We had to carry that sandwich with us. We wouldn't get dinner until much later in the day. So we were constantly hungry.

One day we saw these pigs—a mother pig with her babies. Four or five of the guys started chasing one of the babies, and eventually caught it. One guy had it under his arm—the intention was to kill it and cook it. But the farmer was standing by the fence. He asked, "What are you going to do with that?" We said, "We're gonna eat him." He said, "No, you're not. Let that thing go." So we let it go. [*Laughs.*]

We even chased a sheep once. We had our bayonets out and were going to kill it. There were three of us, but we couldn't catch it. We were running all over this field, chasing that sheep. I don't know how the hell we were going to cook it, but we were going to cook it and eat it. [*Laughs.*]

The best fried chicken I ever ate? We went right up to a farmhouse and knocked on the door. A lady answered. We said, "Could you kill a chicken and cook it for us? Fry it up for us? We'll pay you." She said, "Sure."

You went right up to her house?

[*Nods.*] We gave her ten dollars, which was a lot of money in those days.

Where did she get the chicken?

It was her chicken. She killed it, cleaned it, and cooked it. A little while later she brought it out to us. It tasted so good! We sat under a tree and ate it. Chicken. Fried chicken. [*Laughs.*]

[*Thinks.*] The first time we were out in the field using live ammunition? Our squad was lined up, and as we moved forward we were supposed to maintain that line. We were crawling through tall weeds—a target would flip up, and we'd have to get up and fire at it. So this target flipped up, and I got up on one knee and was about to pull the trigger when this guy popped up right in front of me. I almost pulled the trigger. I would have shot him right in the head. Boy, I dropped that gun. [*Laughs.*]

Did you ever tell him?

No. He never knew.

[*Smiles.*] On another occasion we had to guard German prisoners.

Why?

[*Thinks.*] The military had taken so many young men they didn't have enough to harvest the peanut crop. So they used German prisoners. They put us on trucks and drove us all the way to a place called Dothan, Alabama. We were there for about a week. The way the camp was set up, the Germans were in tents on one side of barbed wire and we were in tents on the other. Each morning they put us on separate trucks and drove us out to the peanut fields. The peanuts had been dug up, and the Germans were given rakes and told to put them in big stacks. At the end of the day, they put us back on the trucks and drove us back to camp.

What I remember was that on the first day, the Germans were eating the peanuts. They'd probably never seen peanuts before in their lives. They kept shelling them and eating them. Raw peanuts. All day long.

What were you doing?

Watching them. We had rifles. And at the end of the day, when we were back on the trucks, we suddenly realized that a lot of them had diarrhea. They were hanging their rear ends off the back, letting it out. [*Laughs.*] We were right behind them, laughing like hell. Isn't it interesting, the things you remember?

What did you think of them?

Well, they couldn't speak English and we couldn't speak German, so there was no dialogue.

But did you think, hey, these are the guys we're going to be fighting?

No. We didn't think of them as the enemy. At night they'd be singing German songs. We'd hear them singing.

[*Smiles.*] While we were there we went to a football game. A high-school football game. At night. I don't know who came up with the idea, but a whole bunch of us went. We were sitting in the stands, and one of our guys got up and started to do some cheerleading. So we all started cheering. "Dothan, Dothan, *pe hea oe!*" [*Laughs.*] We were using Hawaiian words. Do you know what *pe hea oe* means?

No.

It means, "How are you?" "Dothan, Dothan, *pe hea oe!*" [*Laughs.*] All the other people were looking at us, wondering who the hell we were and what the hell we were saying. We cheered throughout the entire game.

[*Shakes his head.*] I've been to a lot of small towns in the South. On weekend leave those were the only places we could go—other small towns in the South. So we'd go to places like Jackson, Mississippi. Jackson, Mississippi! Guys were wandering all over the South. One guy went to Bogalusa, Louisiana. Bogalusa, Louisiana!

Once I went with three guys to this little town—I don't even remember its name. It had a small hotel and a movie theater—we stayed at the hotel and went to a movie. [*Laughs.*] The next morning—this was Sunday—we were sitting on a curb, and one of the guys saw a squirrel and started chasing it. Pretty soon all four of us were chasing it. We chased it until it finally went up a tree. Because we had nothing to do, we sat underneath the tree and waited for it to come down. [*Laughs.*]

Years later, after I was discharged, I was walking in downtown Honolulu and saw this sailor sitting on a curb. He had a bag of potato chips. He was just sitting on the curb, eating those chips. Looking very lonely. I thought, "Gee, that's the way I was."

Another time, in Laurel, Mississippi, they were having a fair. They had a Ferris wheel, things like that. A farmer in coveralls came up to us. He'd been chewing tobacco—you could see the tobacco stain on his chin. [*Draws finger down chin.*] Every so often he'd spit. He said, "What are you boys?" You know, we're in uniform. "We're Japanese," we said. "You're Japanese. Anybody ever call you Japs?" One of us said, "Yeah." The farmer said, "What do you do when they call you Japs?" He said, "We cut off their balls," and reached into his pocket like he was going to pull out a knife. The farmer got so scared he moved away. [*Laughs.*]

Did you ever experience any prejudice?
Did I? No, I didn't.

Why not, do you suppose?
Well, we were a whole regiment. There were so many other guys you didn't feel alone. It wouldn't be like going to the South today and walking around a small town like Hattiesburg by yourself, being the only Japanese American around.

What about when you were with a small group?
Oh, nobody paid any attention to us. We could register in hotels, go to theaters. Nobody bothered us. Mind you, we were in uniform.

Were you aware of the segregation?
Oh sure. If we went on weekend pass to, say, New Orleans, we'd have to go by bus, and at the bus station the restrooms would have signs for

whites and coloreds. The drinking fountains would say "white" or "colored." [*Shakes his head.*] Even the drinking fountains. One for whites and one for blacks.

Which one did you use?

Well, that's an interesting thing. The buses—you can't imagine this—but in front of the last four seats or so there would be a panel. The blacks had to sit behind that panel. The whites were all in the front. But we didn't care where we sat, so if there were empty seats in the back, behind the partition, we'd sit there. One time the bus driver came back. He said, "You boys have to sit up front." He didn't want us sitting with the blacks. We said, "No, we like it here." This made him angry. He said, "If you don't come to the front I'm not moving this bus." We said fine, and just sat there. [*Laughs.*] Eventually he got tired of waiting—he had to keep a schedule—so he went back to the front and drove off.

So that bus driver. He clearly thought—.

That we were whites. Not black.

It's interesting he would make that distinction.

Yes, it is.

The movie theater in Hattiesburg? It had a separate entrance for blacks outside the main building. There were steps that went directly up to the second floor—they couldn't go in through the regular theater. They couldn't sit in the places where the whites were sitting. They had to sit in the balcony. There was a terrible expression for that: "Nigger Heaven." They were sitting in Nigger Heaven.

Did you and your buddies ever talk about it?

Sure. A lot of us talked about it. None of us liked it. It was terrible that they were treated this way. And that persisted for a long time.

[*Thinks.*] Did you know I went back to Hattiesburg? This was years later, during my last scientific meeting in New Orleans [in 1984]. Tad Kanda [friend and scientist from Japan, who worked with Ken at the National Institutes of Health in Bethesda, Maryland] had a car—he had driven to New Orleans with his family—and I asked if he would drive me to Hattiesburg to see Camp Shelby. It's a long drive—about 150 miles—but he did. I remember we stopped for gas outside Hattiesburg, and the gas station attendant asked me what I was. When I told him I was Japanese American, he said that his wife was a war bride from Japan. I thought, "Gee, what a place to come to from Japan." The deep South. No other Japanese around.

What was it like to see Camp Shelby again?

Completely different. When I was there the road between New Orleans and Hattiesburg had only two lanes, but now it's a superhighway. The camp itself is a National Guard training facility—we drove into it and I didn't recognize anything. The main gate that we went through on passes? Completely different. The little wooden barracks we lived in are now cinder block. So it was a big disappointment for me. We stayed about ten minutes. It took us three hours to get there, and we stayed ten minutes. [*Laughs.*] I told Tad, "Let's go. There's nothing for me here."

Did you leave the South at all during your time at Camp Shelby?

Yes. After basic training we were given two weeks furlough. This was in the fall—sometime in October. Gee, that was a big thing. Now we had a chance to see the big cities up north.

But I didn't have enough money. I'd written home for some, and they sent me a hundred dollars—I guess they all pitched in. But I needed more. I thought, boy, a hundred dollars isn't enough for two weeks.

The only way to get more money was through gambling, so I went to a big craps game. You don't know anything about craps, but I was betting on a sure thing. I did it five times, betting twenty bucks each time.

What was the sure thing?

Well, in craps they have what is called "pass" or "no pass." If you win, that's one pass. The odds are very slim that someone will roll three successive passes. So I would wait until someone made three successive passes, and on the fourth I'd bet "no pass." I did this five times, betting twenty dollars each time, and won each time. I made a hundred dollars and quit. So now I had two hundred dollars. [*Laughs.*]

Where did you go?

I went by train to Chicago and New York with a guy named George Teraoka. We'd gone to high school together. He died after the war. But his interests and mine were not the same, so when we got to New York City, he went his way and I went mine. We stayed at the YMCA on 34th Street, near Penn Station. We stayed at a YMCA in Chicago, too, because it was cheap. A dollar a night.

The setup in New York was great for servicemen. They had a central USO, and you could get tickets for all kinds of things. Rockefeller Center. Carnegie Hall. The Metropolitan. All free. I went to several plays.

By yourself?

[*Nods.*] I'd go there first thing in the morning, when it opened. They had a big board that listed all the things for which they had tickets. I'd go down the list and pick out what I liked. I used to like Fred Waring. Fred Waring and the Pennsylvanians—I guess they were from Pennsylvania. [*Laughs.*] He had a chorus and an orchestra, and they'd put on a half-hour show on the radio. So I went to that. It was fun. They performed on a stage. I used to know the names of some of the singers, the women singers.

ALICE

It was an all-girl string orchestra. They came from Sewanee [*spells it, though it's actually Shawnee*], Pennsylvania.

KEN

No. It wasn't all girls.

ALICE

Yes, it was.

KEN

Everything was radio—you know, in those days there was no TV. I guess you never listened to radio shows, so you wouldn't know. But back in those days everything was radio. They had comedy, like Jack Benny and Amos and Andy. And every Saturday afternoon they'd have *The Hit Parade*. The sponsor was Lucky Strikes. They'd have the top ten songs for the week and play all of them, starting with number ten down to number one. [*Imitates an announcer.*] "And number one for this week: 'Wishing,'" or something like that. Then they'd play it. Didn't you listen to that, mom? Music from the Hit Parade?

89

ALICE

I was studying.

KEN

And every day they'd have soap operas. Those were only about fifteen minutes long. They'd always end at a suspenseful moment, so you'd have to listen the next day. "Life Can be Beautiful," that was one.

What kind of music did you like?
 Oh, the popular songs. Jo Stafford. "I'll be Seeing You."

What about you, mom?

ALICE

I told you. I was studying.

Chapter Nine

What do you remember about the day you left?

ALICE

It was Tuesday, April 14, 1942.

But what do you remember about that day?
Nothing. I don't remember anything. I don't remember a thing.

Do you remember the bus ride from Norwalk to Santa Anita?
No.

Was it a public bus?
I don't know. I doubt it. I'm sure they chartered something.

How far is it from Norwalk to Santa Anita?
About thirty miles.

What was Santa Anita like?
It was a big racetrack. Still is.

What do you remember of your arrival?
Nothing. Not a thing.

What about your emotions?
[*Softly.*] Paul, I don't remember anything. It was just so horrible. What do you do? Father's gone, mother's gone. Everything's gone. You're in camp.

April 15, 1942

Dear Papa,

Here I am actually writing from our stable in Santa Anita, which we four have fixed up quite nicely. We have 2 rooms with one room as our bedroom and in the other front room we have our card table and 4 of the school chairs, our cardboard closet and we put up curtains. Each of us got an army blanket, mattress and a half size bed, so we put two together to make a whole single bed.

Mr. Litsey took us to the station and Mr. and Mrs. Scott were out to see us. Although it rained while we were at home and waiting for the busses to come[,] it cleared up and we are having good weather. Mr. Dirks has really been nice to us and helped us very much.

I really miss Jerry so much that I wish we could have all the gay times we used to have together and with Jerry. We were all so busy packing and Jerry knew that something was up because we didn't play with him as much as we used to do. I saw one dog today but I think Jerry would be happier with this nice girl and lots of yard to play on. Only worry is that I hope he does not run away and get lost. Mr. & Mrs. Yates will let us know and go see Jerry for us.

Today we were vaccinated for smallpox and one shot for typhoid. My arms hurt so much that I can barely write and I can't move the rest of the arm. Grace was writing but it hurts so much that she will finish it tomorrow.

Rev. Nicholson is going to Santa Fe for the hearing so he told me that tell the people that your friend is here and that you want him to be at your hearing. Ask the attorney or somebody that you want Rev. Nicholson at the hearing. I certainly hope and pray that we can all be together again real soon. Mother's hearing is going to be this Friday by the Alien Enemy Hearing Board at 9 o'clock A.M. Every one is quite sure of her release since she was only assisting and teaching primaries. Only trouble for her would be that she cannot eat any food made with milk, tomato and those American foods.

Today we saw Rev. Kikuchi and his family, Saikis, Shiraishis. There are thousands of people around here.

Next week we have our second typhoid shot and another one after that. I don't know how it will be after my first shot.

Thursday

Another day ahead with a sore arm. I hope you are feeling alright. We walk so much around here that by the time we get home after eating we are so tired that we feel like eating again. Well I must close now so take care of yourself.

Your daughter,
Marion

What were the living conditions like?

The living conditions were that we lived in stables. We had two rooms—the stall, which was big enough for a horse to stand in, and an inner room. But the walls throughout the building didn't go all the way to the ceiling, so it was open up there. You could hear everything. We had one light per stall.

When summer came it got really hot. We slept on cots, and the floor was tar, and I remember the legs of our cots would sink into the tar. And you know how manure smells.

The mattresses were rough—brown and white lumpy ticking. We didn't have to make them ourselves, though. Other people had to stuff straw into sacks, but we didn't have to do that.

You could see straw sticking out of the walls, because they had simply whitewashed everything. They were in such a hurry—they had to house 18,000 of us.

We were there from April until October. Six months. So we were there when it was hot in the summer and we were there when it turned cold in the fall.

Did everyone live in stalls?

No. There were too many of us. They built barracks out in the parking lots.

What about the infield?

They didn't touch the infield. We weren't allowed on the infield or the track.

I read in *Seabiscuit* that a family named Tanaka [actually Sato] lived in Seabiscuit's stall.[12] It was called the "Kaiser Suite" because one wall had been knocked down to combine two stalls. So the place where he slept was twice as big as the place where five of us [after her mother joined them] slept.

What about meals? How did they feed everyone?

There were about five mess halls, and each one fed three to four thousand people. We were in the first mess hall. They were referred to by color. Ours was the green mess hall.

12. Laura Hillenbrand, *Seabiscuit: An American Legend* (New York: Ballantine Books, 2001), 117.

What was the food like?

Inedible. Literally inedible. Rutabaga stew. You know what rutabagas are? They're like turnips. We were always hungry.

At one point Grace asked Dr. Bruff to get some things for us. I think he got them from the church. He brought a toaster—it had an open grill, and you put two pieces of bread on top. We would bring bread back from the mess hall and toast it.

Who was Dr. Bruff?

[*Fondly.*] Dr. Bruff—Dr. William Bruff—was a practicing physician who lived in Whittier. When the Terminal Island people were ordered to leave their homes within forty-eight hours, he was one of those [with the American Friends Service Committee] who helped them find places to live.

Did you know him before all this happened?

No. He did it out of the goodness of his heart. He did so much for us. He gave scholarships to people—and he was not a wealthy man. Later he gave Grace a job [after she left camp]—she lived with him and his family and worked in his office. I think Grace became a Quaker because of all that he did for us. He and his wife have passed away, but she still keeps in touch with the children.

He was an exceptional man. Exceptional. He came to see us on a number of occasions. He would bring things to us. He brought the diplomas to the [Excelsior] high school graduates. Those two folding chairs in the basement? We stored them in the Japanese school, and he brought them to us. [The chairs, made of wood with leather seats, are still in good shape sixty years later; written in bold, black ink underneath each seat, to identify the family head and number, is: "Grace Imamoto 2183." "Mother hadn't joined us yet," Alice said.] It was a long drive for him, too—over an hour. He was concerned for us.

How did it feel to have someone from the outside visit you?

Well, you were standing there—there was a fence. You were on one side and he was on the other. He wasn't allowed to come into the camp. I don't know how they let us know he was there—we didn't have a telephone. Someone must have gotten us. But I don't know how long he had to wait.

No, I mean emotionally.
I don't remember.

April 26, 1942

Dear Papa,

How are you? I'm so sorry that all of us do not write sooner and more often. We did not hear from you or mother, so we began to worry whether you received our letters or not. We are all in the best of health but after our second typhoid shot we had Wednesday Lily, Alice and I were sick in bed for 2 days. The first shot made our arms sore, but the second one made many sick in the stomach and caused headaches, vomiting, chills, diarrhea and really made us sick. The third and last shot comes on Wednesday again and I heard that it causes chills in the legs.

Lily is trying to work in the hospital, but as yet she can't until she sees the head nurse. Grace is still working in the recreational department teaching and playing the piano for the youngsters. Lily is also teaching Sunday School which is held in the big grandstand.

We are hoping that you are in the best of health. Rev. Nicholson went to Santa Fe, New Mexico or is going so I wondered if you had your trial or hearing yet. Please let us know. We are anxious to hear about your camp life because all the other men tell much.

Yesterday Mrs. Yates and Alice's friend from Norwalk came to visit us and we were certainly happy. She's so nice to us and Mr. Yates wanted to come too but he had to go to a track meet since he is a track coach at Downey High School. We had her buy some crackers, jams and sweater[s] for us[,]so she brought them[,] and Miss Rankins, Vice Principal at Excelsior bought us a box of cookies.

We also saw Harry Murakami and his family and they were so kind to give us a big box full of apples and oranges. Even though we have to go through a lot of trouble to have visitors, it's worth it. We had to walk about 1 mile to the main gate, after we get a permit to see the people.

Rev. Ishikawa still won't say even hello to us so we ignore him. Today Alice had to play for the adult meeting and Ishikawa preached thinking he was a big shot. He told the people so much lies about himself that if they only knew the truth about him, they sure would hate him. He told them that he was so poor that he couldn't even eat breakfast and here they feed him so good. That big liar.

Mother had her hearing already and Rev. Nicholson said that he spoke on her behalf. Order has to come from Washington before they can release mama. Gee it's so lonesome without you and mother that I feel so ashamed for myself for being so sharp tongued and talked back. I know now how bad

I had been and really miss both of you so much that it makes me cry to sleep. I hope and pray that we can all be together real soon.

Mrs. Yates went to see Jerry at this girl's house and said that he is just fine and is getting along fine with the people. Gee I miss him so much, but he's better off there than in here. All the rest of the dogs have been pounded so good thing Jerry is safe.

Today we went to see the Kageyamas and they are all fine. They looked in the paper every day worrying about you and since it was not in the paper they were very happy because they thought mother would be here also and talk about the good times we had before. They are still waiting so that they can see you and mother again. They send their best regards.

Tomorrow is ironing day so I must close and write to mama. Take care of yourself. Please write to us if you can.

Your daughter,
Marion

We got a letter from Itadani-san and he says that you don't write, since you are known for not writing letters. I think the Matsushiges will come here either Tuesday or Wednesday but I'm not sure.

Did you have jobs? Auntie Marion wrote about Lily trying to work in the hospital.

[*Nods.*] I don't know what the hospital was like, but they set up something.

Was she paid?

Yes, but I don't remember how much.

What were some of the other jobs?

[*Shrugs.*] Terry [Kobayashi] said she worked making camouflage nets.

What about bathroom facilities?

To provide showers for that many people? The lines were so long I remember getting up at midnight and walking to the grandstand to take one. The toilets were in a big room, all in a row, with just a board between them. No door, no curtain. So you'd always try to go to the very end. But at the end were knotholes that the boys would try to poke through. Their toilets were on the other side. So there was no privacy.

In order to wash clothes you had to go to the grandstand, which was a mile away, because that's where the hot water was. Marion and mother—after mother joined us—would borrow a child's wagon to carry them.

What about school?

There was no school to speak of. They tried to start one, but I don't remember going to more than two classes. Inside the grandstand? By the betting booths? There was a concrete concourse there, no place to sit, but they tried to hold classes there. The sister of one of my friends tried to teach us. Her name was Lois Asawa—she was Ruth Asawa's older sister. She was Grace's age, so she would have been in her early twenties.

You know who Ruth Asawa is, don't you? She's the artist who did the sculpture in the fountain in Ghirardelli Square. The mermaid? She also did the sculpture at Union Square—scenes of San Francisco in relief.

She was a good friend of mine at Excelsior. We sat next to each other in art class. One time—I told her about this—we had to draw a turtle, and she drew the cutest turtle. [*Laughs.*] I could copy things, but I couldn't create something like that. She was so creative.

She's done a lot of fountains. Her most famous work is in San Jose [the Japanese American Internment Memorial sculpture at the San Jose Federal Building, dedicated in 1994]. It's a long—what would you call a sculpture that's flat? A frieze? It's a frieze. One side depicts prewar Japanese experiences—scenes of farming, kids sitting in front of a schoolhouse, things like that. On the other side are wartime scenes. Relocation. It's our history. It was built at a foundry in Berkeley. She invited us to see it while it was in progress, so I have pictures of it. It's really something.

How many kids were in the class?

About six or seven.

I was reading about Tulare, which was a racetrack in Fresno that served as an assembly center. Apparently they had a well-structured school, so people who went there went right into school. But Santa Anita was just too big. The organization wasn't there.

We did have a newspaper, though. Produced by evacuees. Mimeographed. I don't know how it was circulated. They had some distinguished people on that staff. One of the cartoonists went on to become a professional cartoonist. Some of the journalists, too. You know who still has copies of it? Every issue? Katherine [Matsuki, family friend]. She was there, and kept every copy. They're fascinating. [Katherine Matsuki did, in fact, have every issue, from April 21 to October 7, 1942; the pages, yellowed and crumbling, are kept in a manila folder. "Everything in it was happy," she said. "All good news."]

97

SANTA ANITA PACEMAKER
SANTA ANITA ASSEMBLY CENTER, CALIFORNIA
Vol. 1, No. 1   April 21, 1942

RULES GIVEN FOR OBTAINING LOCAL VISITORS' PASSES
Permits Limited to Blood Relatives, Business Agents

Correct procedures for obtaining visitors' passes were released today in a special bulletin from the office of H. R. Armory, manager of the Santa Anita Assembly Center.

Due to the great number of visitors that are appearing daily at the Baldwin Avenue gate [the bulletin states], requesting permission to see residents of this center, the management has found it necessary to issue the following instructions for the guidance of all.

The following are the only type of visitors that are considered eligible:

1. Immediate blood relatives, fathers, mothers, sisters, brothers, grand-mothers, or grandfathers.
2. Business representatives with proper credentials, proving their identity. . . .

LAUNDRY NOW READY FOR USE

"The present practice of washing clothes in the barracks and wash rooms must be discontinued," center health officials declared today.

"Washing facilities are provided for the entire center at the laundry. Washing water dumped in the residential area creates a nuisance and the fat in the soap will cause odor in the warm weather.

"Therefore, if any individual is dumping water on the ground, it is creating a situation undesirable both to himself and to others. . . ."

BOY! WE REALLY EAT

Imagine spending seven and a half hours to cook rice for one meal! Or try washing 800 pounds of it.

That's the amount of work necessary in cooking rice for one meal at the Santa Anita center.

A typical dinner menu would call for 1300 pounds of baked barracuda, 180 pounds of Japanese pickles, and 225 lbs. of beets, 100 lbs. of onions, and 150 lbs. of lettuce for salad in addition to the rice. . . .

What did you do all day?

Well, *that* I could tell you. The chairs that Dr. Bruff brought us? Two of my childhood friends—Nobuko Endow and her cousin, Esao Otsuki—were there, and the three of us would sit on those chairs and a bed and play rummy. We were all fifteen—we'd gone to high school and Japanese school together. We'd play rummy for twelve hours straight—morning to night. That's why I can shuffle so well. [*Smiles.*] We sat in that stall and played cards all day long.

I asked Terry, "What did you do all day?" She said she just bummed around the stables with her friends.

Did you keep in touch with any classmates from your old high school?

No. But Mr. Burnight got a school annual—I have it downstairs—and took it around for everyone to sign and brought it to me. The whole yearbook is filled with notes. That would have been my junior year.

How did you feel to get it?

Disappointed. That I wasn't there.

Were you able to play the piano?

[*Nods.*] They brought one in and put it up in the grandstand. Can you imagine? A piano at the bottom, with all these rows of seats going up.

On Saturday evenings we had songfests—hundreds of people would be there. We had a song leader, and I used to play. Terry saw me. "I remember a little kid playing the piano." [*Laughs.*] That's what she said.

What kinds of songs did you play?

Oh, gosh. You name it. "I've Been Working On The Railroad." Songs like that. As I said, singing was a big pastime. [*Laughs.*] There was no TV.

Did you ever give concerts?

No. It wasn't conducive to that sort of thing.

[*Thinks.*] The church services were beautiful, though. You'd sit in the stands, looking out over the racetrack, with the mountains in the background. It was beautiful. And the stands would be filled. Hundreds of people. Nothing else to do.

I also took piano lessons from a woman named Ruth Watanabe. She was a USC [University of Southern California] piano graduate. I took violin lessons, too—I used to walk to the grandstand with a friend of mine to take lessons from a man named Mr. Yagura. Tomio Yagura. He was a really sweet man. I don't know where he got the music, but he taught us.

The boys used to say, "Oh, you've got your machine guns." [*Laughs.*]

Who was your friend?

[*Fondly.*] Misako Miura. We went to Excelsior together. She lives in Torrance [California] now, where Kay [Ken's sister] lives. I saw her not too long ago. The Japanese school had a reunion, and she and her husband were there—he since passed away. The reunion was held in a hotel near Norwalk. We all stayed at the hotel and had a two-day reunion. Ruth Asawa was there, too.

[*Smiles.*] You know when you see old, old friends? Misako is someone you could pick up with right away. You wouldn't be talking about old experiences.

I don't even know what her profession was. Whether she went to college or not. It didn't matter.

Is the school still there?

I don't know if the original building is still standing—I doubt it—but there's a thriving community center on the grounds.

Did people talk about their wartime experiences at the reunion?

No. There wasn't time for that. It wasn't conducive to that. And our experiences were different anyway. The other Norwalk people in Santa Anita went to a different relocation camp in Arkansas. They went to Rohwer. We went to Jerome.

Why?

Well, they knew Jerome was going to have a shortage of nurses, and since Lily was helping at the hospital in Santa Anita, she was asked to go there. And, of course, if she was going to Jerome, we were going, too. So we were among the few Norwalk people who went to Jerome. We hardly knew anybody. This Nobuko [Endo]? The one I played cards with? Her sister was a nurse, and Esao's [Otsuki, Nobuko's cousin] sister's husband was a doctor, so they went to Jerome, too. But we hardly knew anyone else.

The people who went to Rohwer left Santa Anita before we did, because Rohwer opened before Jerome. We had to stay until the very end. We had to stay until it closed.

Did everyone in Santa Anita go to Rohwer or Jerome?

No. Terry went to Heart Mountain [Wyoming]. I don't know where the other 18,000 went.

Mom, I've asked a lot of questions about what this place was like, and you've provided a lot of physical descriptions. But I have to ask—is there any way to express how it feels to be treated like this? When you haven't done anything wrong?

[*Softly.*] No.

Why not?

[*Long pause.*] Because we didn't think about it. Nobody thought about it. Nobody thought about how miserable they were. Everybody was in the same boat. So we didn't talk about it.

An interesting thing about Japanese people is that they're fatalists. There's an expression—*shikata ga nai*. It means you can't help it. It can't be helped. It's something mother feels to this day. She's not trying to put the blame on anybody. When you have that kind of philosophy you just take it.

We don't feel like we're entitled to things—that certain things should be ours. "You should do this for me." We don't feel that way. You have to earn things. They're not just given to you.

Mother never said how she felt about the whole experience. It's not something Issei did—talk about themselves. Japanese don't even use the pronoun "I." They imply it in a sentence without using it. So you don't know whether they're talking about one person or two people or ten.

Why is that?

That's just the way it is.

Is it a reflection of the lack of emphasis on the individual in Japanese culture?

Yes, I think so. The individual doesn't count.

You once asked me, "Didn't you complain? Didn't you talk about it with your friends?" No, we didn't. We were surviving. It didn't occur to us to talk like that.

The future was always so uncertain. We had no idea how long we were going to be there. We had no idea what the next week would bring. And under those circumstances, you can't look back. You have to look ahead.

Chapter Ten

You mentioned earlier that you were shipped overseas as a replacement for the 100th. So you didn't go with the 442nd?

K E N

No. What happened was that the 100th had been decimated at Cassino. You've heard of Cassino? The Cassino Abbey? It's near Naples. The Germans fortified the abbey and had a stronghold there. This was in '43. It was a perfect defensive position because it overlooked the entire [Liri] valley, and the allies were attacking from the valley. Not only that, but the general, Mark Clark, ordered them to attack in broad daylight. They also had to cross a river [the Rapido River]. [*Shakes his head.*] They were decimated. They started out with 1,500 men, but by the end they were down to about 700. Half their strength. The rest had been killed or wounded. So they took men from the 442nd to rebuild the 100th. All the replacements were taken from the First Battalion. They were sent over in three groups, 125 to 150 men in each group. I was in the last group.

All 150 of us came up by train. They brought us to Fort Meade [near Laurel, Maryland]. On the way the train stopped—you know the tracks that go over the 14th Street Bridge? It stopped right on that bridge, and when I looked out I saw the Washington Monument. I thought, "Gee, we're in Washington."

We were at Fort Meade for four or five days, being processed to go overseas. And that's where—at age twenty-one—I wrote a will. We all did. It was a standard form, with our name and the name of the person who would get all our earthly possessions if we died. It had to be signed by two other people, so we all signed each other's wills.

Who signed yours?

A guy named Higuchi and a guy named Ishibashi. I don't remember their first names. And I don't know what happened to them—if they survived the war or not. [He subsequently checked the list of those who died and did not find their names.]

Who would have gotten all your earthly possessions?

My father. But I had virtually nothing. [*Laughs.*] When he died [in 1972] they went through his possessions and found that will. My brother sent it to me.

LAST WILL AND TESTAMENT

I, Kaname Takemoto [signed], a legal resident of Kapaa, Kauai, Hawaii, United States of America, now in the active military service as a Pfc., Army Serial No. 30104774, in the Army of the United States, do hereby make, publish and declare this instrument as my last WILL and TESTAMENT, in manner following, that is to say:

1. I hereby cancel, annul, and revoke all wills and codicils by me at any time heretofore made;
2. I hereby give, devise, and bequeath to Yutaro Takemoto, my father, now residing in Kapaa, Kauai, Hawaii, all my estate and all of the property of which I may die seized and possessed and to which I may be entitled at the time of my decease, of whatsoever kind and nature, and wheresoever it may be situated, be it real, personal, or mixed, absolutely and forever;
3. I hereby nominate, constitute, and appoint Yutaro Takemoto, father, of Kapaa, Kauai Island, Territory of Hawaii, as my executor and request that he be permitted to serve without official bond or without surety thereon, except as required by law;
4. I hereby authorize and empower my executor in his absolute discretion to sell, exchange, convey, transfer, assign, mortgage, pledge, invest, or reinvest the whole or any part of my real or personal estate.

IN WITNESS WHEREOF, I have hereunto set my hand and seal to this my last WILL and TESTAMENT, at Ft. George G. Meade, Md. this 7th day of April, 1944.

Signed, sealed, published, and declared by the above-named testator Kaname Takemoto, to be his last WILL and TESTAMENT in the presence of all of us at one time, and at the same time we, at his request and in his presence and in the presence of each other, have hereunto subscribed our names as witnesses, and do hereby attest to the sound and disposing mind of said testator and to the performance of the aforesaid acts of execution at Ft. George G. Meade, Md., this 7th day of April, 1944.

Higuchi   P.O. Box 143 Oahu T.H.
Ishibashi   Lihue, Kauai, T.H.

From Fort Meade we went by train to Norfolk [Virginia]. That was what was called the P.O.E.—the Port of Embarkation. We were there for a couple of days. Then they loaded us on trucks and took us to the docks. At the docks we boarded the ship that would take us overseas.

[*Pauses.*] It was evening. I remember standing on the deck of the ship and looking at the lights of Norfolk. Wondering if I was going to come back. Wondering if I was going to be on the return trip home.

We shipped out the next morning. We were traveling in a huge convoy— there were ships all over. At that time German submarines were still sinking a lot of American ships, so we were escorted by destroyers. They kept circling us, and every so often they'd practice dropping depth charges— we'd hear explosions. Or maybe they actually saw something, I don't know. [*Laughs.*]

What was your ship like?
It was called a Liberty ship. It was one of the big accomplishments of the war—that they were able to produce so many of them. I was on another one when I was shipped from Naples to Anzio.

How many people were on it?
I don't know, but it was crowded. No one was allowed on deck at night— there was a complete blackout—so everyone had to go down below. We slept on bunks stacked five high. It was smelly, hot, and humid, because everything was shut down. It took thirty days to go from Norfolk to Naples. [*Shakes his head.*] Thirty days.

Were white soldiers onboard?
Yes. We were all mixed together.

Do you remember any tensions?
No. No tensions.

No comments about who you were?

No.

Why not, do you suppose?

[*Shrugs.*] We were all in the same boat. Going overseas. Facing the unknown.

Did you have any friends on that ship?

Just the guys I was with. From my twelve-man squad in Hattiesburg they picked only three of us. Henry Nakasone, Nobuo Kajiwara, and myself.

But I did get to know some of the others pretty well, because we'd been together from Camp Shelby to Fort Meade to Norfolk, and now we were going overseas. We were together, this group of about 150 guys, for at least two months. So I got to know quite a few of them.

The guy who won the Medal of Honor? Munemori? Munemori was in our group. Until this year he was the only one [from the 100th or 442nd] to receive the Medal of Honor.

Do you remember him?

Sure. He was a happy-go-lucky guy. Carefree. One day they had an impromptu show on deck—somebody had a ukulele and they were play-ing music. He started dancing the hula. [*Laughs.*] Sadao Munemori. Did you know they named a ship after him? The SS *Sadao Munemori.*

What did he do to earn the Medal of Honor?

He had destroyed two German machine gun nests, and then was in a foxhole with two others when a German grenade rolled in. He threw him-self on top of it—it killed him, but the other two were saved. So if they survived the war, they owe their lives to Munemori.

What else do you remember about the trip?

That there was a lot of gambling. [*Laughs.*] Crapshooting. Meals were served on our mess kits. The toilets were planks with holes cut in them, maybe ten holes in a row. So you'd have ten guys sitting at one time. The crap was removed by water running through a trough underneath—all the droppings fell in the trough and were washed out to sea. One time when I was sitting down some wise guy made a paper boat, set it on fire and let it float down the trough. We all jumped up, one at a time. [Jumps up, laughing.] There were no showers. Once during those thirty days they made us strip and go up on deck—this huge, naked mass—and hosed us down with seawater. You know, soap doesn't produce any kind of lather with seawater. That's how they washed us—hosed us down with seawater. Once. [*Laughs.*]

Were there any stops?

We stopped at Oran, North Africa, for a couple of hours, but they made us stay on the boat. Then we kept going to Naples. I remember standing on deck, looking out at Naples harbor. Mount Vesuvius in the background. They took us by truck to a little town outside Naples called Caserta. [*Spells it.*] We were there for about three days, staying in tents in a big field on the outskirts of town. On the first night a single German plane came over and dropped a single bomb. [*Laughs.*] We all got out of our tents and went into trenches.

What did you think?

I thought, "Boy, we're getting closer and closer to the real action." After that we went by truck back to a Liberty ship and they took us to Anzio.

What was Anzio like?

Well, as I mentioned before, the allies couldn't take Cassino for the longest time. They decided that in order to take it, they'd have to divert German troops away. Like what happened in Korea at Inchon? So they set up an invasion at Anzio, but what happened was that the Germans sent *two* divisions over there.

How many men is that?

About 40,000. So now the American forces were trapped. They went twenty miles inland and that was it. There was a stalemate from January to late May. We landed in April.

Anzio was pretty badly bombed—wrecked buildings and whatnot. But there was hardly any action. The Germans were on one side and we were on the other.

You once told me about a big gun the Germans had used.

The Anzio Express. It was a huge piece of artillery mounted on a railroad car. It could throw shells twenty miles. At night we'd hear them going over—they were bombing the harbor. When I was there a hospital in the back, near the beach, got hit. Guys who were wounded and recovering were killed or wounded again. [*Thinks.*] The shells made a sound very much like somebody rubbing a piece of paper together. [*Picks up a piece of paper and rubs it.*] Like that. On its way. We never heard the explosion, though—it was too far away. We always heard them going over, but we never heard the explosion.

After we took Rome, we were in a town called Civitavecchia [*spells it*] and somebody told me the Anzio Express had been captured and was sitting on a railroad track nearby. So I went to see it. It was just as I imagined it—a big piece of artillery mounted on the bed of a railroad car. The whole car! [*Looks around.*] The length of the barrel must have been half the length of this house. Big!

What did you do at Anzio?

[*Smiles.*] Our cook was from Kauai. His name was Herbert Ishii—he was a good friend of my brother Haruto. Eric Shinseki? [Shinseki was army chief of staff from 1999 to 2003.] Herbert Ishii was Shinseki's uncle. Shinsheki has talked about listening to war stories told by his uncles—Herbert was with the 100th and his brother with the 442nd. Anyway, when we got to Anzio we had to wait to be assigned to different companies—we were replacements, so they needed to tell us where to go—and while we were waiting we had nothing to do, so we played cards. Pinochle. All day long and into the night. Ishii, myself, Kajiwara, and another guy, a 100th Infantry guy, who later became a lieutenant.

What was his name?

Ross Fujitani. Isn't that something? I hardly knew him, but still I remember his name. He got killed. He received his commission, went back to the lines, and got killed. The four of us used to play cards, all day and all night.

When I saw Shinseki [at a dinner following the Medal of Honor ceremony in 2000], I introduced myself to him. I said, "I knew your uncle Herbert. I used to play cards with him at Anzio." He laughed at that. He said, "I heard a lot of stories about my uncles." Both of them were heavy drinkers. Both died of alcoholism. But they survived the war.

[*Long pause.*] Herbert Ishii was the one who told me Kajiwara had been killed. I was marching along and he rode by in a jeep. Somewhere above

Rome. He saw me and yelled, "Hey, did you hear about Kajiwara?" I said, "No, what about him?" He said, "He got killed." [*Pauses. Softly.*] Gee. I remember how shocked I was that he was gone. It was Ishii who told me.

How long did you have to wait before you were assigned to a company?
Not long—a few days. I was assigned to Company B as an infantryman, but after we got to the front they picked four of us to become medics. We became part of what was called the "medical detachment." That meant we were not assigned to any one company. We served the whole battalion.

What did you do when you got to the front?
Well, the first thing we did was dig our foxholes. [*Laughs.*] Survival first!

Did the guys in the 100th say anything to you?
No.

ALICE

They didn't greet you with a round of introductions?

KEN

[*Laughs.*] No.
But it's strange, the things you remember. There was a Nisei officer who was joining the 100th with us. His name was Tsubaki. Kiyoto Tsubaki. [*Spells it.*] I never saw the guy again, but still I can recall his name. What I remember was that he was watching me dig my foxhole. He wasn't digging one for himself—he was just watching me. He asked me, "Is the ground hard?" It was full of rocks and stones—very hard to dig a hole—and I said, "It sure is." I thought, "Why the hell isn't he digging a hole? Nobody's going to dig it for him." If they had started shelling he wouldn't have had a hole to protect himself. But he was watching me dig my hole, and asking me this stupid question.

Did he ever dig a hole?
[*Laughs.*] I don't know. I never saw him again. But I remember his name, and I remember what he said. And I know he made it back alive, because when I looked at the list of [dead] officers, his name wasn't on it.
[*Thinks.*] We broke out late in May. Until then there were short skirmishes, things like that—a lot of shelling, but no real battles. Then there was a

sudden breakout. I don't even know how it happened. You're in your own little world. You don't see the big picture. Then all of a sudden you're moving forward—we'd broken through the German lines. I remember marching through a town called Lanuvio. [*Spells it.*] There wasn't a single building standing. Just bombed to hell. We went right through it. The Germans were retreating so quickly they loaded us on trucks. Now we were *really* moving. When we reached Rome—Rome is, I don't know, maybe fifty miles from Anzio—it seemed like we were the first Allied troops there, but we were told to hold up. We were on the outskirts of the city, just sitting there, waiting. What happened was that General Clark, the same one who ordered the assault on Cassino, wanted to make a grand entrance into the city. He was the head of the Fifth Army. All the cheering crowds? He wanted that. So he rode into the city while we stayed on the outskirts. [*Laughs.*]

[*Pauses.*] I saw a dead German for the first time not long after that. We had taken a break from marching and were eating rations. No hot food, of course. They gave us C rations. Cans? One can was hash—corned beef hash. Stew. We also had K rations—they came in a box. Crackers and cheese. All of it very unappetizing. Anyway, I had opened a can of C rations—we had our own can openers—and was eating it when someone said, "Hey, look at the dead German over there." So I looked over and there he was. Lying on the side of the road. One of our guys—he was sort of morbid—went right up to him. He was one of the four picked to become medics. Kokubun. That's an unusual name. Have you ever heard of that name, Alice? Kokubun?

ALICE

No.

KEN

Thomas Kokubun. Why do I remember these people? I wasn't even friends with him. But I remember Kokubun going over and looking at him and saying, "Right in the head." He'd been shot right in the head. Not long after that we saw a German tank that had been hit and caught fire. It was an inferno. All the Germans had been burned to death inside except for one guy who'd made it halfway out. He was up on the turret. Very badly charred. We all went over to look at him. Kind of gruesome.

Kokubun was a rough character. After I was wounded and left the outfit,

I didn't see him again. But a few years later, after I was discharged and going back to school at the University of Hawaii, I was walking downtown [Honolulu] and along came Kokubun. He recognized me immediately. Called my name. So I went up to him. He had a big gash on his face. Horrible. It went all the way across his cheek. [*Draws finger across cheek.*] I said, "Hey, what happened to you?" He said, "Oh, I was drinking in a bar, and this white guy started a fight with me. He broke a bottle and attacked me with it. Cut my face." Can you imagine?

Did the 442nd join the 100th at some point?

Yes. Right about that time. After we took Rome. Early June, 1944.

[*Pauses.*] And that's when Howard Urabe came to find me. Before his first battle.

He came to find you?

[*Nods. Long pause.*] You know, I just don't know how he did it. I mean, if I wanted to I never could have found him. I didn't know where they were, and he didn't know where I was. It was amazing. [*Looks out window.*] It was as though, say, there were five thousand guys in the hills around here and somebody asked you to go find me—I'm in that group of five thousand. Somewhere in the hills around here. Nobody knows me. How did he ask for me? They didn't know me—I was a replacement. I was a replacement in a small unit, and this unit was together all the time. I didn't know anybody else in the 100th. So how the heck did he find me? It's a big puzzle to me.

What were you doing when he found you?

I was sitting outside my tent. It was about like this. [*Points out window.*] Dusk.

What did he say?

That he had a premonition he was going to get killed. That his father was right. [*Shakes his head.*] I just don't know how he found me. We were in a strange country, nothing but hills. No roads. I don't know how he found me, and I don't know how he found his way back. I wish I had asked him.

How long did you talk to him?

A couple of hours.

What else did he talk about?

He talked a lot about his girlfriend. She was from our town, too. Her name was Elnora.

She was a nurse in Honolulu. When I got back from the war I called her. I called to tell her that I had seen Howard right before he was killed.

What did she say?

Not much. She didn't say much about it.

She had a brother, who was one year below me. I had a couple of fights with him.

He wasn't the one you got into a fight with in front of the Roxy Theater, was he?

[*Smiles.*] Yes. He was the one. Soichi. He was the brother to Howard's girlfriend.

How much longer after he came to see you was Howard killed?

Not long at all. A couple of weeks.

How was he killed?

He was attacking a machine gun nest. They said he got riddled with bullets. [*Voice thickens.*] Right across his chest. He died instantly.

So his father was right.

[*Nods.*] His father was right.

Chapter Eleven

Grandma was allowed to rejoin you in Santa Anita?

ALICE

Yes.

How long was she away?

Almost three months. She was taken from us a month before we were relocated, and we were at Santa Anita for almost two months before she came back. We were relocated in mid-April and she rejoined us in early June.

U.S. DEPARTMENT OF JUSTICE
Immigration and Naturalization Service
Washington

MEMORANDUM FOR ALIEN ENEMY INFORMATION BUREAU
OFFICE OF THE PROVOST MARSHAL GENERAL
WAR DEPARTMENT, WASHINGTON, D.C.

June 3, 1942

In Re: Change of Status
                Detained Enemy Alien

Name of Alien:	IMAMOTO, YOSHI
Nationality:	JAPANESE
Previously Detained At:	San Pedro, California
Date of Change in Status:	June 2, 1942 at 1 PM
PRESENT STATUS:	Evac. Center—Santa Anita, California

(signed) Lemuel B. Schofield
Special Assistant to the Attorney General

Did you know she was coming back?
No.

What do you remember of her arrival?
Nothing.

Nothing?
No. Isn't that awful? I blocked it all out. Good and bad.

June 3, 1942

Dear Daddy,

Mother came home yesterday!! Good news. Gee we were so happy. Mrs. Shizuoka, Kawaguchi, Endow and many other ladies were also released but Mrs. Wada was not and I feel so sorry for Midori-san and Mitsuko-san. I was washing clothes and Sakiye-san came running to tell me that a bus came and mother was on it. Alice and I went running and saw mother.

That was good news, but we went to see Mr. Asawa and he told us the bad news of you. I hope they keep you from being sent to Texas [Seagoville Prison, near Dallas]. Too bad that you did not take the passport at Tuhunga. Now we cannot get it and more proof that you were a student in Berkeley before 1924. [When asked about this, Alice said, "We were grasping at straws. Anything that might help at his hearing."]

When we heard that some men came back from New Mexico, Alice and I ran out to the gate and what a disappointment when I did not see you on the truck. Everybody else was so happy and I was so sad, especially Alice was so sad that she came home and cried.

Now that mother is home, so many ladies come to see her and it's just like the time when you were taken. It takes mother to make our stable look more nicely and more like home. When she came home, we went to get Mrs. Akamoto [actually Okamoto; she and Alice's mother came to the U.S. on the same boat] and was mother surprised. The Mountain View and San Jose people came here. All of Santa Clara County except a few were sent to Pomona.

We're fortunate that we were not sent to Parker, Arizona because the heat is terrible and so many people are getting sick. The temperature goes up to 138 degrees according to Rakumi-san and even with a degree of 108 we suffered terrifically.

There are no more high school classes here and all the boys and girls over 16 and above have to work at making nets for camouflaging. I have been drafted also but I don't know if I will. It's so dusty that it won't be good for me because I'm not too healthy.

There are several people we know who went to Idaho to work in the beet fields, potato and pea fields and they get paid, but I heard that it is a very hard work. Even the women have to work and children over the age of 12. The Sakamoto's from Norwalk, Otsukas, Imaizumi's from Downey and Mr. & Mrs. Nakajima (Miss Yuge). They will work for 5 or 6 months and don't know if they can really come back to this camp again.

When mother came back, Mr. Itano came to me and was very happy that she came back. He has certainly been good to us and told me that if we wanted any help, just ask him and he would do it. He went to speak to mother too.

More people come to visit so I must close now.

Your daughter,
Marion

Did you know how long you would be in Santa Anita?

No.

Did you know where you would be going after that?

No.

Were there rumors?

Rumors after rumors after rumors. Where we were going. When we were going.

What were the possibilities? How many camps were there?

Well, let's count them. Tule Lake and Manzanar [California]. Poston and Gila River [Arizona]. Heart Mountain [Wyoming]. Minidoka [Idaho]. Amache [officially Granada]. Topaz [officially Central Utah, Utah]. And Rohwer and Jerome [Arkansas]. That's ten.

Five of the camps [Amache, Jerome, Minidoka, Rohwer, and Topaz] had under 10,000 people. Some had much more. [Tule Lake was the largest with a population of 21,846; Poston had 17,707, and Gila River had 14,401.[13] The total number—120,313—did not include 219 non-Japanese American spouses who were voluntarily relocated.[14]]

13. U.S. Department of the Interior, *The Evacuated People: A Quantitative Description* (Washington, D.C.: Government Printing Office, 1946), table 2.

14. The Japanese American Legacy Project Web site (www.densho.org).

July 31, 1942

Dear Father,

It's still hot as ever here and I hope you are fine. In the morning it is quite cool but at noon the heat is awful. . . .

We hear so many rumors about where we will go and the last I heard was that Santa Anita and Tanforan will go to Utah. I don't know if that will work since the group is so large here. Grace says that we will go to Arkansas and the Pomona people will go to Wyoming by Aug. 15th. Lily received a letter from Miye and she says that Merced will go to Colorado and 2,000 farmers from Santa Anita by Aug. 31st. That may be true and I know we will all have to go somewhere soon. I hope that by that time we can all get together. . . .

I am still knitting and will be almost finished with my sweater. I know that other states will be cold in the winter so we are all going to knit a warm sweater. It's a good thing we got boots because probably it'll snow and snow. Well[,] we can only hope for the closest state to California. I don't want to get too far so that we can't get back from our relocation center. I will write again so until then take care of yourself. We are all fine so don't worry.

Your daughter,
Marion

When did people start leaving Santa Anita?

A couple of months before it closed. You can't transport 18,000 people all at once. We were among the last to go. It was pretty spooky staying in the stall after everyone had left. The barracks were mostly empty, with just a few people here and there. Then it got cold. October is cold.

SANTA ANITA PACEMAKER
Santa Anita Assembly Center, California
Vol. 1, No. 50   Oct. 7, 1942

FINAL MOVEMENT SET FOR GILA

About 2000 Santa Anitans To Be Relocated to Arizona Project

Starting Oct. 17, approximately 2000 Santa Anitans will be relocated to the Gila river relocation project, it was announced today by Henry E. Scofield, evacuation coordinator. The seventh and final movement in the evacuation of the Center will last for four days ending on Oct. 20, according to the announcement.

In contrast to previous movements, departures in the last movement will start in the evenings instead of in the mornings.

All four departures will begin at 6 P.M. The whole trip is scheduled to take about 18 hours, trains reaching the Gila river project at noon the following day.

Approximately 500 persons will be in each departure of the Gila movement, which is composed of former residents of western Los Angeles and Pasadena.

Family numbers of those in the final movement include 9201 to 9641, 22,851 to 22,860 and 23,151 to 23,550.

GROUP LEAVES FOR UTAH

In the smallest evacuation movement of the Center, approximately 560 left Santa Anita this morning bound for Central Utah. Originally from San Francisco, all persons in the fifth movement departed on one train. The sixth movement will begin tomorrow morning with about 450 scheduled to go in the first departure. The movement will continue on alternate days until it is completed Oct. 16.

A total of 2300 from Santa Anita are to make their new homes at Jerome, Ark.

The last of the Center residents going to Rohwer, Ark., left yesterday.

SEVEN HUNDRED TO REMAIN

Remaining in the Center until the last evacuation movement is completed will be approximately 700 Santa Anitans, it was disclosed today.

Key personnel workers and their families number about 500[,] while the remaining 200 include hospital bases and those awaiting transfers to other relocation centers.

By the end of October, however, all Santa Anitans will have been relocated to the various WRA centers.

Ken Takemoto as high school senior, 1939.

Takemoto family portrait, Kapaa, Kauai, Hawaii, 1936.
Front row, left to right: Minnie (10), Yutaro (50), Ella (12), and Sumi (46);
back row, left to right: Sue (14), Ken (16), Haruto (23), Kay (18), and Fusayo (20).

442nd volunteers from Students' House, Honolulu, 1943.
Ken is seated in the front, second from left.

Ken after induction, Honolulu, March 1943.

Ken (front row, second from left) with fellow wounded soldiers
at the 33rd General Hospital, Rome, 1944.

明治四十年一月二日
於徳山町林燕喬

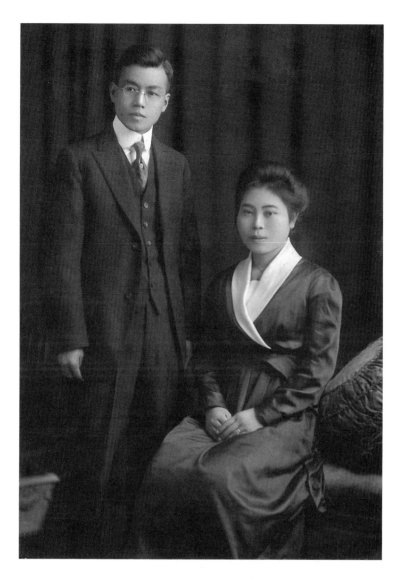

(Facing page, top)
Photo sent from Zenichi to Yoshiko before
their wedding was arranged, 1917.

(Facing page, bottom)
Yoshiko (left) with future sister-in-law, before departing
for the United States and marriage to Zenichi, 1918.

(This page)
Zenichi and Yoshiko Imamoto's wedding photo,
Berkeley, 1918.

Imamoto family portrait, Los Angeles, 1937.
Seated, left to right: Zenichi (48), Alice (11), Yoshiko (39);
standing: Marion (14), Grace (18), and Lily (17).

Alice Imamoto at age eight in Miss Johnston's studio, Fullerton, California, 1934. Her father designed and built the pedal extension.

Dr. Ralph Burnight, Alice's prewar principal at Excelsior High School. This was taken after the war, during a visit to Alice's parents in Washington, D.C.

Alice, Yoshiko, Zenichi, and Marion in Jerome, June 1943.

Yoshiko and Zenichi in Jerome, 1943.

Alice's senior year photo
at Oberlin, 1946.

Ken and Alice in Washington, D.C., 1948.

(Facing page, top)
Ken as visiting scientist at the National Institute
of Health of Japan, Tokyo, 1981.

(Facing page, bottom)
Alice and Ken, September 2001.

The Imamoto sisters celebrating Yoshiko's 105th birthday,
November 3, 2002, Sacramento, California.

8/8/42

Dear Father,

How are you? We're all just fine. We have just found out where we are going. All the doctors, student nurses & registered nurses have been assigned to go to a certain place & Lily has been assigned to go to Jerome, Arkansas. The Norwalk community is going to Rowher, Arkansas[,] but we can't go there because Lily is assigned to Jerome. Teruko Endow, Sue Otsuki [both registered nurses] are also assigned to Jerome. Many good doctors & nurses are going there—Dr. Kobayashi [head of staff here], Dr. Abe, Dr. Fujikawa[,] etc. We are leaving the latter part of Sept. to middle of August. We wanted to go to Gila or Colorado or even Utah in order to go see you[,] but it just isn't possible to transfer like that. Tanforan Center are going to Utah. Mr. Yagura, Okubayashi's are going to Gila River, Arizona. San Diego is going tomorrow to Parker Dam. This Sunday, Santa Clara Valley to Wyoming.

Rev. Tsuchiya came back. I haven't seen him yet[,] but mother & Grace did. We'll have to start packing pretty soon. But maybe Lily will have to stay till the last.

Mr. Takeii is our postman. He made a ring for you out of peach seed & we shall send it to you.

Mrs. Yates is going to come see us again this Saturday.

Mother is at the present time cutting out the handle from wood of shower bags.

I looked up in encyclopedia & it said that Arkansas lies at lower Mississippi & is [a] drainage basin. Has lots of swamps & bayous. There would be lots of mosquitos.

Mr. Nawa is sitting in front of our house on our bench. He tells me to give his best regards to you—he can't write letters[,] so he says for you to be in good health. He seems very healthy—has nothing to do. Please give this other sheet to Mr. Kimoto. Thank him for the pretty wood. I already made a pin out of it & gave it to Hisayo Okubayashi on her birthday. Best regards from everyone.

Your daughter,
Alice Imamoto

What were your thoughts about going to Jerome?

Well, the WRA [War Relocation Authority] said Arkansas would be a beautiful place with green shrubbery and wonderful barracks and this and that. They tried to paint a rosy picture. It was all untrue.

What do you remember about packing?

Nothing. I don't think I did anything. My sisters took care of that.

When did you finally leave?

October 14. Six months after we arrived.

What do you remember about leaving?

Getting on a train. I don't know if there's a track that goes by Santa Anita, but we left by train.

What do you remember about the trip?

I remember that every time we came to a city, we had to pull the shades down. Somebody said it took five days. It was interminable. So uncomfortable. Sitting up for five days.

At that point in the war they were using trains that hadn't been used in a long time. They were shipping a lot of soldiers back and forth. So we had to use trains that had been sitting in railroad yards.

They had rattan seats. Cane? You know how hard those are? They didn't recline. It was just—.

Wed. 6:30 PM

Dear Father,

Thought I would drop a card to let you know that we are fine and on our way to Arkansas. Having a nice train ride, since it is my first and longest. The others are just fine. Went through Beaumont, Indio and passed the Salton Sea. There are 2 engines pulling 10 cars, 2 diners. Sometimes it gets so rocky that I cannot write. It'll probably be a long trip so I'll try to write often. It was very sad leaving the camp and our friends. Since some of the L.A. people bound for Gila has to go to Jerome, we might see some of the St. Mary's people like Mr. Yagura or Okubayashis. I must close now.

Bye,
Marion

Chapter Twelve

KEN

After the 442nd joined us, we were three battalions again. They turned the 100th into the equivalent of what the First Battalion had been. But the 100th had made such a name for itself the men didn't want to lose their identity. You asked me why it was called the 100th Infantry Battalion/442nd Regimental Combat Team. That's why.

The men of the 100th were very proud of what they did. In fact, I heard later that they looked down on the replacements.

Did you sense that yourself?

No, I never had that feeling. I guess because my stay with them was very short, and we didn't have time to get to know the rest of the company. We only knew the guys we were with. In combat—that's the way it is. You don't know what's going on with the rest of the company. You don't know where they are or what they're doing. All you care about is what's immediately in front of you. Especially the Germans. [*Laughs.*]

Do you consider yourself more a part of the 100th, since you fought with them?

No. I have no attachment to the 100th, because outside of our small group I never got to know any of them. Also, I joined the 100th in March and was wounded [for the second and last time] in mid-July. So I was with them for only four months. The only friends I had were the few guys I came with.

[*Thinks.*] The first big battle after the 442nd joined us was pretty disastrous. They were inexperienced, and the 100th ended up bailing them out. The 100th captured a lot of Germans and equipment—tanks and whatnot. Just wiped them out.

Where was this?

A place called Sassetta. [*Spells it.*] Actually, there were two towns—Sassetta and Belvedere. This was someplace past Rome—I can't say exactly where. But that was where the 100th got its first [of three] Presidential Unit Citations. [The 100th/442nd received eight Presidential Unit Citations, which are the unit equivalent of the Distinguished Service Cross. Individual medals included 21 Medals of Honor—including the 20 awarded on June 1, 2000—33 Distinguished Service Crosses, 559 Silver Stars with 28 Oak Leaf Clusters—the latter in lieu of a second award—4,000 Bronze Stars with 1,200 Oak Leaf Clusters and 9,486 Purple Hearts.[15]] So, in my records I have a Presidential Unit Citation.

What were the circumstances of the battle?

[*Shakes his head.*] I have no idea. In a battle you have no idea what's going on. Your only thoughts center around survival. You don't know who's around you, what the battle alignment is, where the Germans are really situated—you don't know any of those things. It's a complete blank. You're just going. Following everybody. Going along with the fighting. So when you ask what the circumstances were, my recollection is that I was getting shot at and scared to death. I didn't even know we were wiping out the Germans. Another company lay in ambush, and when the Germans came along, they opened fire and knocked out tanks and a whole company. Took a lot of prisoners. It was over before I knew it.

How did the 442nd mess up?

I don't know. All I know is that we had to go immediately into battle. We were supposed to be held back, but they rushed us in.

In combat do you actually see the enemy?

[*Firmly.*] Oh, yes. Yes, you see them. Yes. Yes. And there were a lot of times when I was fired at and *didn't* see them. Just heard bullets flying by. And of course there were times when we were being shelled by mortars and artillery that came from so far away we *couldn't* see them. All we could hear were the shells coming in.

15. *Go For Broke Educational Foundation* Web site (www.goforbroke.org).

How long do these situations last? These moments of combat?

It's hard to gauge. You have no awareness of time. It's just the action. We underwent some pretty heavy bombardment by artillery, when it seemed like we were being bombarded for an eternity, but in actuality it might have lasted only a couple of hours. But it seems like forever, because all you're doing is lying there, waiting. Waiting for the shells, and hoping one doesn't come right at you.

[*Thinks.*] That's an odd thing about living in such precarious circumstances. That you have no awareness of time. It's strange, isn't it? Because all other human activities involve time. You know how long it takes for certain things to happen. But in combat you lose all track of time. It seems like a long, long time, but things are happening so fast the time may in fact be very short. [*Pauses.*] The overwhelming emotion is fear. Fear. That at any moment you're going to get it. And you don't know where it's going to come from. But it's not the kind of fear where you're shaking all the time. It's the constant thought in the back of your head that at any moment you're going to get it. The future is so uncertain. You don't know if you're going to be alive the next day or not. It's hard to describe. All of a sudden you have a guy firing at you from a matter of twenty or thirty yards away. Bullets flying all over the place. Or mortar and artillery shells exploding all around you. It's an indescribable feeling. The fear. And yet you go! You move! You're not so scared that you can't function. And that's the basic thing about the human spirit. That even under those conditions you can still function. You can still go.

ALICE

But there must have been some guys in the 442nd who didn't hold up. Who weren't able to function.

KEN

Yes. I've seen people so scared they couldn't move. Paralyzed. I saw an officer who couldn't function. I saw an officer—he was a medical officer— who was so scared he would take off. When he heard a shell coming he would just run. One time we were in a building and a shell landed maybe fifty feet away. Pretty far away, considering. But he was so scared he hid under a table and wouldn't come out.

[*Thinks.*] The first time we were shelled I was with Henry Nakasone. We were completely out in the open, and the Germans started dropping shells all around us. Artillery was exploding everywhere. I was lying flat on the ground, and I heard Henry yell, "I'm hit! I'm hit!" I thought, well, I have to go see what's wrong. I didn't want to leave my position [laughs], but I crawled over to him. He was sitting up. I said, "Where are you hit?" He said, "My neck." He went like this. [*Wipes the back of his neck and looks at his hand.*] No blood. So he did it again—no blood. I said, "Henry, let me take a look." He had a great big burn on his neck, and on his helmet, an inch from the bottom, was a hole this big. [*Makes a circle with his thumb and forefinger.*] A shell fragment had gone right through it, and that saved him, because when it hit his neck it just bounced off. Shell fragments are very hot, so it burned him, but that was all. I said, "Henry, it went right through your helmet. Look at your helmet." He took it off and looked at it. We were both amazed. Just amazed.

[*Looks out window. Lost in thought. Softly.*] You know, I've always hated the sound of the German language. I've always hated it.

Why?

Well, a lot of that is my association with what went on when Hitler was in power. Those speeches. "Sieg Heil!" [*Raises arm.*]

You won't remember this, but when you were young we went to Yellowstone [in 1962]. We were waiting in a long line to register for cabins, and here came this German man with a Coke. There was a gap in the line, and he slipped into the gap. Butted in line. So I went up to him and tapped him on the shoulder. I said, "Back of the line." He said, "Oh, I went to get this Coke." Heavy German accent. I said, "I don't care what you did. Get in the back of the line." He did.

Did you hate them when you were fighting them?

No. In combat—they were getting killed and we were getting killed. They were in the same boat. Just other human beings.

You didn't hate them?

No. I hated the language, but I didn't hate them. On several occasions I saw prisoners up close. Once we were at an aid station and there was one sitting on the ground. He was very young—only about fifteen or sixteen. He hadn't even started shaving yet. I think he was one of those Hitler youth. He'd been shot right through the mouth—the bullet went in one side and came out the other. Tore out the inside of his mouth. He was in extreme pain. I felt so sorry for him. He was in so much pain that—just for something to do—he was grabbing clumps of grass and pulling them up. [*Makes pulling motion with hands.*] Just grabbing them and pulling them up. Face all contorted. There was nothing we could do. Nobody had any morphine. I never forgot him.

[*Lost in thought again. Smiles.*] This has nothing to do with anything, but once when we were going after the Germans—they were retreating—we came upon a very nice house in the middle of a field. A woman was inside. She had a grand piano in the living room.

She was alone?

Yes. And it must have seemed like an odd request—here's this foreign soldier—but I asked her to play. Now that I think of it, gee, that must have been strange for her. A bunch of soldiers barging into her house, and one of them asks her to play. But she sat down and played.

Do you remember what she played?

The same one that mom used to play. [*Laughs.*] No, I don't remember what she played or how long she played. But she played, and we listened.

How long had it been since the Germans left?

They had just gone through.

Was she scared?

I'm sure she was.

Why did you ask her to play?

[*Shrugs.*] I wanted to hear some music.

Chapter Thirteen

What was your first impression of Jerome?

Well, I think there was a stop called Jerome, but there was nothing there. There was no town. If I remember correctly, we had to walk to the camp. It was cold.

We all had diarrhea—I think from the food on the train—but the washrooms weren't open yet in our block, so we had to go to the next block. It was muddy, rainy. We were wearing *getas* [Japanese sandals] that were made by father's fellow inmates at Lordsburg, and they kept getting stuck in the mud. It was miserable.

The camp was comprised of blocks. Within each block you'd have a mess hall and a washroom. The mess hall was in one building and the washroom was in another. The washroom had bathrooms and washtubs to wash your clothes and brush your teeth. There was no running water in the barracks. The barracks were lined up on either side of those buildings. Six on one side and six on the other.

How many people were in each block?

About four hundred.

We were in 18–10–A. Eighteen was the block, ten was the barrack and A was the unit. We were on the edge of the camp.

Block 18–10–A
10/20/42

Dear Father,

How are you? Here we are in Jerome[,] Arkansas. It took us 4 days & 4 nights for the trip. We don't know if we passed through Lordsburg or not because it was in the night that we went through lower New Mexico. We passed through Arizona, New Mexico, Texas, Oklahoma, Arkansas, crossed the Mississippi over to Memphis, Tennessee, crossed back into Arkansas & came to Jerome 3:30 A.M. morning!

We received nice big room for 5 people but there is enough room for 6 people too. The houses are black but they have white doors & white windows. We have a closet, a little porch, screen windows and chimney. It is very warm in the afternoon, much more warmer than Santa Anita. Mother likes it a lot over here. I'm sure everyone does. We have been getting good food. The Otsuki's & Endow's live very close to us. [In the same block.] The Saiki's live in the next block[,] but quite near to us. Sadako-san had remained in Santa Anita after her folks left, & she has left for Gila River Project because her husband might be able to go there because that climate is good for his health.

We live pretty far from the Kitahata's, Masuda's, Yamada's, Taniguichi's, Ouchi's, Takii's & from the Suzuki's (the man was with you in Santa Fe, N. Mexico).

School hasn't started and I don't know when it'll begin.

This camp isn't completed yet. Only 2 groups from Fresno have come in. Our block's mess hall, shower etc. aren't finished[,] so we have to go to another block even for a drink of water & that's quite far. But after everything is completed, things will be fine. The camp is very very large. 1 mile wide & 1 mile wide of the buildings.

We are 26 miles southwest of the Mississippi River[,] so they say. Let's hope it won't overflow.

Mother is at the present time sewing curtains & busy putting it up. We have 5 great big windows. We have a few tall trees around here. In other blocks, there are no trees at all.

There are a great many snakes—especially around here where the trees are. We haven't actually come upon one but different people have told us so. There aren't very many mosquitos as we thought. All in all, this is a very nice place and I know you'll like it when you get here. It is hotter than California & colder than California. Here it is October but it still is quite warm in the afternoons when Wyoming is having snow. Mother is really glad that we came here. Colorado is pretty bad place. Gila River is overcrowded with people & not enough living quarters[,] so maybe one group of people from Santa Anita that is scheduled to go to Gila may come here. And if they do come, maybe Mr. Yagura, the Rev. Yamazaki's & Nobuko Kadowaki may come here[,] because they are in that group. But this camp isn't all ready yet either. I hope Mr. Yagura comes here. I hope the Yamazaki's come here too. As it is, we don't have any ministers—not one. Maybe someone is coming from Fresno—Rev. Hideo Hashimoto.

I hope you could come home soon. This is really like a home compared to those horse stables.

I received that letter from Mr. Tamura—I'm glad he likes the stockings. I hope he could come here.

Last night for supper we had roast beef. This noon we had veal & was it good! My, the food is delicious!! Tonight we had stew just like the way mother cooks it. I'm very glad that we came here—I think Rohwer and Jerome are the 2 best camps of all. It doesn't have any dust storms as most other camps do.

Well, I shall close this letter now. Please say hello to Mr. Tamura, Mr. Ikezaki, Mr. Kitahata.

Your daughter,
Alice

Each barrack held six families. The end rooms were twenty by twenty-five [feet], and the middle four were smaller. The five of us stayed in one of the end rooms.

The walls were plywood covered with black tar paper. That was it. No insulation. During the winter it went down to thirteen degrees. It was almost like living outside. Plywood and tar paper. [*Shakes her head.*] It was freezing.

What about heat?

We had a potbellied stove, but they didn't give us coal. Marion had to cut wood, and that's what we burned. We didn't have any boys in our family, so Marion was the one who did that.

[*Leaves, returns with high school yearbook from Jerome—The Denson High Victoria—and opens it to a page with an aerial photo of the camp.*] Here's a block. This is the mess hall, and this is the washroom. See? There are six barracks on each side of those buildings, and six units within each barrack. Those two windows? The room inside was twenty by twenty-five [feet]—that was our unit.

What was the physical layout of your room?

The physical layout of our room was that we had five beds. [*Laughs.*] We also had a card table, and when it was cold mother put the toaster underneath it. The toaster Dr. Bruff brought us? We put the toaster under the table and a blanket over it, and we'd sit there to keep warm. So our legs would be warm. It's a Japanese style called *kotatsu*. It was the only way we could keep warm. I think the real *kotatsu* style is with an urn filled with hot coals under the table.

Did you have any paintings on the walls?

What? No.

Were there any partitions in the room?

No. It was just one room. The barracks did have walls that went all the way to the ceiling, so they were better than the stables in that regard. But you could still hear everything.

Each unit had a door to the outside. All the doors were on one side of the building. There were a few steps down to the dirt. You didn't go for walks—there was no place to go. Nothing was paved. It was just dirt—hardened dirt.

Was the camp surrounded by barbed wire?

Oh, yes. And towers with armed guards. The towers were along the edge of the camp. I never went near them. One was just like another.

What was the surrounding landscape like?

It was rich with swamps. Pretty flat.

The older men would go to the swamps that were within the camp and get cypress trees. They'd dig up the roots, soak them in a washtub and scrub them. They'd see figures in the roots and make sculptures out of them.

There was hardwood, too. Marion made a table out of it. The furniture that we had? She made it. She also made a coffee table—a beautiful hardwood coffee table—and some kind of chest to put our things in. Someone must have taught her how to do this.

Was it difficult not having any boys?

Yes.

[*Thinks.*] One of the families that lived in our unit had a bunch of boys. We were on one end and they were on the other. There were about four of them. They were real—do you know what *yogore* means? Rough. I don't even know if they had parents. My memory is that they were fishermen from San Pedro, and in most of those families the fathers were gone.

Gone?

Arrested. They knew the coastline, so they were considered particularly dangerous.

But they were good to us. They were in their early twenties. They had an older sister with them—dad, do you remember the older sister? She was married to Tomita? Kats Tomita? We met them at the Nishi's house.

KEN

No.

ALICE

Whenever they went to the bathroom to brush their teeth or whatnot they had to go by our door. And if there was heavy work to be done—carting things—they did it for us. They had this rough exterior, but they were nice. All of them. Our father wasn't there and we didn't have any brothers, and they sort of looked after us.

What happened to them?

I have no idea. That was the thing about camp—you left and lost touch with people. You had no idea where they went.

[*Thinks.*] You didn't see much of your neighbors. You didn't sit in front of your barrack, and you went to the washroom only if you had to go. If you had classmates, you didn't play in each other's homes. There was no place to play—it was just a narrow room with beds. Marion made a screen, so when you walked into the room it hid some of the beds. But there was nothing but beds. It was not conducive to play.

One time a friend of Grace's came over. His name was Vance Oyama. They were talking, and he wouldn't go home. Finally mother told him, "Go home!" We wanted to go to sleep, and we couldn't as long as he was there. There was no sitting area.

[*Pauses.*] But I remember these people who came from Hawaii. They lived close by—their block was near ours. There were about five hundred of them. These were families of men who had been taken—the fathers had been arrested and the families were sent to Jerome. And, oh, when they came it was cold—*cold*—and yet they were wearing sandals and thin, flowery shirts. I felt so sorry for them. They all came at one time. There wasn't a massive evacuation from Hawaii, so this was the biggest group. Five hundred people. Whole families without the father. [*Shakes her head.*] You wonder what ever happened to them.

Did you have any friends?

The friends I had were the two from my hometown. The two I played cards with at Santa Anita? Nobuko Endow and Esao Otsuki. But we didn't play cards at Jerome. Mother was there, and she didn't play cards. [*Laughs.*]

I did become good friends with May Ishimoto's [family friend] sister. Her name was Aiko. Very sweet girl. Just a wonderful human being. We became friends in school. She lives in Palos Verde.

What about activities?

Well, I belonged to that girls' club. There were a lot of us—maybe thirty. Mary Nakahara? She was the leader. I only knew her about half a year, but I still keep in touch with her.

[*Thinks.*] She became a real activist. After the war she went to New York City and lived in Bedford Stuyvesant. Do you remember when Malcolm X was shot? There's a picture of Mary right there with him.

Whenever I went to New York after the war I looked her up. Dad and I would go to her apartment. She married a 442nd guy who was in K Company with Hank [Kobayashi, Terry's husband]. Her married name is Kochiyama, and she goes by her Japanese name now, Yuri. She's about eighty, so she would have been in her early twenties when she started that girl's club. She must have realized there was a need for that kind of thing. She was a very giving person. A ray of sunshine.

But other than that, we didn't have any fun. Isn't that sad? I didn't go to dances. I didn't date. I was too young, too shy. I went to church. I knew all the ministers.

What were mealtimes like?

We always tried to eat together. You'd get in line and sit at the closest table that was free. The benches were attached to the table. My sisters said we had a lot of oysters—oysters after oysters, and I don't eat oysters. I can't think of a good meal there. But it wasn't as bad as Santa Anita— at least we didn't go hungry. And we did have rice, because they grow rice there.

You'd leave as soon as you were finished. You'd scrape off your plate and put your silverware where it was supposed to go.

Who washed the dishes?

Whoever had that job.

If you were a doctor, you got nineteen dollars a month. If you were a teacher you got sixteen dollars. A dishwasher got twelve dollars. Those were the three pay levels. Professional at the top, sub-professional in the middle, and non-professional at the bottom.

All of my sisters had jobs. Lily was supposed to be a nurse, but she was offered a job as the block manager's secretary, so she did that. Marion worked as a secretary at the high school. I don't know what Grace did. [Grace taught music in the elementary school. "I had no books," she said. "I had to teach them by rote."]

Lily didn't work in the hospital?

No. So she didn't take the job that was the reason we went to Jerome in the first place. She took the secretary job because it was right there in our block. The hospital was far away.

What about grandma?

[*Shakes her head.*] The Issei women didn't work. There weren't any jobs for them. As the younger people left, though, jobs opened up.

What about living supplies? Where did you go to buy things?

There was a canteen, which sold the bare essentials. Toothpaste, stuff like that. No food or clothes. It occupied one half of a barrack.

Terry worked in the canteen [at Heart Mountain]. She said that one time a young guy came in and wanted condoms, and she didn't know what they were. She said, "Well, tell me what they are. Describe them to me." [*Laughs.*] She's only sixteen, you know. Trying to be so helpful. "I'll look for them. Just describe them to me."

What if you needed more than the bare essentials?

We had a Sears Roebuck catalogue. They gave us a clothing allowance—something like $2.50 a month. We had a Montgomery Ward catalogue, too. So whatever you wanted had to come from the Sears or Montgomery Ward catalogue.

Mother taught me how to knit, and I remember ordering yarn from the Sears catalogue—they didn't have wool, because all the wool was going to the soldiers—but we were able to get this alpaca yarn and I knitted it. I made a sweater. We saved peach pits for buttons. The seeds? We'd split them in half and drill holes in them. Shave them down. People were ingenious with everything they had. The end of a toothbrush? The handle? People would chop it off and file it down to make miniature *getas* [sandals].

The knitting—that's how the exhibit at the Textile Museum [in Washington] came about, four or five years ago.

Tell me about that.

It was all about looping and knitting from ancient times. B.C. to the present. I had just come back from visiting mother and was having lunch with a group of friends. One of them had been in my weaving group— Ginny Friend—and I was telling her about mother. She's one of the donors to the Textile Museum and the Renwick [Art Gallery]. I didn't know this. But she started asking questions. "Did your mother knit?" It turned out she was on the search committee for the Textile Museum, and for the last panel of this exhibit they were looking for something contemporary. She said, "How would both of you like to have your things included in an exhibit at the Textile Museum?" So one day I took a bunch of stuff—baskets of things I had knitted and one of mother's sweaters—to the museum. The planners took pictures and selected what they wanted.

The basis for the story was that mother learned how to knit in prison and taught me how to knit in a relocation camp.

She learned how to knit in prison?

Yes. She knew how to tat—that's like a fine lace-making, except you have this little shuttle that you keep flipping back and forth—she knew how to crochet, she knew how to embroider, and she knew how to sew. But she didn't know how to knit.

Who taught her?

One of the thirty-three women at Terminal Island. They had nothing to do, and they prevailed upon one of the friendlier guards to bring them materials. Knitting needles, things like that. And somebody taught her how to knit.

When she returned to us at Santa Anita, I had nothing to do, so she taught me how to knit. That was the story.

What about medical needs? What was the hospital like?

Well, they called it a hospital because there were beds there.

Was it in one of the barracks?

Everything was in the barracks. The hospital, the school. Everything.
[*Thinks.*] I had to have my tonsils taken out. I remember sitting up while the doctor took them out with local anesthetic. He just clipped them out. I laid there for the rest of the day.

Was he Japanese American?

Yes. The hospital staff included internees. The camp doctors were good.

OUT PATIENT PROGRESS RECORD

Surname:	Imamoto	Given Name: Yoshiko	
Date of 1st visit: 11/4/43		Address: 18–10–A	
Age:	46	Occupation: Housewife	
Sex:	F	Race:	
Date:	Nov. 4, 1943		
Service:	Slipped on pavement & back hurts.		

Pt slipped on wet mess hall floor & struck on elbows & buttocks. No contusions on elbows. Rx Epsom salts—hot compress.

R. S. Howell

What about school?

Well, the schools weren't finished when we got there. We arrived in October, but didn't have school until January.

One block was set aside for the school buildings. They weren't heated, so it was cold in the winter. In the summer it was so hot we started at seven in the morning and walked to school carrying umbrellas to shield us from the sun.

Dear Father,

Thank you very much for [the] letter. All of us are healthy & well. How are you? The weather is quite chilly. Our stoves were installed this morning[,] so we get the warmth for the cold mornings & evenings. We are able to cook things on the stove because the top is flat. People cook go-han on it, toast bread, boil water etc. The trouble is to haul kindling wood to our house. We will not get coal & there isn't enough chopped wood. People don't like to be wood choppers or cutters [passage censored; Alice said she didn't know outgoing letters were being censored, but letters from her father had portions blacked out].

Anyway those are the circumstances & if there aren't more men to chop the trees in small pieces, we all may suffer severe inconveniences during the cold winter.

School starts this Wednesday. I'm not at all sure what my subjects will be. I would like to take Senior Problems (required)[,] Latin II, Advanced Algebra, English Literature, P.E. (Physics ?) & also a period of piano. Next semester, I have to take 1/2 semester of Chemistry because I dropped it in Excelsior. This is why I dropped it—Mr. Hawley gave us so much work to do, & after March 13, I didn't attend school everyday since I went to see you & mother & I didn't study. The quarter exam came a few days later & I was so behind in the work, I couldn't take the test & I was absent that day anyway & instead of getting a very low grade in Chemistry, I dropped it. So there maybe I won't take Physics. What I should have done was to take 3 years of French. I'm not sure if they teach Latin II. Anyway these teachers act & talk [passage censored] that I'm not sure if we'll learn as much as I did in Excelsior. The school buildings aren't made at all so school is to be held in a block. It is very far from our place. Especially when it rains, it'll be very hard on walking & possibly they might have [a] bus system for those who live far away—maybe not. Grace & Marion won't have to walk at all because they are workers. Grace says that the text books are all brand new ones. I don't think there are any chairs at all in school[,] so we'll probably have to sit on the floor. The chemistry book is the same as the one I used. Grace checked it out for me[,] so I have it at home now. I'm glad that school is starting—our summer vacation has been too long for anyone. I will write again after school starts about all of my subjects.

Your daughter,
Alice Imamoto
18–10–A
Jerome

I see by the yearbook that the school was called Denson High. Why Denson?

[*Shrugs.*] That was the closest crossroads. There wasn't anything at Jerome.

What was the faculty like?

We had a white principal and mostly white teachers. [According to the faculty photos, eighteen of the forty-three teachers were Nisei.] The white teachers were the dregs from the nearby school system. Really the dregs. [It should be noted, though, that the Mississippi Delta region of Southeast Arkansas was—and still is—one of the most impoverished areas in the country. Camp teachers were paid a civil service salary of $2,000 per year, nearly three times what they would have earned in the public school system. Also, some teachers, such as Mabel Rose Jamison Vogel, who taught art at Rohwer High School, became very close to the Japanese community and had a strong positive influence on their students.] I had a Latin teacher who was horrible. When I look back on it now—you wouldn't employ her anywhere. Least of all as a high school teacher.

And yet in this lousy Latin class—in any class—there was so much competition. Isn't that weird? We had no equipment and hardly any books, yet all the students competed to get good grades.

[*Looks at photos.*] But this was a terrific lady. Mary Kasai. She was a very good music teacher. Wonderful person. She was from Fresno. We kept in touch—exchanged Christmas cards for years.

Were there any extracurricular activities?

We had a band. [Yearbook photos show a nineteen-member band and a fourteen-member orchestra. The conductors stand with their backs to the camera, arms raised, before students sitting on wooden folding chairs arranged in semi-circles in the dirt. Barracks are visible in the background.]

Organized by Mr. Robert Head, early in the year, the Denson High Band has progressed rapidly. Although handicapped by lack of instruments, the small brass ensemble has already made public appearances. . . .

The orchestra is constituted of experienced players from the west coast schools and they play very excellently as an ensemble.

Being a fine group of musicians, they have appeared before a number of audiences throughout the center, a few of them being: Commencement exercises at the High School, Baccalaureate Services, for distinguished visitors and faculty, style show, Mother's Day program, and others. . . .

What about sports?

We had basketball. Baseball.

Who did you play against?

The other camp. Rohwer High School. We only played each other. The basketball team played three games.

Fighting valiantly for the Black and Gold, the Denson High's varsity teams came through the year with flying colors.

Beginning the season with basketball, coaches Norikane and Kunishima built a deadly potent casaba team. Twice, Rohwer High invaded Denson but met disastrous defeat each time. And again they met defeat when Denson chalked up another win at Rohwer High School.

Coming of cowhide season saw coaches Kunishima, Norikane and Kusakai rounding out a star-studded baseball nine. But Rohwer presented a superior team and consequently Denson met three defeats in three encounters.

So the season closed, leaving on the records a dead-lock of three wins each for Denson High and Rohwer High School.

["Outstanding seniors" are shown a few pages later. Alice is one of eight pictured individually. Her caption reads, "No nickname, just 'Alice.' Very active and talented in music, also active in community affairs, friend to all."]

[*Laughs.*]

[Next are the "Denson High Beauties"—Akiko Yamanaka, Masako Nobuto, and Akiko Shiotani.]

Aren't they pretty?

During a class meeting held by the Senior A class[,] 19 students were selected because of their outstanding characteristics. In our opinion even Hollywood's movie actors and actresses cannot vie with the chosen students for profile, personality, attractiveness, figure, physique, etc.

Most Popular Boy:	George Nakashima
Most Popular Girl :	Akiko Yamanaka
....	
Intelligent Girl:	Alice Imamoto

Intelligent girl?

[*Laughs.*] See? Show that to dad.

It looks like they tried to make things as normal as possible.

They tried. But I was so disappointed with the whole thing I didn't even stay for graduation. School started late, so it was extended through August. But I didn't stay to the end. I left to go to Oberlin.

What about music? Did you have a piano?

They brought one in. One of the mess halls—those were the biggest buildings—was used for a church. They put a piano in there, and I played for church services.

What kind of church was it?

It was interdenominational. There were several ministers. They would take turns using the church.

[*Thinks.*] About a month after I arrived—this was around Thanksgiving—I was asked to go with a white minister to one of the larger towns nearby and play for his church. A white church. I was one of the first to be allowed to leave camp. I had to have a special permit.

So I played for his church and afterwards was invited to the minister's house for tea. I remember the flouncy, flowered tablecloth. [*Pauses.*] It just seemed so nice. Because we had none of those amenities. And being in this home with all of those things. . . .

What town was it?

I think it was McGehee. That was the nearest town of any significance.

Were you allowed to leave at any other time?

I was allowed to leave on two other occasions. The second time was with two Caucasian women. We drove for hours to some kind of church conference, and again I played.

What I remember about that was that as we were driving on this unpaved road a cloud of dust was following us. [*Laughs.*] I don't remember anything else. Not a thing. Just that. The cloud of dust.

The third time I was allowed to go to a Girls' Reserve conference in Gulfport, Mississippi. We went by bus.

What was Girls' Reserve?

It was sort of like the Girl Scouts. I went with a bunch of girls from camp. We stopped overnight in New Orleans, and I remember sleeping on the floor of a gymnasium.

Were the other girls white?

Yes. We were the group from camp.

What was it like to be around them? The white girls?

[*Pauses.*] Well, I was shy. Very shy. So it was hard for me to interact with anybody. I mean, even with people in my own classes.

You asked me about the piano. Here's a funny story about that. They had some famous speakers—ministers—come to Jerome, probably making the rounds of camps. This man came—his name was Page. Kirby Page. He lived in California, but traveled all around. Now, I knew all the hymns by memory, but as I was playing my eyes strayed from the page. I started looking at people. And this piano was way out of tune. There was no heat, it was cold. It was so out of tune that it was pitched one whole tone lower. If you hit a C, you'd get a B. It wouldn't have mattered if I didn't have perfect pitch, but because I have perfect pitch, I started hearing the actual notes when I looked away from the page, not as they were written down, and when I looked back they didn't look right anymore. So I started to transpose in another key. Everyone was singing, and I threw them into another key entirely. [*Laughs.*] I was so embarrassed. That never would have happened anywhere else.

But this minister—somehow he knew what was going on, which was kind of remarkable. He said something to everyone about how it wasn't my fault. Saved my—what's the word? Now *that* I'll never forget.

What about weddings?

Yes, weddings were held there. [According to War Relocation Authority figures, a total of 2,120 weddings were held in the 10 camps, 103 in Jerome, and 153 in Rohwer. There were no divorces.] Dances. And people died, though I don't remember playing for any funerals.

Were they buried there?

Yes.

I wonder if they're still buried there.

Sure they are. [A total of 1,862 Japanese Americans died in imprisonment during the war. Seventy-six died in Jerome, and 168 in Rohwer.[16]]

What about holidays? What was Christmas like?

Pretty dismal. I don't remember.

December 25

Dear Father,

A very merry Christmas and a Happy New Year to one we miss very much this Christmas.

I do hope you will have a nice Christmas despite the fact we observe it under different circumstances and in a different surrounding. For some reason Christmas this year does not seem so real to us in this camp. Perhaps it's the atmosphere but anyway we all try to make the best of it.

To me this year its better than last year because I am with the other members of the family except for you.

We had a nice Christmas dinner in the evening with a short program and gifts for the little children. Through the kind efforts of our [C]aucasian friends the small children were not forgotten this Christmas. Both the Christian and the Buddhist children were given something.

In the evening the young people gave a very nice program. Will send you the program so you can get a better idea what it is. . . .

Your daughter,
Lily

16. *The Japanese American Legacy Project* Web site (www.densho.org).

Mom, can't you say anything about the absurdity of all these people being stuck behind barbed wire in the middle of nowhere?

[*Pauses.*] No. I can't voice it. I just know that I was miserable, and I wanted to get out of there as fast as I could.

[*Softly.*] See, while I was going to Excelsior I was so active. And this would have been my senior year. You looked forward to your senior year, because your senior year was the big year. Your senior year was everything. And what did I come to? Jerome.

Chapter Fourteen

Why were you picked to become a medic?

KEN

They had run out of them. See, the Germans were shooting them. Killing or wounding them. Right before we got there one of our men had been killed, and the body was out in no-man's land. There was nothing they could do—they couldn't send anyone out, because the Germans would shoot them, and there was no point in risking anyone's life, since he was dead. Finally, after a couple of days, the coast was clear and they sent out a four-man team [of medics]. But the Germans had booby-trapped the body, and when they moved it they set off the explosives. They were all blown up.

We were the fresh recruits, so they came around and picked four of us. You, you, you, and you. Henry and I happened to be standing next to each other, so they picked us along with two others. Thomas Kokubun? Him and another guy. The other guy was from the 100th—he was sort of the leader of the team. His name was Hayashi—I don't remember his first name.

[*Thinks.*] Henry and I were in training together, we were sent overseas together, we joined the 100th together, and we were picked as medics together. We were together throughout the whole thing.

Did you wear a red cross?

Yes. We had armbands with a red cross on it. One guy would carry the Red Cross flag.

What were your duties?

We had to go out in the middle of fighting to pick up bodies. Whenever somebody was wounded or killed we had to go out there, pick up the body, and bring him back.

[*Pauses.*] It was hard work. It was tough because bodies—especially dead bodies—are dead weight. Stiff. Very hard to carry. And it's a scary thing to be doing, because it ended up that both sides were shooting each other's medics. All it took was one guy getting shot—and it could have been accidental—and they would think he had been shot deliberately. So they would retaliate.

Were you armed?

No. That's another thing—we had no weapons at all. We couldn't shoot back. They took our guns away.

Did you treat the wounded?

Yes, but we didn't get any training.

What did you treat them with?

Bandages, things like that. Stop the bleeding. It was just temporary.

[*Long pause.*] There was one guy—this is among the things I have never forgotten. He was very badly wounded. We brought him into a farmhouse. He had been attacking two German machine gun nests in another farmhouse, and destroyed both of them. By himself. Crawled up to the house and killed the Germans manning the machine guns. But there were other Germans in the house, and as he was approaching a window—he was about to throw a grenade—one of them threw a grenade first. It exploded right in front of him. Blasted him. We brought him back to the farmhouse. It was in the afternoon.

Do you remember his name?

Yes. Koda. I don't know his first name. [*Goes back to the list of the dead. Looks it up.*] Here it is. Koda. Kiichi. [*Spells it.*] There's only one Koda, so this must be him. He got the Distinguished Service Cross for that action.

We had him in that farmhouse for several hours. Couldn't get him out. Couldn't get him to an aid station—the Germans had surrounded the whole area. What they call crossfire? Interlocking? Any movement and they'd start firing immediately. Shells would start coming in. So we were stuck in that farmhouse.

How many guys were there?

Five of us. Four of us [medics] and him.

I remember looking at him. He was wounded all over. Even down to his big toe. Shrapnel—just blasted with shrapnel. I doubt he would have survived even if we had gotten him back. He was just too badly wounded. But he never complained. Every so often he would ask for water. Someone would give him a sip and he'd lie back down. And then all of a sudden he sat up. He said, "I'm going to pretend that I'm dead," and laughed. He gave a loud laugh, like he was making a joke, and flopped back down and died.

Isn't that weird? He knew he was going to die. He said, "I'm going to pretend that I'm dead," like he was making a joke, and died.

What did you do?

We covered him with a blanket and said the Lord's Prayer.

[*Voice thickens.*] I tell you, these guys. I've seen a number of them die. And they were all real brave men. They never cried. They never complained.

[*Emotional.*] It's a terrible feeling to see your own men dying or dead. One time we were marching up in the hills, following this path, and we saw that someone had placed one of our men on a big rock. Carefully laid him there. I went up to the body and looked at him. He had been killed recently, maybe only a half hour or so earlier, but already the features were getting swollen, and when I first looked at him I thought he was somebody from my hometown. I was shocked. Looking at his face he looked just like this guy I knew. So I picked up his dog tag and looked at the name, but it wasn't him. It wasn't anybody I knew.

Who was the guy from your hometown?

Nakamoto. Yukio Nakamoto. And this guy wasn't Nakamoto. Nakamoto survived the war.

Did you ever tell him?

No. He never knew.

[*Pauses.*] Another time we were trying to evacuate an officer. He had a Japanese name, but he was only half-Japanese. I think he was from New York. His name was Takagi. Boone Takagi.

Boone?

Boone. Like Daniel Boone? [*Smiles.*] He was a big guy. Heavy. Over 200 pounds. We were trying to get him to the aid station. He was badly wounded, in deep pain. He had a bullet in the belly. We were having a tough time. Going up and down hills. Every so often we had to stop, put him down, and rest, because we were so tired. And I remember feeling very badly about it, because we needed to get him back quickly. It meant his survival. Yet we couldn't go. And then we got lost. Completely lost. We didn't know where the German lines were, where our lines were. It would have been easy to go in the wrong direction and get captured. It's happened. So we stopped. We were looking around, asking each other, "Which way should we go?" when he kind of propped himself up and looked around. He said, "That way, boys." He pointed in the direction he thought we should go, and he was right. We went in that direction and found the aid station. We waited while the doctor went over him. And, gee, within five minutes the doctor came out and said, "He's gone." [Emotional.] I felt so bad. So bad. I thought if we'd only gotten him back sooner he could have been saved.

Did you know him?

I knew of him. He was an officer in the antitank company, and I had good friends in that outfit. So I knew who he was.

[Looks at list again.] It's surprising to me that so many officers got killed. Takagi was just one. I was going through this list, marking the names of all the people I knew who had died in action, either friends or people I had gotten to know. I counted about twenty-two. And I realized that a lot of officers had been killed. Do you see the circles?

Those aren't Japanese names.

No, they're not. So you know they were officers. I became curious as to how many officers in the 442nd had been killed, so I started picking out all the English names and putting circles around them. I counted twenty-four. That's a pretty high number.

I'd like to ask how you were wounded.

How I was wounded?

Yes.

[Thinks.] Well, the first time was from a mortar shell. We were in back of a small Italian farmhouse. I had taken off my helmet and was leaning against the wall. The chaplain was with us. He was standing in front of me, and all of a sudden a mortar landed close by. Bam! Dirt and everything was flying all around. When things cleared up I felt something on my throat. I was bleeding. A shell fragment had gone right underneath my chin and gashed me. That's all I had. They gave me a Purple Heart for that. [*Laughs.*]

The chaplain had a shell fragment go right between his chest and his arm—it cut him just like the other one had cut me. He had a gash, too.

Do you remember his name?

Oh yes. His name was Chaplain Yost, from Pennsylvania. Chaplain Israel Yost. He was a Lutheran minister.

Do you know if he's still alive?

[*Smiles.*] He's alive. The Smithsonian exhibit? "A More Perfect Union"?[17] They held a reunion of the 442nd to coincide with the opening of that exhibit, a dinner at one of the big hotels in Washington. So I went. Outside the dining room was a list of everyone in attendance. I was looking down the list and saw "Israel Yost." So I started asking around, "Does anyone know Chaplain Yost?" Somebody said, "Yes, he's here. I just saw him. He was standing outside." So I went outside and, sure enough, there he was. He had changed, of course. His wife was with him. I went up to him and said, "Chaplain Yost, you won't remember me, but I was with you through a great part of the fighting." He asked me my name and I told him, but of course he had no recollection. I said, "Do you remember the time a mortar shell landed about five feet from us and I got cut underneath my chin and you got cut between your chest and your arm? It went right through?" He said, "Oh yes, I remember that." [*Laughs.*]

He was an amazing man. There were times when we'd be very tired, we'd finally rest after marching for a long time, and here he'd come. Singing! Singing these Hawaiian songs the boys had taught him. And skipping! [*Gets up and starts skipping.*] Like this. I remember him passing me by, singing this Hawaiian song. [*Sings.*] "I was strolling nonchalantly in Hawaii. Never dreaming sweet romance was on its way. Then the unexpected happened in Hawaii. On a Honolulu hula holiday." Singing that song and skipping along, you know, just trying to get our spirits up.

17. As part of the celebration of the bicentennial of the U.S. Constitution in 1987, the Smithsonian's National Museum of American History established an exhibit called "A More Perfect Union: Japanese Americans and the U.S. Constitution."

I told his wife that. I told his wife that I remember him skipping along and singing these Hawaiian songs. She said, "That would be just like him. That would be just like him."

[*Pauses.*] You know, we'd all be so tired. Very discouraged. And here he'd come. Smiling and laughing. [*Emotional.*] Singing. Just trying to keep our spirits up.

What was he like?

He was tall. A nice-looking man. We talked at the reunion about what he did after the war. He said he had a chance to serve at a ministry in Hawaii for two years, so he went to Hawaii and spent two years there.

He was right there at the front with us. Administering last rites, comforting the wounded. Things like that. He was right there with us.

Was he assigned to your outfit?

Yes. The 100th Infantry had Chaplain Yost. The 442nd had three Nisei chaplains. Two were from Hawaii—Chaplain Higuchi and Chaplain Yamada. The third was from the mainland—Chaplain Aki. George Aki.

ALICE

I knew him. He was in our camp.

He was in Jerome?

Yes. He was a minister in Jerome.

KEN

At Camp Shelby we had a chaplain from the South. Chaplain West. But when the 442nd joined us in Italy, I didn't see him. I asked someone, "Where's Chaplain West?" They said he had been transferred out. He was overheard to have made some derogatory statement about Japanese Americans.

Kind of un-chaplain like.

[*Laughs.*] Yes. So they got rid of him.

What about the second time you were wounded?

You want the circumstances of the second time I was wounded?

Yes.

[*Long pause.*] You know, I knew the name of the town, but I can't recall it now. It was very near—have you heard of the Arno River? It was very near the Arno River.

The Germans had been cleared out, so we had the town to ourselves. We were in a building, and it was getting dark. It was summertime. The Germans threw in several artillery shells, which landed fairly close, but were hitting other buildings. It was strange, because they were shelling us, and I should have been in a safer place in the building—against the wall, say, or under a table. All I remember is hearing this loud crash. A shell came in and hit the building next to us. The next thing I knew I was down on the floor. I didn't feel any pain. Then Henry was standing above me.

Were other people there?

There were a couple of other guys there, but I don't remember who. Henry was saying, "Get up. Get up. It's over." But I couldn't move. I couldn't move my arms. Couldn't move my legs. Couldn't move anything. I was totally paralyzed. I said, "I don't know what's wrong. Maybe I was hit." At that moment I felt wetness on my back. By then the other guys had come over, and I said, "I think I got it in the back." So they turned me over and pulled up my shirt. One of them said, "Yeah, you're bleeding." They patched me up and called for an ambulance. I had to wait a long time, several hours. It was about 11 o'clock at night when the ambulance finally came. I couldn't move at all. Henry stayed with me until the ambulance arrived. He watched them load me onto the ambulance, and then he said goodbye to me. [*Voice thickens.*] I said, "Henry, take care of yourself. Be careful." That's what I remember saying to him.

Were you in a lot of pain?

[*Shakes his head.*] I was in no pain. No pain at all. But they must have given me a shot of morphine, because I went to sleep. I don't know how long it took to get to the field hospital, but the next thing I knew I was lying on a cement slab and this guy was going to take an X ray of my back to try to locate the fragment. I remember him saying "Can you move up a little?" but when I tried to move up I passed out. I don't remember anything else. They operated that night and flew me out. That field hospital, by the way, was in a town called Siena. I think Siena is known for its marble. It's near Pisa.

I woke up the next morning. I was still in no pain, just total numbness. I was lying on a cot in a big hospital tent—all the wounded were in there. And this is odd, but when I opened my eyes the first person I saw was a guy from my hometown. He was about ten feet away, and had a big bandage around his head. He had an unusual name. Kazuso. Kazuso Nishimoto. I tried to call him, "Kazuso!" But no sound came out. I tried again, "Kazuso!" Nothing. That tired me out, so I closed my eyes. When I opened them again he was standing right beside my bed. The nurse had seen me trying to call him, and led him over to me. So we talked. He told me he'd been hit in the head, and that they put a big steel plate in there. He was never the same after that.

I saw him after the war. I should have talked to him, you know? I was in a public building in Lihue [Kauai], using the restroom. And there he was. He was an ordinary janitor, mopping the floors. I didn't want to embarrass him, because he was doing this menial work. But I should have talked to him. That was in '45, maybe '46. Then I heard he died. He was sort of deranged. Haruto told me he approached him once with a knife.

[*Thinks.*] You know, it wasn't until after the war that I found out what I was doing when the shell hit. Before that it was all a blank. But in '46 I met Henry in Honolulu, and we talked. He asked me, "Do you remember what we were doing when you got hit?" I said no. I said, "I know you were right with me, but I don't remember." He said, "You had your pants down, and I was picking fleas off your body." [*Laughs.*] See, it was summertime, and we used to sleep in barns and farmhouses. We were full of fleas! My trousers, where the crease is? It would be lined with fleas. We were scratching all the time. We were filthy. We never took baths. One night, after we'd been marching for hours, they finally said, "Okay, we're going to stop here." It was pitch black, and I couldn't see anything. I was feeling around, trying to find a place to lie down and go to sleep, and I came upon this big mound of something. I thought it was straw—it was nice and dry. Soft. So I just flopped into it and went to sleep. The next morning when I woke up I discovered I'd been sleeping in a big pile of dried chicken manure. [*Laughs.*] You'd get so tired you didn't care about anything.

What happened to Henry after you were wounded?

We talked about that, too. I lost track of him. I never wrote to him, and he never wrote to me because he didn't know where I was. I don't know why I didn't write to him. I used to think about him, but I never wrote to him. I should have, but I didn't.

I asked him if he ever got wounded aside from the time the shell fragment went through his helmet and burned his neck. He said no, but that he had a lot of close calls. He said one morning he dug a hole to do his business and was squatting over the hole when a mortar shell came in and landed right in front of him. It was a dud. He said, "I must have jumped six feet in the air!" [*Laughs.*]

Even during our time together we had a lot of close calls. Once we got way ahead of everybody else—ahead of the whole regiment. The four of us. I don't know how it happened. We cleared the top of a hill, and a German machine gun on the other side opened up. Bullets were splattering all around. So we took off down the hill, out of the line of fire, toward this little town, and when we got there the fourth guy was missing. See, we worked as a team, and we needed him. He didn't join us until much later that night, and when he did we gave him hell. We asked him, "Where the hell were you? Why didn't you come down with us?" He said, "I was so scared I ran back." He was the only guy I ever knew who ran back. He showed us his shovel—we all carried a small shovel with a wooden handle. A bullet had knocked the handle off. [*Laughs.*]

Where is Henry today?
He's gone.

He died?
Yes.

When?
About three years ago. He had cancer—throat cancer. He was a smoker, and I don't think he ever quit.

Where did he live?
Honolulu. He received a PhD from [the University of California at] Davis in agriculture—plant pathology, something like that. He was interested in agriculture, so he went to Davis.

What did he do for a living?

He taught at the University of Hawaii. He got married. We kept in touch for a while, but then we stopped. Just like everything else.

So you have two Purple Hearts?

I have two Purple Hearts. When you have two they call it a Purple Heart with an Oak Leaf Cluster.

And you have a Bronze Star?

Yes.

What did you do to get that?

Oh, they were giving Bronze Stars to everybody. [*Laughs.*]

Chapter Fifteen

When did grandpa join you?

ALICE

In February of '43. He was gone almost a year—from March of '42 to February of '43.

Did you know he was coming back?

No. We actually thought he'd be gone longer, because he was a prisoner of war. We didn't think we'd see him for the duration of the war. He was one of the first prisoners of war to be allowed to rejoin their families.

Why did they let him go?

Did you read the letter I wrote? I wrote a letter and sent it to the War Relocation Authority. Mother and father said it was because of that letter that he was allowed to come home.

To the Authorities of the Lordsburg Internment Camp,

I am the youngest of four daughters of Zenichi Imamoto who is interned in your camp for the duration of the war. I am 15 years old and am writing this letter to you straight from the bottom of my heart to tell you how I feel about the fact that my father can't be returned to all of us. We have tried for a rehearing, asking our many old friends to rewrite affidavits for father's sake. We had sent quite a few to District Attorney Wm. Fleet Palmer's office, waiting day after day for any kind of a response. It has been almost 2 months but we haven't had any reply. My high school principal, Mr. Ralph Burnight of Excelsior High School in Norwalk, California, who is a very prominent and brilliant man[,] had tried to get in touch with Dist. Attorney Palmer or his assistant, Mr. Gault, many times but wasn't able to do anything about the rehearing. Recently we heard that District Attorney Palmer had passed away and so I decided to write to you right away since I know those affidavits didn't do any good.

We have just been relocated from Santa Anita, California[,] to Jerome, Arkansas[,] and we were all busy packing away everything the past few weeks. We have no brothers or no relatives at all, and all the freighting and heavy packing had to be done among us girls.

All through my life[,] since I could remember, my father has been a tolerant man, kind in his thoughts and doing everything possible for all of us. He never touches tobacco or liquor and has been a very faithful member, a possessing Christian of the church. If he did scold us, he only did it because he loved us and wanted us to do the right thing.

Father has taught the Japanese language for several years. I was in his class for a few years & he never has taught the students subversive things. The sole purpose I went to school was to be able to talk better to my parents & to other parents who speak Japanese. Some children have to speak to their parents in English and[,] in turn, the parents speak in Japanese. In that way, there can't be much of an understanding between the children and parents. Father has brought us up to be loyal citizens of America. Here I am, born in America and possessing all the luxuries of living the American Way of Life & I am more than grateful for it[,] for no other country could give it to us. My sisters and I, we don't know what Japan is like, none of us have ever been there and we have no thought of going. My father and mother have never returned to Japan since they arrived in America so very long ago. Father had come here when he was still in his early teens and has lived here ever since, attending Berkeley Hi School and University of California summer session. Because he is an oriental, he can't take out citizenship papers so that he could become a real citizen. America has been his mother country since he has been here. He is no different from any of you—just because he has black hair and yellow skin. It wasn't his fault that he was born an oriental. Even though his appearance is different from yours, his heart has the same feeling and thoughts about America as any of you loyal citizens do. He has been very interested in all of our education—my 3 sisters have all graduated High School taking College Preparatory Courses. The oldest sister would have graduated U.C. of Calif. this year except that she came home suddenly before her mid-terms in April when father and mother were both arrested because my 18 year old sister and I were the only ones home. My other sister was also up north, attending a nurses' training school in San Leandro. They both quit and came home the day before the curfew law was enforced, and then evacuation began. When dad and mother were both arrested, that was the saddest day in my life—we didn't know what to do—we hardly ate or could do anything since mother had always done things for us. We had no relatives to go to and until my sisters came home, the two of us endured it for 2 weeks with the help of friends. We didn't want our eldest sister to come home[,] because she had only 2 months to go[,] but she did come home anyway because of worries for us, and she didn't receive her B.A. degree.

Father always encouraged us to take part in school activities such as student government etc. I played the Hammond organ for many of the school assemblies. Father let all of us learn to play an instrument, piano, violin, cello. Father was a P.T.A. member every year from when my eldest sister was in lower elementary grades. He not only was a member by name but attended the meetings and always was the only parent of all the Orientals present.

He helped the Red Cross Drive tremendously and the Japanese School Board of trustees all went to the faculties' homes and collected funds. Under the direction of my father, they all had collected over $1000.00 from the few farmers around our town who had to toil in the fields from early morning to night to make their daily bread.

Father had worked daily for about two weeks with a Lieutenant Ellis of the Norwalk Sheriff Station to go around and make a survey of every single person of Japanese race in about 4 little towns around Norwalk. Though he was not well in health due to stomach ulcer, he offered to work all day for this period of time without any pay at all.

Every time I think of my father, it makes me sad and lonely and tears soon come out and I can't hold it back. We don't know how long this war is going to last and I don't know how much longer I can stand it if father doesn't come back to us. My father is so soft hearted and he couldn't harm a thing and that makes me more sad for the fact that he's interned in camp without the family. Why is father interned? Please tell me that—I see no reason why he is interned. You accuse him of things that he doesn't even do. We have lived longer with father than anyone else in the world, we are the ones to know if he had done anything against this country[,] of which I know he hasn't done at all. I guess there isn't much to do to get him back to us—we have tried every way possible. If he can't come back, please all of us would like to be with him there in Lordsburg. I will offer with all my heart and soul to be the supponser [sponsor] of father if you will let him return[,] and I will guarantee to all of you that father's character and conduct will be the most kindest and satisfactory one. Father gets along well with everyone—both those of Japanese race and his many friends of Caucasians. Please won't you let him return—I plead with you—we know father the most of anybody and he would never do any harm.

Do you know how it is to have your only one dear father be taken away from you when you are only 15? I envy others who have their fathers and mothers with them when our father is just as innocent as they are. We were just shocked when we heard that father was interned. The fact that he is interned is worse than being in jail, not because of the surroundings and life there but because we aren't able to visit him and see him[,] since we are in camp too. I know father is treated very good there[,] and I have no worries about him to that respect[,] but we all are lonely because he isn't with us and we don't know how long the war will last until we will get to see him again.

A man in camp with him had drawn a picture of father and had sent it to us[;] we have it hung up where we could see it the most. I look at it and while I am lying in bed to sleep, I always think of father every night and have to cry. I pray and pray to God that he may be able to return. Do you believe you are doing justice to all of us by breaking up our family and interning a man who is innocent? So many men have come back from those detention camps and I don't see why they get to come back and father doesn't. Don't you think you have made a grave mistake?

Won't you all please think this matter over carefully and study over our case and take it to heart? You won't be making a mistake if you let him return. Haven't you found him kind and sincere?

I pray that you could do something for us so that he may be able to return to us soon.

I shall be anxiously waiting for a reply from you soon.

Sincerely yours,
Alice Imamoto
18–10–A
Jerome Relocation Center
Denson, Arkansas

Did you get a response?

I think the response was that they let him go.

JUSTICE DEPARTMENT ORDER

File no. 146–13–2–12–1580
In the matter of (James) Zenichi Imamoto, Alien Enemy

The above-named alien enemy having been interned by order dated May 20, 1942; and a rehearing have been had herein; and the Alien Enemy Hearing Board having recommended that said alien enemy be paroled; NOW, THEREFORE, upon consideration thereof and upon reconsideration of all the evidence bearing upon this matter,

IT IS ORDERED that said order dated May 20, 1942, be, and the same hereby is vacated and set aside; and it is

FURTHER ORDERED that said alien enemy be transferred to a Relocation Center and paroled in the custody of the District Parole Officer for the District in which said Relocation Center is situated; that the parole be conditioned upon the alien enemy's reporting his activities to his sponsor weekly; and that the said parole be further conditioned upon the execution of and compliance with the sponsor's and parolee's agreements provided by the Immigration and Naturalization Service.

(signed) Francis Biddle
ATTORNEY GENERAL
January 8, 1943

IMMIGRATION AND NATURALIZATION SERVICE TRAVEL AGREEMENT

Feb. 4, 1943:

I, JAMES ZENICHI IMAMOTO, in consideration of my release on interim parole from the Army Internment Camp, Lordsburg, New Mexico, agree to proceed directly to the Jerome War Relocation Project, Jerome, Arkansas, and to report my arrival at that project, within twenty-four hours, to the Chief District Parole Officer, Immigration and Naturalization Service, Pere Marquette Building, New Orleans, Louisiana.

I further agree to abide by all rules and regulations governing the conduct of alien enemies while traveling from Lordsburg, New Mexico, to the Jerome War Relocation Project, and further agree to abide by such rules and regulations while I am a resident of that relocation project.

I understand that if and when I am released from the relocation project it will be necessary to obtain a sponsor for me prior to such release, to whom I will make weekly reports.

(signed) JAMES ZENICHI IMAMOTO
Witness:
(signed) Donald B. Burnett,
Chief District Parole Officer

U.S. DEPARTMENT OF JUSTICE
IMMIGRATION AND NATURALIZATION SERVICE
U.S. COURTHOUSE
P.O. BOX 1650
EL PASO, TEXAS
February 4, 1943

James Zenichi Imamoto
Army Internment Camp
Lordsburg, New Mexico

Dear Sir:

This will serve as your authority to travel from Lordsburg, New Mexico, to the Jerome War Relocation Project, Jerome, Arkansas, following your release on interim parole from the Army Internment Camp.

You will depart from Lordsburg on the Southern Pacific train at approximately 6:30 A.M., arriving at El Paso, Texas, at approximately 9:50 A.M. You will leave El Paso on the same day at 9:20 P.M., traveling via the Texas & Pacific Railway, and will arrive in Little Rock, Arkansas, at 11:55 P.M. You will depart from Little Rock at 2:15 A.M. on the Missouri Pacific Railroad and arrive at Jerome, Arkansas at 5:09 A.M. At Jerome you will be met by a representative of the Jerome War Relocation Project who will convey you to the Project.

This travel authority must be surrendered by you upon your arrival at the relocation project, and must not be considered as authority for any travel other than that outlined above.

Respectfully,
For the District Director:
(signed) Donald B. Burnett,
Chief District Parole Officer,
El Paso District

(signed) James Zenichi Imamoto

Personal Description: Japanese, male; age 53; weight 120 pounds; height, 5'4"; brown eyes; black-grey hair; wears glasses; burn scar on right hand across knuckles.

PROJECT DIRECTOR   Lordsburg, New Mexico
JEROME WAR RELOCATION PROJECT   February 5, 1943
DENSON, ARKANSAS
JAMES ZENICHI IMAMOTO FORMERLY INTERNED ARMY INTERNMENT
CAMP LORDSBURG RELEASED ON FEBRUARY 5 TRAVELING VIA T&P
AND MISSOURI PACIFIC. EXPECTED TO ARRIVE JEROME, 5:09 AM FEB-
RUARY 7. PLEASE ARRANGE TO MEET ALIEN AND TELEGRAPHICALLY
VERIFY HIS ARRIVAL.

DONALD B. BURNETT
CHIEF DISTRICT
PAROLE OFFICER

IMMIGRATION AND NATURALIZATION SERVICE PURCHASE ORDER

Appropriation: Salaries & Expenses, alien enemy
VENDOR: Dining Car Steward, Texas & Pacific Railway, en route El Paso,
Texas to Jerome, Arkansas
Article or Service: Please furnish one dinner to the Japanese alien enemy
JAMES ZENICHI IMAMOTO
Quantity: 1
Unit: meal
Price: 1.00

What do you remember of his return?

Oh, I was happy. I don't remember much more than that. I don't remember anything specific. But we were so happy to have him back. He'd been
away for so long.

Did he talk about what he went through?

Not that I remember. I asked Grace if she remembered father saying
anything about prison, and she said no, he never talked about it. Mother
didn't talk about it either.

Why not?

The same reason I never talked about my camp experience.

And what was that?

[*Long pause.*] Well, when you have something bad done to you, you get to thinking *you* were bad. That it was your fault. That's the psychology. And that's what I thought. So I never talked about it. I'm also very sensitive— if nobody wants to listen, I'm not going to talk. It was painful.

Even now, if the subject comes up in conversation, I try to get a sense of whether that person really wants to listen or not. If they have a sympathetic ear or not.

How could you think it was your fault?

[*Long pause.*] It's hard to explain. You feel ashamed.

I think a lot of victims feel that way. [*Indicates she has nothing more to say.*]

What kind of life did grandpa settle into at Jerome?

He got a job. He worked for the social services.

Doing what?

It was like social welfare. Counseling. You know, people needed help.

WAR RELOCATION AUTHORITY
Jerome Relocation Center
ENLISTEE SERVICE AND PAYMENT RECORD CARD
FISCAL YEAR 1943

Identification No.: X-951–F   Name: Imamoto, Zenichi
Address: 18–10–F   Sex: M

E.O.D. Date	Division	Designation	Rate of Pay
5–17–43	Com. Ser.	Welfare-Case Worker	16.00

CHARACTERISTICS OF PERFORMANCE

NAME: Imamoto, Zenichi
DATES EMPLOYED: 5/17/43—present
TITLE: Counseling Aide
WAGE RATE: $16 [per month]

Mr. Imamoto's schooling in the United States was better than the average. His experience was that of a leader among the Japanese. He made wide acquaintances in connection with his work as secretary of the Strawberry Growers' Association. In spite of all this training and good experience, Mr. Imamoto never became fluent in English. Japanese was always his language and his difficulty with English is no doubt his chief handicap as a Counseling Aide.

Mr. Imamoto was hired a month or two after his parole from internment [at Lordsburg]. He was recommended as a person who commanded the respect of everyone and neither he nor those who knew him claimed that he had any special skills which would apply in counseling. That general recommendation proved accurate.

Mr. Imamoto is one of the most polite and mannerly men imaginable. He is extremely considerate of the other person and he has never been asked to do anything which he was not willing to try. However, he does not have the drive and resourcefulness required for an effective case worker or counseling Aide. It seems that he resists making decisions which involve any degree of judgment. His failure to eventuate in case situations may not be so much a fear of making decisions as lack of understanding caused by his limitations in English.

Mr. Imamoto is interested in social work and he would have a good start at Rohwer because he knows so many people and they undoubtedly have high respect for him. If he could collaborate with a younger bilingual person who would help him translate and record and make sure that he understands the technical parts of instructions, I think he would be reasonably productive. As we have worked here without any close supervision or much assistance from a Japanese-speaking person in detailing instructions to him, he has often failed to grasp the significance of an assignment or a case problem and his work has not been quite analytical and thorough enough to meet the need. At the same time, as mentioned above, none of his contacts have ever caused any embarrassment except as a result of some omission. He has never committed any serious errors in his positive activities.

In summary, I would like to re-emphasize that Mr. Imamoto is Americanized in his attitude and one attribute is that he is considered a leader among the Christian groups. He has much in his favor as an individual in the community, but he isn't strong as a professional counselor.

J. Lloyd Webb, Counselor
May 26, 1944   Community Welfare Section

WAR RELOCATION AUTHORITY
Rohwer Relocation Center
ENLISTEE SERVICE AND PAYMENT RECORD CARD
FISCAL YEAR 1944

Identification No.: 8369   Name: Imamoto, Zenichi
Address: 24–10–E   Sex: M

E.O.D. Date	Division	Designation	Rate of Pay
6–22–44	Fire Program	Fireman	$16.00

He was also a fireman?

Well, counseling proved to be too much, so he became a fireman. He liked that. There were no fires. [*Laughs.*]

How do you think the whole experience affected him?

Oh, it ruined him. It did. The whole thing was rough on him.

[*Thinks.*] See, before the war, as the principal of a Japanese school, he was the leader of the community. *The* leader. People came to him for advice. And he had a very strong feeling of responsibility for those people. He had civic pride. He always went to PTA meetings—he was the only Asian who did. He was straight as an arrow. There was an expression mother used to describe him: *Baka shojiki.* It means you're so honest you're dumb. [*Laughs.*] *Baka* means "dumb" and *shojiki* means "honest."

But after the war, after relocation, he was cleaning a house. He had a record, and the only job he could get was as a domestic. Mother had more status than him—she was a cook. Just think what that would do to you. He was fifty-four. That would be you in ten years. Think about what would happen to you if you had to leave everything you've been building up to. When he left camp his total worth was thirty dollars. That's what his personal belongings were worth, all that he owned. Thirty dollars. Mother's was eleven.

Was he a pacifist?

[*Firmly.*] Yes. Yes. Very much so.

He couldn't kill a chicken. Literally. We had chickens, and if we were going to kill one, Lily had to do it. That was father.

What about grandma? Do you feel that the experience ruined her?

No.

Why not?

Because she never looks back. Between the two of them, mother was stronger.

[*Thinks.*] She's had to rebuild her life so many times. She had to rebuild it when she first came to this country, and when the war broke out and we had to go into the camps. Then the war ended and she and father came to Washington to work as domestics. Then they went back to (Compton) California to teach [at a Japanese] school again [in 1954]. Then they retired from teaching and moved up to Berkeley [in 1963]. Then she was widowed [he died of colon cancer and pneumonia at the age of 90 in 1980]. And then, at the age of 100 [in 1998], she went into a nursing home—that was an especially hard time for her. But Grace said she never talks about Berkeley, which was her home for so many years, despite the fact that when she lived there she said, "I can live in this house even if I'm blind." She loved that house. She didn't want to go into a nursing home. But now that she's in a nursing home, she never talks about Berkeley. She doesn't look back.

She never talks about her war experiences?

No. We [the sisters] want to find out as much as we can, but she won't talk about it. She says, "Oh, that's past history."

Chapter Sixteen

Where did you go after your surgery in the field hospital?

KEN

I was flown to a big hospital in Rome. The 33rd General Hospital. I spent three months recovering there.

The hospital had a main building and a lot of large tents set up around it. I was in one of the tents. As I recall, there were three rows of cots in each tent, and each row had about twenty cots. So that's what—twenty, forty, sixty men.

Actually, when I was first brought in I was on a stretcher in a hallway in the main building. A nurse gave me a shot—I think it was morphine again, because it put me out—and when I woke up I was in one of the tents.

Much of those first few weeks is vague. I remember a doctor and a nurse would come by every once in a while to change my dressing. Since I was injured on my back, they'd have to put me on my stomach. One time the guy next to me watched them change my dressing, and after they left he said, "You know where you got hit? Right in the middle of your back. It's amazing you're not totally paralyzed." But I could barely move for at least two weeks. All I did was lie there, all day long, with my eyes closed.

Was he Japanese American?

No. He was white. They were mostly white soldiers. I have a picture that somebody took of me with six or seven of them.

Did you become friends with them?

I became good friends with one of them. Tony Lehner. [*Spells it.*] Jewish guy. He was from New York. When they discharged me from the hospital, he knew I was going home instead of back to the front, so he told me, "If you're ever in New York City, I want you to call my parents. I'll give you their names and phone number. Please call them. You may be home before I do." So I had his family's name and number in my wallet, and when I landed in New York that was the first thing I did. I went to a phone booth and called his family.

Who did you talk to?
   His father. I told him who I was and why I was calling—that I knew his son when I was in the hospital, and he'd asked me to call them.

What did his father say?
   I don't remember. They were happy to hear from me, though.

Where was Tony Lehner wounded?
   In his foot. It wasn't a serious injury, so in all probability he went back to the fighting.

Do you know if he survived the war?
   No. But when I called his family it was three or four months after I'd last seen him, and they didn't say anything about him being dead.

What do you remember about him?
   That he was a nice guy. We didn't do much talking about personal things, though, so I never found out what he did before the war or anything about his family.
   [*Thinks.*] I still remember my nurse's name. Isn't that interesting? After all these years? She was a very nice woman. Kramer. [*Spells it.*] She must have been Jewish, too. That's a Jewish name.

What was her first name?
   I didn't know her first name. But she was a second lieutenant.

What do you remember about her?
   That she was very nice. Very pretty. Plump.
   There was another nurse—I don't remember her name. But she woke me up in the middle of the night to ask if I knew what *besame mucho* meant. She woke me up to ask me that. [*Laughs.*] She thought I was Spanish.

Why did she want to know that?

It was the name of a popular song. I knew what it meant, so I told her and went back to sleep.

What does it mean?

It means "Kiss me a lot." [*Laughs.*]

Did you ever tell her you weren't Spanish?

No.

Why not?

[*Shrugs. Laughs.*]

Were there other Nisei in the hospital?

Yes. There was another guy from Kauai, a good football player. His name was Doi. Wally Doi. He'd lost his leg. A grenade exploded right at his feet. Destroyed his ankle.

Somehow I heard he was there. So I went looking for him. This was about a month after I arrived—by that point I could walk. I found him in one of the beds.

He told me that because of football, he'd always tried to protect his legs in combat. He felt that his legs were the most important part of his body. But what he feared the most was exactly what happened—he lost his leg. They amputated it below the knee. So as far as sports were concerned it was over for him.

Was he a good football player?

Oh yes. He played guard for the University of Hawaii.

He was a tough guy. A judo black belt. He told me that even after basic training the Nisei were getting in fights. He said that in Norfolk, just before they shipped out, there were a lot of fights between whites and Nisei. He wanted to put an end to it, so one day he approached the leader of the white group and said, "You pick a man, any man, and the two of us will fight it out. Forget the other guys. We'll settle this." He said nobody wanted to fight him. [*Laughs.*]

What happened to him after the war?

He ended up living in Salt Lake City. He had a tiny store. Mom and I drove through Salt Lake City years ago and stopped to see him. But he wasn't there. He'd gone fishing. I don't know why was he was living in Salt Lake City. He was married, and maybe his wife was from there.

He had one of those mom and pop stores, where they sell all kinds of things. Ice cream and candy. Things like that.

Is he still alive?

No. He died of a heart attack at the age of 45.

[*Thinks.*] There was one other Nisei in that hospital. He was at the far end of the tent, but he wasn't very friendly. He could walk, but he never came around to talk to me, so I didn't get to know him. But he wasn't seriously wounded—he got discharged and sent back to the front.

Were any of the white soldiers curious about the 442nd?

No. Nobody talked about the war. Nobody talked about the fighting.

Not even to say, "Where were you?"

No.

Why not?

[*Shrugs.*] It was too close to us.

[*Thinks.*] Until I was able to move around on my own, the doctors were worried I'd have permanent paralysis. They kept pricking my leg, my foot, different places, asking if I could feel it. They'd come around and check on me.

Did you have physical therapy?

No, there was no therapy. There were no facilities for that.

After I could move around I was transferred to the main hospital and spent another month there. Most of the men in there had pretty much recovered from their wounds and were waiting to be discharged. Then one day, when I was getting around pretty well—I remember I could play ping pong—a nurse came to my bed and told me to come with her. She didn't say why.

She took me to a room where there were four or five doctors sitting at a table. It was like an examining board. They asked me to do a bunch of different things. Walk to the end of the room and back, bend over, side to side. Simple things like that. It lasted only a couple of minutes, and then they said, "That's it. That's all." So I went back to my bed. A short time later the nurse returned and said, "Congratulations." I asked her why. She said, "You're going home."

[*Emotional.*] Wow. Boy. See, all that time I thought that after I recovered I was going to be sent back to the front.

You did?

Yes. But she said I'd been reclassified as unfit for combat duty. This meant I wasn't going to fight anymore. It meant I was going to live.

A few days later they told me to get dressed and get all my belongings together. I was loaded on a truck with fifteen to twenty guys. They took us to a train station and put us on a train. Didn't tell us where we were going, what we were doing. No information at all.

We were loaded into a boxcar. No seats, nothing. Just a plain, empty boxcar. We rode in that thing all night long. It was cold as hell—this was October. We were freezing. No blankets. What we did was huddle together and try to sleep.

When we woke up the next morning we discovered that we were in Naples. I was right back where I started from. [*Laughs.*] We were in a big camp that had been converted from a racetrack—a huge place, full of tents. It was called a replacement depot. This was for people who were transient, either on their way to the front or going home. I was there from October to December—almost three months. Bored to death. Nothing to do.

Did you know anybody there?

There was one other Nisei—he was in the same tent. Sakamoto, was his name. I think his first name was Harold. He was being sent home, too. I have a picture of him. He and I went to Naples for the day, and we came across a street photographer and had our picture taken. So I have a picture of the two of us in Naples.

We also went to Pompeii. We took the train. I was fascinated with Pompeii—it was so interesting. But he didn't think much of it. So he and I separated—I think he went home early. I wandered all over. Today you can only go certain places, but in those days you could go anywhere. I wandered around so much that by the time I was ready to go back it was dark, and I couldn't find the train station. [*Laughs.*]

I didn't have any money—they didn't have my records, so I wasn't getting paid. See, I'd been in two different hospitals and then was shipped down to Naples, so my records never caught up to me. I'd go to the Red Cross and they'd give me ten dollars so I could buy cigarettes and Cokes and whatnot, but I got so desperate that one day I bought two cartons of cigarettes—a carton was fifty cents—and sold them on the black market in Naples. Italians were always asking, "Cigarette? Cigarette?" I sold each carton for twenty dollars.

[*Smiles.*] One time Sakamoto and I got hungry for rice, so we went into town and bought some rice. Then we bought a fish—a fresh fish—and asked the guy to clean it. Now we had rice and a fish. We went back to camp and found two empty gallon cans in the kitchen. We cooked the rice in one and boiled the fish in the other. Rice and fish! It was so good.

The food they served was so bad you didn't want to eat it. They had these big barrels—after we were finished eating we'd scrape our uneaten food into them. Later I'd see Italians coming into the camp and going through those barrels and picking out food we had thrown away. They were starving, and we were throwing food away.

I was so bored I volunteered to work in the post office. Just to have something to do. I spent my days sorting mail. Otherwise I would have gone crazy.

After combat, weren't you grateful for the boredom?

[*Laughs.*] No, I wasn't grateful. I was bored.

But I *was* glad to be in a tent with a cot and a warm blanket, because it was already beginning to get cold. In the morning the inside of the tent would be covered with frost. I was thinking of the guys out in the field, sleeping on the ground with nothing around them.

Did you know how long you were going to be there?

No. But part of me expected to be reassigned to some kind of duty in Italy. Something clerical, nothing strenuous. Norman [Ikari, family friend] was wounded, but they didn't send him home. He'd had some training as a medical technician, and they put him to work in a hospital.

Then one day they called me and again I was told to get all my belongings and assemble at a certain spot. Here were all these other wounded Nisei from the 100th and 442nd. Twenty-six of us had been called out. All of us had our bags packed.

Did you know any of them?

I knew two of them. One was a high school classmate. He was from Lihue. His name was Suzuki. Mitsuo Suzuki.

The other was a guy from my squad at Camp Shelby. Paul Tamura. He was young—I think he was only nineteen when he volunteered. I asked him where he'd been wounded, because his voice sounded funny. He said, "Here" and showed me his throat. He had a scar this long [*holds fingers about two inches apart*]—he'd been hit by shrapnel in the throat. That's why his voice sounded funny. He said, "I tried to call for the aid man, but I couldn't talk. Only gurgling sounds came out." He said he passed out, and when he woke up he thought he was dead. He got up and looked around and thought, "Hey, when you're dead everything's the same. You can still see trees. Nothing's changed." [*Laughs*].

[*Pauses.*] But with these guys, too, nobody talked about the fighting. Nobody talked about their wounds. One guy had his shoulder almost completely blown off. He was in pretty bad shape. Others were badly wounded as well, and some had relatively minor wounds. There was one guy who could have been sent back to the front. His finger got shot off—the middle finger. [*Laughs*.] That was his wound. He could still shoot, but they sent him home. I remember kidding him. When we went to the john I said, "Hey"—what was his name? I forgot his name— "when you pee, how do you hold your thing? I bet you pee all over yourself."

It turned out that all of us had been classified as "limited-duty." That meant we couldn't fight anymore. They loaded us on trucks and took us to the docks. There was a huge ship there. They told us we were going on that ship. They told us we were going home.

167

Chapter Seventeen

How long were you in Jerome?

ALICE

Ten months. October of '42 to August of '43.

I left to go to Oberlin. Oberlin didn't start until October—they went on tri-semesters—but I couldn't get out of Jerome fast enough.

You were allowed to leave?

You were allowed to leave if you had an outside contact. If you had a job or were going to school.

Apparently they determined you were no longer a threat.

Right. They realized we were not dangerous. I think the government finally realized it was all a mistake.

You know, I'd be curious to know whose idea the whole thing was in the first place.

Oh, it was people like [Lieutenant General John L.] DeWitt. I think Roosevelt was pressured to sign that executive order. [Inaccurate: Roosevelt ended the debate on the forced evacuation of those with Japanese blood by giving Secretary of War Henry L. Stimson the authority to take whatever "reasonable" action was deemed necessary. Roosevelt "deserves censure for not providing moral and constitutional leadership. Although his duty as president of the United States was to protect the constitutional rights of all citizens, he repeatedly subverted the rights of those of Japanese descent. His decision to sign Executive Order 9066 was made casually, with no consideration or weighing of the racial or constitutional implications of that action. . . . He refused to take steps to permit internees to return immediately to their homes even after the government endorsed their loyalty.

On the contrary, he prolonged the internees' confinement for several months after he knew there was no military justification for it."[18] Walter Lippman, the columnist, was in favor of it. Even Supreme Court Justice [Earl] Warren. And Abe Fortas. He became a Supreme Court justice, too.

[*Thinks.*] Did you know I went to his house? Abe Fortas's? Twice. This was back in the seventies.

Why?

To play. To play and have dinner. A sit-down dinner for the musicians. He placed me on his right. [*Laughs.*]

He was an amateur musician. A couple of my friends used to go and play with him.

What instrument did he play?

Violin. We played piano quartets. Either quartets or quintets. My friend Barbara Winslow—she's played with a lot of famous people. She asked me, "Would you like to play chamber music at Abe Fortas's house?" He must have been retired, because he was pushing seventy. He lived right in Georgetown. Beautiful house. Semicircular driveway. Right across from Dumbarton Oaks. Another man played the cello, and Barbara plays the viola. Afterwards we ate in a formal dining room, with someone serving us.

What was he like?

Very charming. Very nice. He made us feel at home. He made us feel as if it was his pleasure to play with us. But we were better than him anyway. [*Laughs.*]

We went again on his seventieth birthday. He didn't want a party—he wanted to play chamber music. Again I sat on his right.

Why did you sit on his right?

I don't know. But the others sat on his left. [*Laughs.*]

Did the thought go through your head that he had been in favor of forced relocation?

Oh yes. Yes it did.

18. Greg Robinson, *By Order of the President: FDR and the Internment of Japanese Americans* (Cambridge, MA.: Harvard University Press, 2001).

What did you think?

I thought, gee, you know, this is very nice of him to treat me this way. [*Laughs.*]

Did you feel any bitterness toward him?

No.

Why not?

[*Pauses. Softly.*] I don't get bitter about those things, Paul. It would ruin me. If I had that attitude it would ruin me.

When he died [in 1982] I went to the Kennedy Center for the service. It was open to the public. Isaac Stern and two others played The *Archduke* Trio. That was one of Beethoven's later trios. It has a slow movement that's really beautiful.

Why did you go to the service?

I just felt he was someone I had known, however briefly.

Getting back to Oberlin—how did you end up going there?

I got a full scholarship from the Southern Baptist Convention.

What's that?

You don't know about the Southern Baptist Convention? It's all the Baptist churches—they have their own convention. I used to go to Baptist churches, and they were all part of the Southern Baptist Convention.

The man who was the head of the whole thing—his name was Thomas, Dr. John Thomas—gave me a scholarship to go to Oberlin. The Southern Baptist Convention paid for my tuition.

How did you know him?

He was one of the [Baptist] leaders who came to speak at the camp.

Why did he give you a scholarship?

Well, I had played in Baptist churches from the time I was little. Twice a year they had what was called a "five-point Baptist rally," in which five churches would get together, and I'd play for them. Sometimes it would be a "seven-point rally." So a lot of the ministers knew me.

We were all looking for scholarships. Otherwise we wouldn't have been able to go to school. Without *question* we wouldn't have been able to go to school. This Dr. Thomas knew me, and gave me a scholarship.

How would you describe your feelings toward people like him? People who helped you?

[*Simply.*] They formed my whole life. The generosity of these people.

What about your sisters? What did they do?

They had already left by that point. They left in the spring—I think in April—to go to Minneapolis. Minneapolis was considered a friendly city.

What do you mean by a "friendly" city?

Cities that welcomed—we called ourselves "evacuees." Chicago was also considered a friendly city. Philadelphia. Washington. These were places where we could get jobs. Once word got around that jobs were available, people would congregate there. So you'd hear, "Oh, Minneapolis is a friendly city."

Why did you call yourselves "evacuees"? By definition, evacuees are people who are removed from a place of danger for their own protection. But in this case you were supposedly the cause of the danger.

The government came up with that term. It sounds so much nicer.

"Relocation," too, means, simply, to move to another place. It doesn't mean to move by force.

No. The government came up with that term also. But in this case it meant imprisonment.

Why do you still use those terms?

Because I was brainwashed. But when I hear about people who were in prison, I think, "Hey, wait a minute. So was I." It's taken a long time to realize that.

MEMORANDUM TO: All Staff Members
SUBJECT: Use of the terms "Japanese," "Camps" and "Internment."

The words that we use in correspondence, in reports, and in conversation with the evacuees exercise a great deal of influence in determining the attitude of the evacuees and of the American public toward the activities of the War Relocation Authority. It is, therefore, distinctly worthwhile for employees of the Authority to make an effort to avoid using certain terms that are misleading and inappropriate.

It is inaccurate to refer to the persons who have been evacuated from the West Coast as "Japanese." The Japanese are the people who live in Japan. The persons who have been evacuated from the West Coast are people of Japanese ancestry, but they are not "Japanese" in all cases. With a few exceptions, they have come to the United States because they want to live here, and two-thirds of them are citizens of the United States.

It is even more objectionable, of course, to refer to the evacuees as "Japs." They do not like the word; nor would you if they were an American of Japanese ancestry. "Japs" means the subjects of the Japanese Emperor, living in Japan.

The term "camp," when used to refer to a relocation center, is likewise objectionable. It leads people to confuse the relocation centers administered by the War Relocation Authority with the detention camps and internment camps administered by other agencies.

The evacuees are not "internees." They have not been "interned." Internees are people who have individually been suspected of being dangerous to the internal security of the United States, who have been given a hearing on charges to that effect, and have then been ordered confined in an internment camp administered by the Army.

In lieu of the misleading, question-begging, and emotion-laden terms "Japanese," "Japs," "camps," and "internees," employees of the War Relocation Authority should refer to the persons who have been evacuated from the West Coast as evacuees, and to the projects as relocation centers. Some people have been referring to the evacuees as "colonists." This term is not objectionable, but the term "evacuee" seems preferable. Where the context makes the meaning clear, the term "resident" is, of course, also acceptable.

I should appreciate your calling the contents of this memorandum to the attention of the members of your respective staffs.

[signed] D. S. Meyer, Director
[signed] Elmer L. Shirrell, Project Director

In order to leave [camp], you had to make the [outside] contact yourself, as well as all of the arrangements. And, of course, the camp had to let you go. I have papers saying I'm going to be released on such-and-such a date. Where I would be going and who I would be staying with. What I would be doing.

WAR RELOCATION AUTHORITY
Jerome Relocation Center
Denson, Arkansas

August 31, 1943

Mr. Dillon S. Myer
Director
War Relocation Authority
Barr Building
910 17th Street, N.W.
Washington, D.C.

Dear Mr. Myer:

Enclosed please find Form WRA-130 for Miss Alice Setsuko Imamoto of Block 18–10–A. Attached to same is a copy of letter of acceptance from employer, Mrs. H. E. Dulmage, 67 South Professor Street, Oberlin, Ohio. This domestic job offer has been confirmed and approved by Mr. Harold S. Fistere, Relocation Supervisor of Cleveland, Ohio.

Indefinite leave has been issued under Section 60.4.3, Paragraph C, of the Administrative Handbook on Issuance of Leave.

Sincerely,
[signed] John L. McCormick
FOR Paul A. Taylor
Project Director

What did your sisters do in Minneapolis?

They all went into private homes to work for families. Grace and Marion used the money to go to the University of Minnesota. Lily also went to see Ken [Matsuoka, her late husband], who she married a couple of months later. Ken was in the army—he was teaching at the MIS language school [at Camp Savage, Minnesota]. His father was interned at Jerome, and he met Lily when he was visiting his father.

Why did you pick Oberlin?

If you backtrack—in Santa Anita I was taking piano lessons from Ruth Watanabe. The USC piano graduate? She left camp to become a librarian at the Eastman Conservatory in Rochester, New York. People say that she's a walking encyclopedia. You mention her name to any musicologist in the country and they'll know her. She's that brilliant. Anyway, I heard she was up in Rochester and wrote to her. This was how you made contacts. I asked her where I might be able to go to music school. She suggested Syracuse, which is nearby, and also Juilliard. But at the same time I heard through the grapevine that Oberlin had a Nisei student body president, and that's what clinched my decision. That's all I went on.

What was his name?

Kenji Okuda. When I heard a Nisei was the student body president I thought, "That must be a friendly school." That was my sole reason for wanting to go to Oberlin.

Did you ever meet him?

No, but Grace knew him. She went with him on several occasions to talk to different groups about evacuation. Schools or civic organizations.

But Oberlin had to accept you first.

Yes, and that's interesting too, because they didn't even have a tape of me. It was all based on a recommendation from Dr. Thomas. Years later my teacher at Oberlin—Dr. Frank Shaw, the director of the conservatory—told me he just took a chance on me.

[*Thinks.*] Did you know Oberlin has a thousand applicants for next year's class? And only about 20 percent get in. Marjory [Hanson, friend and former classmate] and I were talking the other day and we said, "Boy, if we applied now, we probably wouldn't get in." [*Laughs.*] I think there was a shortage of students back then. That's my guess. Why else would they take an unknown from a camp?

174

How did you pay for school?

I had the scholarship, which paid for tuition, and for two months before the semester started I worked as a domestic for a family named Dulmage. I don't remember how I heard about them. I think there was an office in the camp where opportunities were posted.

WRA-130
Budget Bureau No. 13–RO26–43
Approval Expires 7–31–43

WAR RELOCATION AUTHORITY
APPLICATION FOR INDEFINITE LEAVE

Note: This application will not be accepted
unless an application for leave clearance has been earlier
filed on Form WRA-126, or accompanies this application.

Relocation Center: Jerome
Family No. 2183
Center address: 18–10–A

Name: IMAMOTO   ALICE   SETSUKO
      (Last)   (First)   (Middle)

What is the purpose of the proposed leave?
Indefinite Leave has been issued under Section 60.4.3, Paragraph C, of the Administrative Handbook on Issuance of Leave.

If you plan to attend any education institution, state its name and address:

    Oberlin College   Oberlin, Ohio
    (Name)   (Place)

Has your leave been taken up with the National Student Relocation Council?
No.

Have you arranged for any employment?
Yes.

Name of employer: Mrs. H. E. Dulmage
Address of employer: 67 South Professor St., Oberlin, Ohio
Occupation of employer: Housewife
Your prospective occupation: Houseworker
Salary: $12.00 a week plus room and board

How much money are you starting out with?
None.

Have you property providing an income?

No.

What arrangements have been made to meet your expenses while on leave?
From salary earned from employment.

Upon arrival at the first destination of this leave, I undertake within 24 hours to report to the Director of the War Relocation Authority in Washington, D.C., my arrival, and to confirm my business or school and residential addresses. In case of any change of school, employment, or residence, I will give prompt notice of such change.

[signed] Alice Setsuko Imamoto
August 24, 1943

August 20, 1943
Oberlin, Ohio

Dear Alice:

We shall look forward to having you in our home. Our present maid leaves us the seventh of September. You and your sister are welcome to come at any time on or before the seventh. I think it would, in fact, be a good idea for you to come early and get settled in your room, rested, and get acquainted with Oberlin before you start to work.

Our present maid comes to work at 9 A.M. and works until 6:30 or 7 P.M. She is free Saturday afternoon and all day Sunday. Our house has eleven rooms which we clean thoroughly once a week. We go over the downstairs each day to keep it neat and free from dust. We will have six freshmen students beginning the next semester. They take care of their own rooms with the exception of the weekly cleaning. The salary for this kind of help is twelve dollars.

I sincerely hope your train ride will not be too difficult. I feel sure you and your sister will enjoy Oberlin.

Cordially yours,
Mrs. H. E. Dulmage
67 South Professor St.
Oberlin, Ohio

What were your feelings about leaving camp?

Oh, I had mixed emotions. I was happy about leaving camp, but I wasn't happy about leaving mother and father. This was the unknown. So I was scared. Really scared.

[*Pauses.*] There was a woman at the train station, a Nisei woman who was leaving camp at the same time. There was maybe a half dozen of us. She was wearing a winter coat—she must have gotten it from a catalogue—and she hadn't removed the label. The label on the sleeve? It was still there. And she never took that coat off. It was hot—this was August in Arkansas—but she never took it off.

Did you know anyone?

Ken Matsuoka's father was there. Ken's sister lived in Chicago, and he was going to see her. I didn't know him very well, but at least I wasn't alone.

[*Thinks.*] There was no place to sit. A lot of soldiers were traveling. It was packed. I had a little suitcase, and I sat on it in the aisle.

[*Pauses.*] You go into a crowded train and the faces are all—no one's friendly. All white.

So many things I've pushed away, but certain things I can't remove from my memory.

Were white people intimidating?

Sure. Oh, sure.

What did grandma and grandpa think of your leaving?

They never made me fear anything. If they worried about me, they never showed it. That's something, isn't it? That they had confidence I could do whatever I had to do?

So I was fairly independent from early on. I was sixteen when I left Jerome.

Chapter Eighteen

KEN

Do you know what ship I came home on? The *Queen Mary*. You've heard of the *Queen Mary*, haven't you? It was a luxury liner before the war— the biggest liner in the world. [*Shakes his head.*] The *Queen Mary*. It was filled with soldiers. All of them going home.

So again I was standing on the deck of a ship and looking out at the Naples harbor. And again I could see Mount Vesuvius—it had erupted earlier that year, and smoke was still coming out of it. I remember looking at Mount Vesuvius, looking at Naples, thinking, gee, I'm going home. I made it through the war.

Was it pretty?

No. I never thought Naples was pretty. [*Laughs.*]

I also remember thinking that I would never see Italy again. Not that I didn't want to—I just didn't think I ever would. And, of course, I ended up going back for [scientific] meetings twice, to Padova and Florence.

What were your feelings when you went back?

Well, after the meeting in Florence [in 1975], mom and I took a tour— we went by bus to Rome, and then to Naples. As we were approaching Naples, the bus driver stopped and pointed out Cassino [Abbey], which had been rebuilt. He asked, "Does anyone want to see the monastery?" I said, "Yes, I'd like to," but the others weren't interested. So he kept on driving. [*Laughs.*]

We also went through the town of Caserta, which was where we spent a few days before we were shipped to Anzio. That's where the single German bomber came by and dropped a single bomb. But it didn't bring back strong memories of the war. All I thought was, well, I was here. This is where it all started. But we didn't go near the battle sites, so I didn't have strong feelings.

Would you like to see the battle sites?

I'd like to see the town where I was wounded. Orciano. I couldn't remember the name of it before. I can recall a lot of fairly large buildings, and, of course, being in one when the shelling started. But I don't know if I could find that building again. It's not easy to find those places.

I'd also like to go to Anzio. I was told they have a monument there—a monument to the allies. I'd like to see it.

So we sailed out of Naples and through the Mediterranean. On the first day I was told to report to the captain's office. I don't know why they picked me, but they put me to work doing paperwork. Now I was in comfort! All the other guys were stuck in crowded holds in the bottom of the ship, but I had my meals served to me. [*Laughs.*] I worked on records for the whole trip.

Were you in a convoy going home?

No. By then most of the submarines had been destroyed, so they were no longer a threat. Also, the *Queen Mary* was very fast. It took only nine days to cross instead of thirty. We landed in New York just before Christmas, 1944.

What was that like?

[*Long pause.*] We were all on deck. It was very foggy—you couldn't see anything. You couldn't see the skyscrapers. Everything was fogged in. You know, in a fog it's quiet, so everything was quiet. The ship was moving slowly. Then all of a sudden the fog cleared, and there was the Statue of Liberty. [*Voice thickens.*] Right there. Boy. Guys started crying, seeing that. Coming back from the war. Many of us wounded. We made it through the war, and there was the Statue of Liberty.

When we got off the ship, carrying our bags, the Red Cross ladies were there to greet us. They had coffee and milk. Everybody drank milk. [*Laughs.*] We hadn't had milk in forever. It tasted so good! It was such a good feeling. Milk! They had doughnuts, too. Coffee and milk and doughnuts.

They loaded us on trucks and took us to a place called Camp Shanks. I have no idea where that was in relation to Manhattan—all I know is that it was Camp Shanks. [Camp Shanks was located in Orangeburg, New York, about twenty-five miles north of Manhattan; it was built to process the massive number of troops deployed to Europe, opening in January 1944 and closing in July 1946.[19]] We got there just about dinnertime, and I remember I was so happy to be on land, to be in America, that I was running to the mess hall with my mess kit and my aluminum coffee cup, oblivious to the fact that it had snowed and was icy, and I slipped on the ice and everything went flying. [*Laughs.*] But this was my first day back home.

They gave us passes to go into the city, and some of us went to a Japanese restaurant called the Miyako. It was on the second floor of a building close to Central Park, about 56th Street. We had a great dinner there. My first Japanese food in over a year.

[*Thinks.*] Downstairs was a small Japanese grocery store. A young woman was working there, and I gave her twenty-five dollars and told her to pack up a box of Japanese things—canned goods and whatnot—and send them to my friends in Italy. I told her to buy whatever she thought was good and save some of the money for postage. She asked me for my address, so I gave her my home address in Kapaa. And what do you know, a couple of months later, back in Kapaa, I got a check in the mail from her for a dollar and fifty cents, and a note saying it was left over from the original twenty-five dollars.

Did you know her brother lives around here? I met him one night at Norman's [Ikari] house. He was in the same company with Norman. He was a medic, too, and when Norman got wounded, this guy went out and patched him up and brought him back.

See, Norman was the second point man. These guys go ahead of everybody else, out in front of the whole company, and they're there strictly to draw fire from the Germans so the rest of the company will know their location. They're like clay pigeons. In Norman's case, the Germans let the first guy pass, and along came Norman and they shot him. He got hit in the left thigh, and as the bullet passed through his thigh it veered downward, came out, and lodged in his other leg near the ankle. He was wounded in both legs by the same bullet.

So there he was, out in the open. This guy—Kelly Kuwayama, is his

---

19. *63rd Infantry Division Association* Web site (www.63rdinfdiv.com).

name—went out and patched him up. And what Norman said was that as he was patching him up he looked around kind of casually and said, "Hey, I guess we should get the hell out of here." [*Laughs.*] Norman is very grateful for that. The guy risked his life for him.

His family was so nice. They invited a few of us to their home—they had a car and drove us to their place. I have no idea where they lived, but it was Christmas Eve, and we went to a Christmas program put on by the Japanese community.

We were at Camp Shanks for four or five days, and then they loaded us on a Pullman train for a trip across country. A Pullman train! Boy, that was fun. It was very comfortable—we had nice accommodations. All twenty-six of us were in one car. We played cards all day long. Waited for meals. At night they pulled the bunks down, top and bottom. There was a ladder for the top bunk.

The trip lasted six or seven days. The only place I recall stopping was Denver—they let us out for a short while. I don't recall any discomfort or unpleasantness about that trip. [*Smiles.*] We ended up in Marysville [California], near Sacramento.

The only thing I remember about that place—we were there for three or four days—was that there was a fight. Some of the guys went to drink beer at the PX [post exchange] and got into a fight—a big fight, involving a lot of people. Afterwards we were all restricted to our barracks. [*Laughs.*]

What was the fight about?
I have no idea, but it was against some whites.

After that they sent us by train to Monterey, to a camp called Fort Ord. We were there for about three weeks. On our very first morning a captain came by and said we were going to be put to work building roads. Heavy construction work. Everybody howled. We let him know we were on limited duty, that we weren't supposed to be doing heavy work. He said, "Those are the orders." We said we weren't going to obey the orders. He threatened us with court martial, and we told him to go ahead and court martial us. At that point he gave up. He knew we weren't going to work on roads. We spent the rest of the time there playing cards. [*Laughs.*]

From there we were shipped to a camp near Seattle—I don't remember its name. We were there for about a week.

There doesn't seem to have been any rhyme or reason to your movements.

No. It was kind of silly. But I think the difficulty in knowing what to do with us stemmed from the fact that our final destination was Hawaii. We could only go when ships were available, and if no ships were available from, say, December to February, they had to accommodate us until one was ready. So we went to Marysville and then to Fort Ord and then to Seattle before we were finally loaded onto a ship for Hawaii. The whole thing took about two months.

What do you remember about the ship?

Well, I don't remember what kind it was, but it went by itself because by that point in the war there was no threat of Japanese submarines. Seattle is like a harbor, so that area was calm, but as soon as we hit the open ocean the boat was going up and down and sideways. We had to eat standing up. We put our trays on tall tables, and I remember hanging on to my tray. They had fifty-gallon drums all over the place for people to vomit into. Fortunately I never got sick.

What were your feelings?

That I was finally going home. That I had made it through the war. That feeling came up quite often.

The trip lasted eight or nine days. It smoothed out after a while and was calm the rest of the way.

[*Pauses.*] I remember the first sight of land. Diamond Head? We came around that. We could see Diamond Head, and then Waikiki. The Aloha Tower. We were all on deck. Some of the guys had tears in their eyes.

Was anyone there to greet you?

No. Nobody knew we were coming home, so there was no one to greet us. No band music or people waving or anything like that.

We were given one month's furlough, so I went back to Kauai.

What was it like to go home?

[*Thinks.*] Well, today the airport is in Lihue, which is only eight or nine miles from Kapaa, but at that time it was clear on the other side of the island. They moved it during the war to a place called Kekaha. Waimea? It was beyond Waimea. So I landed there. No one was there to greet me, because they didn't know I was coming home, but at the airport a man from Kapaa saw me and offered me a ride.

Now this was strange, because he had two sons in the 442nd, but he didn't ask me anything about the war. He didn't ask me anything about why I was back. It was pretty much a silent ride all the way home.

Were his sons still overseas?

Yes. And I don't know if he had influenced their enlistment, but they were not pure Japanese. They were half Hawaiian and half Japanese. The father was Japanese—his name was Morita. The younger one played football with us—David Morita. Since he wasn't pure Japanese, his nickname was "German." [*Laughs.*] Here German was fighting the Germans.

He dropped me off in front of the family store [owned by his brothers; Sam ran a photography studio and Haruto made and sold jewelry; his father, retired, helped out]. I got out of the car and thanked him for bringing me home, and then I walked into the store. There was my sister Kay. [*Voice thickens.*] She saw me and started to cry. My mother came out. My father. They were all there.

My father didn't say much, but he was so happy I was back he wanted to have a big party and invite people to celebrate my return. He went out and got all the materials. He was going to put up a tent with tables and benches, so all the friends could come and celebrate my return. But I didn't want that.

Why not?

I told him it wasn't good because a lot of boys had been killed and there was still fighting going on. It would have been terrible for the families to find out we were celebrating my return. They had sons who were never coming back. I said, "It's not good. Don't have it." But my father was pretty insistent. Finally I had to threaten him. I said, "If you have a party I'm leaving. I'm going back to Honolulu." He gave up on the idea when I told him that.

He just wanted to do something to celebrate. But I didn't think it was appropriate. It was a difficult time. A very difficult time.

Chapter Nineteen

What do you remember about the trip to Oberlin?

ALICE

I remember changing trains in St. Louis.

I didn't go straight to Oberlin—I went to Chicago first and met Grace there. As I said, Ken's father was going to Chicago to see his oldest daughter, who was living at the Robie House. Frank Lloyd Wright's famous house? It's now a showplace, but at the time it was being used as a University of Chicago dormitory. We stayed there for four days. Then Grace and I took a train to Cleveland, and another train from there to Oberlin.

Why did Grace go to Oberlin?

To take care of me. To look after me. She paid for my room. I helped pay for it the first two months by working for the Dulmage's, but after school started I worked only for board. Nobody worked for room and board—it took too much time. So Grace paid for the room. She was a cook's helper at the Graduates' House, which was a dormitory for graduate students.

What did you do for board?

I washed dishes in the dining hall for regular students. I remember the dishes would be piled up to here [*holds hand high in the air*], and I would be scraping them. I did that every meal. That's how I got by.

Did Grace take classes, too?

Yes. I think I mentioned earlier that when she had to leave Cal [to go to Santa Anita] she was three credits shy of graduating. She got those last three credits at Oberlin. But Cal wouldn't let her get her degree from Oberlin, so she got it from Cal.

She stayed at Oberlin for three semesters, long enough for me to get settled, and then returned to California to work for Dr. Bruff. She lived with his family and worked in his office, and when she'd saved up enough money she went to UCLA for her teaching certificate. California required a fifth year if you wanted to teach.

[*Thinks.*] Grace gave up a lot of her life to put me through school. The only reason she went to Oberlin was because I went to Oberlin. It's amazing. And it was something she did on her own. Mother and father didn't ask her to do that. I don't know what I would have done without her.

Where did the two of you live?

At the Dulmage's. They had a big house—Mrs. Dulmage had five or six students living there—and in the back was a tiny little room that had just enough space for a double bed and a dresser. That was our room. Grace and I shared a double bed for the entire year.

Were the Dulmages nice to you?

No. They had a daughter who was younger than me, and that daughter was very nice. But there was nothing much pleasant about living there. Mrs. Dulmage was not nice to me. I have no warm feelings toward her at all.

The Sound of Music? Well, that family, the von Trapp family, came to sing at the college, and two of the girls stayed at the Dulmage's house. It was half a block from the center of campus. I met Maria. She was huge! A huge, ugly lady. [*Laughs.*]

Other students lived in that house, too, and during my second year, the year Grace left, I roomed with two of them in a dorm. Grace stayed for one semester that year, at the Graduates' House.

Were you friends with them?

Not really.

Why not?

I was shy. It took me a long time to make friends. It was hard for me to make friends. I didn't have much fun in school—I didn't have a social life. It was all hard work.

185

Did you talk to your parents about this sort of thing?

No. They had no idea what my fears were. I couldn't unload anything on them. I didn't want to burden them. They had a lot to deal with themselves. And language was a problem. That's how most of us felt. Terry [Kobayashi] and the rest of us.

Did coming from a camp set you back?

Oh sure. Absolutely.

[*Pauses.*] I think that was why I didn't make friends with some of the other students. I didn't have a feeling they were sympathetic to that. But I was wrong. I exchange Christmas cards with another student to this day, and in one of them she expressed tremendous sympathy and respect for what we had gone through. It was just that I felt so self-conscious.

[*Thinks.*] With the Worcesters, though, I knew right away that they were sympathetic.

Tell me about them.

[*Fondly.*] Kenny Worcester delivered milk to the Graduates' House—his father owned the Worcester Dairy. He and his wife, Libby, had three daughters who were about our age, and Grace became friends with all of them. Before she went back to California he said it would be nice if I knew a family in town, so they invited me over for dinner.

Now, I had such allergy problems in the dorm I could hardly sleep. In the springtime it was so bad I couldn't get my rest. And because of that they invited me to live with them, which I did my junior year. They had a little room for me—they cleaned it, stripped all the rugs, and even used an allergen-free mattress cover. I had a bed and an old rolltop desk. [*Smiles.*] I loved that desk.

They treated me like I was their fourth daughter. That summer they took me on a cross-country trip—they wanted me to see my sisters in California. We went in a brand new Ford that Kenny bought from his brother-in-law. It was one of the first cars to roll off the assembly line toward the end of the war—production had stopped prior to that. There was a photo of us in the Oberlin paper standing in front of the car. That was hometown news. [*Laughs.*]

Did you ever talk to them about being in a camp?

No. We never talked about it, because you never talked about those things. But I knew they were sensitive to it.

[*Thinks.*] You know, they didn't have much money. They lived in a very modest house. But after father and mother left camp and were living in Washington, they wanted me to be able to spend one of the holidays with them—to go by train—and tried to give me twenty-five dollars. I didn't take it—they couldn't afford that. That's like two hundred dollars now. But that's how sweet they were.

Libby passed away about three years ago—she died in Kenny's arms—but I still keep in touch with him. He lives in a retirement home in Ashland, Oregon.

So I lived with them my junior year. My senior year I moved back into the dorms—I wanted to be more a part of campus life. And that's when I finally made some friends in school. For the first time. A girl named Leni Weissman, now Baxter—Eleanor, was her real name—lived across the hall from me, and she and some of her friends would invite me over. I had a single room. They were in the college, not the conservatory. Leni also invited me to stay with her family in New York City during breaks, and I did that twice. Her roommate was Margo Yokota, now Matsunaga—she came from a relocation camp, too, and my parents knew her parents before the war. So we all became friends. I made lasting friendships with these people.

Did you like Oberlin?

At the time I didn't know if I liked it or not. It was so hard. My first semester, for example, I took eighteen units—my major was piano, so they were all music courses. My average was an A-minus. But all I did was work and study. Nothing else. I also practiced three hours a day.

Did you ever go back to Jerome?

Grace and I went back in the summer of '44 to visit mother and father, but by then Jerome had closed and they were living in Rohwer. That was the only time I ever went back to Arkansas.

What do you remember of that trip?

[*Pauses.*] That it was horrible. A miserable train ride. I don't remember how long we were there or what we did. Most of the young people had already left.

What were your thoughts?

Well, we were going to see mother and father, so I guess my thoughts were with them. What they were going to do. We didn't know what would happen to them. No idea.

It wasn't—it wasn't a pleasant trip.

Chapter Twenty

What was it like to be home?

KEN

[*Smiles.*] I remember playing cards with my family. My mother and father and sisters. We were playing blackjack for money. Now, in the army every other word is a swear word. I went over twenty-one and said, "Fuck." My sister Kay gasped. [*Laughs.*]

[*Long pause. Softly.*] But you know, one of the things I wanted to do when I got home was visit the families of friends of mine who had died. At that point there were three. Two were in Kapaa. One was Howard Urabe's. I went to see his family first, because he was my friend and we had gone off to the war together.

I saw them unannounced. I just walked in. They had a little store, and I went into their store. His mother and father were there. I didn't say a word. I just walked in, and his mother looked at me and burst into tears. She burst into tears and turned around and ran out of the room. They lived above the store, and that's where she went. So there I was alone with the father. He was as surprised by her reaction as I was, so he couldn't say much either.

[*Voice thickens.*] I didn't know what to say. I didn't know what to say at all. We just looked at each other. Then he said, "It's too hard to talk. Why don't you come back later." So I said okay and left. But I didn't go back. I never saw them again. Because I thought if I went to see them again they would have the same reaction.

It was too soon after he had died. It was only a matter of months since he'd been killed. It was just too soon.

[*Emotional.*] I still think about it. I should have gone back. I should have gone back, because I could have said things to them about their son that

189

might have given them comfort. I could have told them that I had seen him two weeks before he was killed. That he had come to see me, and that we'd had a long talk together. I think it would have helped them. But it's all over now. They're both dead now. They're gone.

[*Pauses.*] Howard was killed attacking a machine gun nest. My understanding is that he was going to fire a grenade. There's a thing called a grenade launcher—you fire it and the grenade is propelled right to your target. Instead of crawling close to a machine gun and throwing a grenade, it's safer to fire a grenade with a grenade launcher. So that's what he was trying to do. But as he got up to fire, the Germans fired first, and he was killed. I was told bullets splattered across his chest. He died instantly. He got a Silver Star.

All the guys who died affected me, but he affected me more than any of the others. [*Emotional.*] I felt honored that he would come to see me before he was killed.

When did you decide to name me after him?
It was something I thought of right before you were born.

How come you never told me about him? Even when I used to make fun of that name?
[*Shrugs.*]
So that was Howard's family. The other family in Kapaa was named Yamashiro. They were Okinawan. He was a year below me in high school—Gordon Yamashiro. He got the Distinguished Service Cross in the battle where he was killed. Again, he was attacking some German machine gun nests. He had destroyed two and was going toward the third when they opened fire and killed him. He was up for review last summer for the Medal of Honor, but he didn't get it.

[*Pauses.*] It was very difficult to do this. Extremely difficult. I knew it was going to be a difficult thing. I went with somebody else to see the Yamashiros—I don't recall who it was, but there were two of us.

Another GI?
Another GI.
His father was outside in the yard. We approached him. Now, the Okinawan language is very different from Japanese. It's a totally different language, and this was what he spoke. I don't know how we were able to convey

the information that we were there to extend our sympathies for the loss of his son, but he knew. He got very angry. Extremely upset that his son had died. He was jabbering something in Okinawan that I couldn't understand. He went back and got the Distinguished Service Cross and showed it to us, all the time saying something to us in an angry tone. What I think he was saying was that he didn't want the medal, he wanted his son back. That the medal was useless. He threw it on the ground.

There was nothing we could say. I couldn't talk to him in his language. I just wanted him to know that we were there because we were very sad about the loss of his son. I wanted him to understand that. I don't know whether we succeeded or not.

But he wasn't angry at you.

No, he wasn't angry at us. He was angry at the whole thing.

What was he like? Gordon?

He was a good athlete. A lot of them were good athletes—sports were very important when we were growing up. He played football for the high school team.

So those were the two from Kapaa. The third was from the other side of the island, a town called Hanapepe. I drove over there. His name was Daniel Betsui. I knew he had a brother who was a dentist, so I went to his brother's office. He was working on a patient when I walked in. I told him who I was, that I was a friend of his brother, and that I was sorry he was killed. I didn't stay very long. He had a patient there the whole time, but thanked me for coming. Maybe I should have asked about his parents. Maybe I should have gone to talk to his parents, but it would have been very difficult for me to do that.

How was Daniel Betsui killed?

He was in the engineers. He got killed by accident. [*Shakes his head.*] It was an accident. The engineers were putting on a demonstration in Italy of different types of explosives that had been confiscated from the Germans—mines, booby traps, grenades. Things like that. They put on this demonstration in back of the lines—I think it was during a rest period—and afterwards they were loading the truck. He was on the truck, putting away the explosives as they handed them to him. Something happened. It was a mistake—somebody made an error, a safety device was not put in, something—and the whole thing blew up. Blew up the whole truckload, and he was right on it.

Anyway, those were the three that I knew, but a number of guys were killed after that. In the town of Kapaa a total of five were killed. One was in the 100th. He was two years older than me. Growing up, I considered him a much older person, like an older brother. But we did some things together. Once he asked me to go fishing with him. We got a group of guys and put our nets in the ocean and drove the fish into the nets. This was at night.

What was his name?

Minami. Yoshio Minami.

How did he die?

I saw him—where was it that I saw him? Anzio? I was walking through this town and ran into him. We stopped and talked for a short while. He was in intelligence—his job was to interrogate German prisoners. That's what he did. I don't know where he learned German [*laughs*], but he did the interrogations. They had captured about ten Germans, and he was in a house talking to them, interrogating them, when a German shell smacked right into the house. Killed him and a number of Germans. That's how he died.

He was a nice guy. He played basketball, and he was a pitcher on the baseball team. Pretty good pitcher, too.

It's curious, isn't it, that so many of the guys who died were good athletes? You didn't know Haruto's first wife, Mitsuko—she died before you were born. Her maiden name was Naito. She had a brother who was a year above me. Kaoru Naito. They were from Lihue. He was an athlete, too—played on the high-school football team. Good halfback. Tough guy. But he got killed. He was drafted and served in the 100th Infantry and got killed early in the war.

The fifth—I don't know if I mentioned this before, but we had the same last name. Iwao Takemoto, but nobody called him Iwao. We called him by his nickname—Blondie. It was from that comic strip. *Dagwood?* There was a Blondie, and we called him Blondie.

Why?

I don't know. [*Laughs.*] He was a tough guy. I remember watching him play football—he was on the high school team—and boy, when he hit guys, he really smacked them. A hard hitter. He was fast, too—ran the sprints. He was a year below me.

But he got killed. I don't know how. Now, the way the army notified the families was through a Portuguese guy who had also been my classmate. He was the one who delivered the bad news. He would come driving up in a jeep, and if they saw him coming in that jeep they knew it was bad news.

What was his name?

Medeiros. Abel Medeiros. And one day he showed up at my parents' house. He said, "I have bad news for you. Kaname died."

Who answered the door?

I don't know, but he handed them the telegram and they looked at it and saw that it wasn't me. When Medeiros saw the name Takemoto he assumed it was me and brought it to my house. But it was this Blondie. It was him that got killed.

So when I was wounded Medeiros showed up again, and this time they thought, well, it can't be a mistake. He can't make the same mistake twice.

[*Thinks.*] There are these coincidences. My family told me that the night before Medeiros delivered the news, my father dreamt about it. He had a dream I was wounded. When he woke up he told my mother something had happened to me, and he turned out to be right. That day Medeiros showed up with the telegram.

How did Medeiros get that job?

I don't know. The bearer of good tidings. [*Laughs.*]

So five died from Kapaa, and about ten from the whole island. Far more— probably about a hundred—served with either the 100th or the 442nd.

[*Thinks.*] There were some sad cases. The older brother of a good friend of mine was in the 100th. He got married shortly after he entered the army, and while he was in training his son was born. Then he went off to Italy and got killed, so he never saw his son. I read an article a while ago about the [Go For Broke] Monument in Los Angeles—they interviewed some of the people who went to the dedication [June 5, 1999], and one of them was the son. [The monument was erected by the Go For Broke Educational Foundation, a nonprofit organization dedicated to educating the public about Japanese American veterans.] He was there because he wanted to see his father's name—they have the names of all who served on a wall. My name is on that wall. Randy [Toji, nephew, son of Kay] went there and saw it.

What was the father's name?

Sato. Shukichi Sato. He was the oldest of four Sato boys who served in the army. I knew one of his younger brothers, Harry. We went in the army together.

Maybe that's something I should mention, too—that some families had more than one son serving in the military. The family that had the most was Min Nakada's [late family friend]. Nine of them served. [*Shakes his head.*] Nine boys. The youngest ones served in the Korean War, but during World War II there were five or six of them. Two were in the 442nd. Min was in the interpreters.

What did you do when the furlough was over?

Well, the war [with Japan] was still going on—this was in the spring of '45—so I was given an assignment on Kauai. I remember being a little upset by it. I didn't want to be on Kauai. There was nothing to do. It was boring. [*Laughs.*]

What was your assignment?

My assignment was with the—I don't know what you would call it. It was an investigative office, and its main purpose was to keep track of Issei to make sure nothing subversive was going on. It was crazy, especially when you consider that the war was at the point where we were ready to invade Japan. The Japanese navy was destroyed. There was absolutely no possibility of the Japanese invading the Hawaiian Islands. It was stupid to have an office like that. They had all these records on harmless Issei. It didn't make sense.

The office consisted of five individuals. Three of us were in the army and two were civilians. Of the three in the army, one was what I considered to be an old man—he was thirty-eight. [*Laughs.*] I don't know how he got into the army at that age. He was a sergeant. Caucasian. But the main investigator was a lawyer from Chicago. Another Caucasian. Rather stocky. Always dressed in civilian clothes. For the longest time I thought he was a civilian. He was the one who interviewed the Issei and wrote up the reports. The two civilians were women, and one was my brother's classmate—she was part Hawaiian and part white.

194

Were you the only Japanese person?

Yes.

Would Issei get called into the office?

No. They never came to the office. The investigator would go to their homes. I wish I could recall his name.

What did he ask them?

The basic information on all the Issei had already been acquired, so it was just a matter of keeping track of their activities. Where they went, and when. What they did. These were harmless people, like my father. It was so stupid, harassing them like that. All I did was type reports, but never on my father.

By design?

I don't know. But I knew they had a file on him. I was never able to get into it, of course.

Did you want to see it?

I wanted to see it, but it was impossible. I was never alone in the office. I suppose I could have asked the principal investigator, but that would have put him on the spot, so I never did. But I wanted to.

I wanted to know why they had my father on restriction. He couldn't travel more than fifteen miles from home. He couldn't go to, say, Waimea, which is on the other side of the island. The whole thing was ridiculous. And that restriction was in place until the end of the war. He kept a suitcase packed the entire time. Just in case they took him.

[*Thinks.*] But the principal investigator and I became good friends. He was actually a staff sergeant in the army—he told me this after I got to know him. We used to have lunch together. Every day. We'd go to different restaurants, usually small Japanese restaurants, and I remember he loved to eat steamed fish. Steamed mullet. He'd order that all the time. I can hear him now, answering his grandson. "Grandpa, what did you do in the war?" "Oh, I ate steamed mullet and kept track of Japanese civilians in Hawaii." [*Laughs.*]

Did he ever ask about your service?

No. He never asked me about it.

195

Did he know you were a combat veteran?

No. I don't know if anyone knew.

So I did that for six months, and then the [Pacific] war ended. The war in Europe had ended long before that—May 8th. The Pacific war ended on August 14th.

Do you remember what you were doing when you heard the news?

I was in the office in Lihue. Somebody said the war was over. But there was no big celebration. I don't recall any people yelling or tooting horns, anything like that. It was rather subdued.

What were your thoughts?

Oh, I was so glad. I hated the army.

No, I mean in terms of the end of the war.

[*Shrugs.*] I didn't think about it.

After V-J Day they had a parade. By then quite a few of the 100th veterans had been discharged, so they had a parade. I was in it. It was in Lihue. All I remember was that we marched through town, and then we sat in a park somewhere while people made speeches. I don't remember what they said.

When were you discharged?

October. I don't know why it took so long. Maybe because they had to set up the facilities to discharge a large number of veterans. For that I had to go back to Schofield Barracks.

[*Thinks.*] I was so happy. It was such a great feeling to be free of the army. October 15. October 15, 1945. [*Smiles.*]

[*Long pause.*] You know, I was very antimilitary. Very antimilitary. It's a total waste of lives. I'll tell you about one incident to show how strongly I felt. This was at Schofield Barracks, right before I was discharged. I was walking along a road—there was a ball field to one side—and coming from the other direction were four colonels. Full colonels, with all their ribbons and badges and whatnot. Now, in the army you have to salute officers, and for me that was such a degrading thing, to salute someone just because he was an officer. I said to myself, "I'm not going to salute these bastards." It was a silly thing to do—it's just raising your hand—but I said, "I'm not going to do it." So I kept eyeing them, and they kept eyeing me, and as they came up to me I turned my head—I looked away and walked past them. One of them yelled for me to come back. He said, "Why didn't you salute us?" I said, "Oh, I didn't see you. I was watching the game." [*Laughs.*] He took out a pad and said, "What's your name?" I gave him my name. "What's your outfit?" I gave him a fictitious outfit. "Six thirty-fifth infantry division." He told me they were going to court-martial me, and I said okay and walked away. Of course they never did anything. But that's how strongly I felt about not saluting them. I just couldn't do it. A slave bowing to the master.

[*Thinks.*] That feeling is why I never joined any veterans' organizations. After my discharge I vowed I would never get involved with any of them. I wanted to stay away from any group that would glorify war. I'm still holding on to that. You know, they have a local 442nd veterans' organization here. I went to the first meeting and that was it. I couldn't get a satisfactory answer as to why they were organizing a veterans' group. I want something solid. Not just social. I'm not anxious to get together just to get together.

I didn't keep anything that would remind me of the army. My dog tags? I threw them away. My uniforms, too. Some guys kept everything. I didn't want anything. Some guys like to talk about the war. I don't. When I went to talk to Molly's [granddaughter] class on Veteran's Day [2000], that was the first time I ever talked about it. And it was very brief and directed toward third-grade kids. [He went at her request, and spoke very simply about where he was from, where he had fought during the war, and some of his friends who had died. Afterward, the teacher had tears in her eyes.]

But now I wish I had kept my uniform. Size twenty-six waist. [*Laughs.*] You know how much I weighed when I got out of the army? A hundred and twenty-five pounds. I was that way for a long time, too. [*Laughs.*]

What about the guys you served with? Did you see any of them after the war?

Not really. You know, it's interesting. The twenty-five guys I came home with? We were together for almost three months, we became very close, but once we got discharged we never saw each other again. I did see Paul Tamura once—he invited me to a picnic with his friends. This was about a month after I got discharged. But after that I never saw him again. I went back to school and didn't keep up any of those friendships.

Why not?

[*Shrugs.*] We went on with our lives. Most of them got jobs—they weren't thinking about education. None of the other twenty-five were the type to go to college. Except one—Melvin Nagasako. He'd been in college when the war broke out. He was the one who later drowned while fishing.

[*Thinks. Smiles.*] But I did run into one of them years later. In Japan, of all places. This was about 1975. I spent a week at the University of Kyoto [for a scientific meeting] and stayed at the faculty house. The faculty house was near a famous temple called the Golden Pavilion. Beautiful place. One morning after breakfast I decided to walk up there, and as I was approaching the shrine, a bus pulled up. All these guys started coming out—typical Hawaiians. [*Laughs.*] The loud shirts? Typical Hawaiians. I thought, hey, I might know some of these guys, so I waited. And sure enough, here came this guy, he'd been one of the twenty-six, and with him was a guy I knew from high school, who'd also been in the 442nd. He was a year below me. The name of the guy who was one of the twenty-six was Nishida, Sadao Nishida, and the other guy's name was Okutsu, Yukio Okutsu. I said, "Hey, Nishida!" He looked at me, very puzzled. Of course, this was thirty years since I'd last seen him. I gave him my name. I said, "I came home with you from Italy. We were on the same ship." He didn't remember me. [*Laughs.*] No recollection. I said to the other guy, "Hey, Okutsu, I know you, too. You went to Kauai High School, didn't you?" He said yes. I said, "You came from Koloa?" He said yes. But he didn't remember me, either. [*Laughs.*]

Okutsu got the Medal of Honor this past summer. He destroyed two or three German machine gun nests—attacked them all by himself. He was a sergeant—pretty brave guy. At the ceremony I went up to him. I congratulated him and told him that I knew him in high school. He didn't remember me then, either. [*Laughs.*]

What about other guys? Those who weren't part of the twenty-six?

[*Smiles.*] I saw Butch Takei. The boxer who was being picked on by the guy named Bragger in basic training? After his discharge he stayed in Hawaii while he was waiting to reenter Berkeley—he'd been a student at Cal before the war. He had a few months to kill, and he used to call me all the time. "Hey, let's go out." But I was already in school [at the University of Hawaii], and I'd say, "Butch, I have to study." He kept talking about going drinking, but, you know, I'm not a drinker. He said, "When is your final exam? I'm going to call you after your final exam." I told him, and, by golly, he called me the night after I finished my last exam. He came by and picked me up, him and another guy, and the three of us went to a bar in downtown Honolulu. I ordered a drink, but just sipped it. Just to keep them company. There were some sailors in the bar, and one of the sailors threw a glass of ice at us. Butch jumped up, ready to fight. [*Laughs.*] We dragged him away before we could get into any trouble. That ended the night.

But that's not the end of Butch Takei. In '47, when I came up [to the mainland] to go to school, I stopped off in San Francisco. I stayed at the St. Francis Hotel. I knew two guys who were living in San Francisco, both from my company. One was Butch, who by then was back at Cal, and the other was George Yamasaki. He was from San Francisco. I knew Yamasaki's address, so I looked him up first. I said, "Let's go see Butch." Yamasaki had a car, so we drove over to Berkeley. Now the tables were reversed—Butch had to study while I was free. [*Laughs.*] He couldn't spend much time with us. So we just talked a little while and left so he could study.

That's still not the end of Butch Takei. When I first met Tomio [Sakurai, late husband of Alice's sister Marion]—this was in the early fifties—I asked if he knew them, because he'd grown up in San Francisco and went to Cal. He said, "Oh, I know both of them!" Through the years he'd always tell me, "You know, you ought to see those guys. I can arrange it." But I'd say, "Ah, the war's over. They've got new friends. I'm doing different things. Better to let things lie." And that's the way it was.

But the last time I saw Tomio, right before he died [in 1996], he said, "I made arrangements for us to have lunch with Butch Takei and George Yamasaki. We're going to meet in Japantown and have lunch." He did it on his own. He was an amazing guy, Tomio. He wanted me to see those guys again. So we met them at a Japanese restaurant in Japantown. We ended up talking for three hours. Yamasaki brought a whole bunch of pictures of guys from our company. He didn't remember some of their names. I told him, "Oh, this is so-and-so, and that's so-and-so." I remembered their names.

You know, when I saw Butch in Honolulu after we were discharged, we never talked about the war. Never. And in the restaurant I suddenly realized I didn't know what happened to him once we got overseas. So I asked him how he made out. If he was ever wounded. He said he wasn't, but that he went through a lot of scary times. He said the worst was the rescue of the Lost Battalion. It was wintertime, cold and wet, and they were trapped in foxholes full of water, being shelled by Germans. His feet got frozen. Trench feet. He said that even today, on cold days, his feet hurt. He has trouble walking. Another time they were crossing a river—they couldn't get their rifles wet, so they were holding them above their heads—and Germans on the other side started shooting at them. Bullets were whizzing all around, and they couldn't shoot back. [*Laughs.*] But he made it through okay. He made it through the whole war.

Did you recognize them after all those years?

Oh sure. Yamasaki, you could never mistake him for anyone else. He was short, with thick glasses. His eyes were so bad he never went overseas. They wouldn't let him go. But he was a feisty little guy, only about five feet tall. About the size of mom. [*Laughs.*]

During training we had to go out in the fields for a week. Sleep in tents. We shaved and brushed our teeth out of our helmets. One morning I heard him saying, "Who took my glasses? Who took my glasses?" Patting the ground all around him. They were by his side the whole time.

He was always doing things. Once we were at the PX. There were a lot of white soldiers in there, and I was standing in line behind one of them. Pretty soon someone pushed me, so I bumped into this guy. It was Yamasaki, trying to start some trouble. [*Laughs.*] Pushing me so I would bang into this guy.

Another time, a white soldier said to him, "Hey, what are you, anyway?" Yamasaki took off his army cap. "I'm Irish," he said. "Can't you see? I'm Irish."

What did they end up doing in life?

Yamasaki became a mailman. There were a lot of guys—I guess they hadn't been trained for anything. So they were doing simple things. I don't know if he ever got married. He didn't say anything about that.

Did he seem happy?

Sure. He was always a pretty happy guy.

What about Butch Takei?

Butch finished college. I think he went to work for the government, but I'm not sure.

[*Pauses.*] But you know, after we had lunch they didn't ask for my address and I didn't ask for theirs, so I don't know where they are.

Why not?

I don't know. I just never did.

[*Pauses.*] It's not that you dislike them or anything. It's just—. It's just that there's nothing to hold you together.

Chapter Twenty-One

Were grandma and grandpa ever allowed to leave camp?

ALICE

Mother left once to help Lily, who had just given birth to Karen. Karen was born on September 14, 1942. But after that she had to go back.

Telegram from Immigration and Naturalization parole office to Ray D. Johnston, Project Director, Rohwer Relocation Center, Sept. 12, 1945:

PERMISSION GRANTED YOSHI IMAMOTO TO TRAVEL TO WARRENTON VIRGINIA PERMIT AIRMAILED TODAY TELEGRAPH US DATE SHE DEPARTS YOUR CENTER

By that point Lily and Ken were living at Vint Hill Farms, which is near Warrenton, Virginia. Ken had been transferred to a unit that decoded and translated Japanese documents. His Japanese was very good. He was a master sergeant. He was in charge of about twenty people, all of them Nisei or Kibei. "Kibei" means they were educated in Japan.

Why was his Japanese so good?

He had gone to one of the top Japanese schools, the Compton [California] Japanese School. It was really high-powered. Run by a husband and wife—Mr. and Mrs. Endo. They had no children of their own. Mrs. Endo was one of the thirty-three women who were arrested, and Mr. Endo was taken before father. They wanted to be repatriated—early in the war, people who wanted to be repatriated were shipped to Japan. They were on the first boat that left for Japan. But they never made it. They got as far as the Philippines. I don't know what happened, but mother said something to me years later about their having met a tragic end. She said something about them being killed by some Filipinos.

Mother was still considered an enemy alien, so she had to report to the War Relocation Authority and the INS [Immigration and Naturalization Services] while she was helping Lily. I have a paper that says she is going to be released from Rohwer to go to Vint Hill. They have Ken's name, the reason why she's going there, and an itemized account of her possessions.

But, in time, of course, it got to the point where they *wanted* everyone to leave. They realized it didn't make any sense to keep these people in camps. So they decided to close the camps. Never mind that they weren't going to help anyone find employment or places to live—we had to do that on our own. And that was really hard on people who had no [outside] contacts.

See, that was the thing. You couldn't go back to where you were from, because nobody was there and everything you had was gone. So *everyone* was shiftless. And that's what was so terrible about it—that all these people were uprooted from their homes, confined to a camp, and when the government decided they were not disloyal, they were pushed out with nowhere to go. Dates were set. "This or that camp is going to close on June such-and-such, 1944."

Some people even said they weren't going to leave. Isn't that horrible? They were protesting because they had nowhere to go.

Federal Bureau of Investigation
United States Department of Justice
510 South Spring Street, Room 900
Los Angeles, 13, California
December 6, 1944

Mr. E. F. Owen
Evacuee Property Officer
Rohwer Relocation Center
McGehee, Arkansas

>Re: YOSHIKO IMAMOTO, with aliases
>Yoshi Imamoto, Yoshi Inamoto, Yoshido Imamoto
>ALIEN REGISTRATION #5554617

Dear Sir:

This office is transmitting to you under separate cover by registered mail certain personal property belonging to the above named person which was procured from him [her] by Special Agents of this Bureau at the time of his apprehension. This property is listed in inventory form on the Property Receipt Forms attached, one copy of which is for inclusion in your files.

It is respectfully requested that your office, at your discretion, release this property to the above named individual, and at the time of delivery have him execute his signature on the original Property Receipt Form attached. A self-addressed envelope is enclosed for your convenience in returning the receipted form to this office.

Your cooperation in this matter is appreciated.

>Very truly yours,
>[signed] R. B. Hood
>Special Agent in Charge

100–12003
Enclosures [2]

PROPERTY RECEIPT

This is to certify that I have received the following described property belonging to me which was voluntarily released to Special Agents of the Federal Bureau of Investigation:

6 religious pamphlets published in Japan

1 book on information of Los Angeles published in Japan

1 high school text book of physical education published in Japan

3 exercise books published in Japan

1 book of the Daughters of the American revolution published in US

1 Japanese language text book published by Japanese Language School Federation of San Francisco

1 book on research of goodness published in Japan

2 home work books published

1 letter

1 book on minutes of Nanka Japanese language school Federation

It is my understanding that any contraband materials which I may have released have been placed in the custody of the United States Marshal.

[signed] Yoshiko Imamoto
12/13/44

Jerome was the last camp to open and the first to close. [It subsequently housed German prisoners of war.[20]] After it closed [June 30, 1944], mother and father moved to Rohwer, where the remaining people [from the two camps] were consolidated. They could have left if they had jobs, but they didn't have any contacts. So they were in Rohwer until it closed in September of 1945, more than a year later. [Tule Lake was the last camp to close, on March 20, 1946; the War Relocation Authority program

20. *The Japanese American Legacy Project* Web site (www.densho.org).

officially ended on June 30, 1946.[21]] All told, mother and father were imprisoned in one form or another from March 13, 1942, until Sept. 14, 1945. Three and a half years.

McGehee, Arkansas
June 5, 1945

Mr. Dillon S. Myer
Director
War Relocation Authority
Barr Building
Washington, D.C.

Attn. B. R. Stauber, Chief, Relocation Planning Commission

Dear Mr. Myer;

Your letter of May 26, 1945 in regard to the application of James Zenichi Imamoto, Alien Registration No. 5554616, for release from parole has been received. I submit the following statement based on records and interviews.

Mr. Imamoto came to the United States in 1908. He has never made a return trip to Japan. He has never applied for repatriation. He has no plan to return to Japan any time in the future.

He speaks very good English. He dresses well and has very pleasing manners. He has a high degree of Americanization.

He has four children. Lily Matsuoka is living in Warrenton, Virginia[,] in order to be near her husband who is serving in the United States Army. Grace is attending business college at Whittier, California. Alice is a sophomore at Oberlin College, Oberlin, Ohio. Marian is a sophomore at the University of Minnesota, Minneapolis.

Mr. Imamoto states that, if he had any sons, he would be perfectly willing for them to serve in the armed forces. He insists that he is ready to make any contribution he may be called upon to make to the war effort. He is unwilling to answer definitely the question: Do you want the United States or Japan to win the war? He says that he wants peace.

Prior to evacuation, Mr. Imamoto was a language school teacher at Norwalk, California. He has no definite plans for relocation. He may return to California, or he may relocate to Ohio to be near his daughter, Alice.

Mr. Imamoto was originally a resident of the Jerome Relocation Center. A copy of a letter from Mr. J. Lloyd Webb, his supervisor there, is attached. He was transferred here approximately a year ago. He has been employed as a fire inspector. A copy of a letter from his present supervisor, Mr. John Mailes,

21. Allan Bosworth, *America's Concentration Camps* (New York: W.W. Norton & Co., 1967), 257.

is attached. Mr. Imamoto has also been President of the Parent-Teachers' Association and a copy of a letter from the High School Principal, Mr. William M. Beasley is attached.

There are no adverse reports in his record. He has been placed on the "all cleared" list by the Commanding General of the Western Defense Command.

It is recommended that Mr. Imamoto's application be given very possible consideration,

Sincerely yours,
RAY D. JOHNSTON
Project Director

It looks like they were preparing to leave camp about a month after Japan surrendered.

I guess so.

Do you remember what you were doing when you heard the news that Japan had surrendered?

No. I don't.

Why not?

[*Thinks.*] Well, those things would be very vivid for someone who was older, but I was young. That was just before my junior year. You also have to remember that I was cloistered in the conservatory building. And I mean *cloistered*.

What were your thoughts about the war being over? This war that had caused so much suffering for your family?

[*Shakes her head.*] I don't remember. I just don't. I suppressed everything.

ROHWER RELOCATION CENTER
McGehee, Arkansas
RESETTLEMENT STUDY
Prepared by the Rohwer Relocation Welfare Section

RE: IMAMOTO, Zenichi James
Family Number: 2183
Center Address: 24–10–E
July 2, 1945

Problems Affecting Relocation:

Mr. and Mrs. Imamoto want to return to California but since they are excluded from the West Coast they have been unable to think in terms of relocating elsewhere. [The Army rescinded the order that excluded those with Japanese blood en masse from the West Coast in December 1944, but continued to issue individual exclusion orders. The Army decision came within days of a Supreme Court ruling that Mitsuye Endo, who filed a petition for a writ of habeas corpus asking to be discharged from Tule Lake, was "entitled to an unconditional release by the War Relocation Authority." In its opinion, delivered by Justice William O. Douglas, the court said, "A citizen who is concededly loyal presents no problem of espionage or sabotage. Loyalty is a matter of the heart and mind not of race, creed, or color."[22]]

Family Composition:

Mr. Imamoto, age 55, was born in Japan and came to the United States when he was 20 years old. He has never been back to Japan. He completed 12 years of normal school education in Japan. After coming to the United States, he spent six years studying. He is especially interested in education and educational opportunities for his children. He was a teacher prior to evacuation.

Mrs. Imamoto, age 47, was born and attended school 12 years in Japan. She came to the United States with her husband [incorrect; he came to the U.S. in 1905] in 1918 and has never been back to Japan.

Grace, age 25, returned to California on the first special train that went back in May. She had just completed her AB degree in Oberlin College and was planning to continue with graduate study, majoring in social work. Dr. and Mrs. Bruff in California invited her to their home. She is in their home now and is taking part time work in a commercial college. Lillian, age 24, married and is with her husband in Warrenton, Virginia, where her husband is stationed in an army post.

22. U.S. Supreme Court, *Ex Parte Mitsuye Endo,* 323 U.S. 283 (December 18, 1944).

Alice, age 21 [16], is relocated in Oberlin, Ohio, where she is attending college, majoring in music.

Health:

Mr. Imamoto has a very delicate stomach condition which bars him from manual labor. He had a nervous breakdown in 1920 and has never been quite as strong physically since.

Mrs. Imamoto is very strong and healthy.

All the other members of the family have generally good health.

Alice had infantile paralysis when she was a child, and the family has spent practically everything they had on her health. She does not wear a brace now. However, she is not able to use her leg in playing the pipe organ as well as she had hoped; therefore, she expects to major in piano instead of pipe organ.

Religion:

The family are members of the Baptist Church and have always taken a very active part in church work. In fact, their lives have been influenced a great deal by their church activities. Each member of the family displays a great deal of interest in the welfare and health of each other and their religious faith is often referred to as the strength that has been their guiding influence through all trials and tribulations.

Employment:

Mr. and Mrs. Imamoto have always taught in Japanese language schools. The daughters had never worked outside of the home prior to evacuation. The parents are most anxious for the girls to have liberal education and be able to enter the professional world and earn their living by their professional training.

Residence and References:

The family lived at 765 N. Gridley Street, Norwalk, California, for five years prior to evacuation. Eight years before that they lived in Garden Grove, California.

The following were listed as references:

Mr. and Mrs. Allen, Garden Grove, California

Mr. and Mrs. George Scott, 3230 Euclid Avenue, Lynwood, California

Dr. and Mrs. Bruff, 512 E. Berkeley, Whittier, California.

Relatives:

The family have no relatives in the United States.

Finances and Property:

The family own no real estate and have spent what cash resources they had on hand sending the girls through college since evacuation. The personal goods and household property were stolen from the home after the parents were interned and the girls had been evacuated to the Assembly Center. The family have never been able to get an authentic report regarding their household equipment since they have been in the Relocation Center.

The girls have no cash resources[,] as each has been working her way through college up to date.

Suggested Plan:

Mr. and Mrs. Imamoto plan to relocate to Washington[,] D.C. They are interested in obtaining housing and employment there. They will except [sic] employment as domestics if housing can not be taken care of otherwise.

They expect to request assistance from the WRA in completing their plans after they arrive.

Grandma and grandpa went to Washington?

Yes. Mother went to Virginia first, this time to help Lily with Kenji [Lily's second child], while father continued on to Washington. He lived on Washington Circle.

In an apartment?

No. Certain cities had a—what's the word? A hostel. In Washington the Quakers set up a hostel near George Washington Circle.

For Japanese Americans?

Yes. They could stay there temporarily and look for jobs. The camp would get notice of where these hostels were located, and people would go there.

Why did they pick Washington?

I think because it was the closest city to Lily and Ken. I was in Ohio, which wasn't all that close, but at least it was in the same part of the country.

Had they ever been to Washington before?

No.

So they were facing a lot of uncertainty.

Sure. But you know, I never had any inkling of what kind of stress they were under. What their worries were. They never let on.

ROHWER RELOCATION CENTER
McGehee, Arkansas
Sept. 10, 1945

Mr. Emery Fast
Relocation Officer
Barr Building
910 17th Street N.W.
Washington, D.C.

RE: IMAMOTO, Zenichi
Family Number: 2183
Center Address: 24–10–E

Dear Mr. Fast:

Attached you will find two copies of the Family's Resettlement Study and two copies of WRA Form 329 which gives the family background and relocation plans.

Mr. and Mrs Imamoto expect to leave the Center September 12, for Washington, D.C. However, they will stop in Oberlin, Ohio, and in Warrenton, Va. to visit their daughters.

They will expect assistance from WAR [sic] in locating housing and employment in Washington.

Sincerely,
Cornie Key
Relocation Advisor

U.S. DEPARTENT OF JUSTICE
Immigration and Naturalization Service
208 Hutching Bldg.
939 D St., N.W., Washington, D.C.

REPORT OF ALIEN ENEMY

Name: IMAMOTO   YOSHI   JAPAN
           (Last)   *(First)*   *(Nationality)*
Alias: Imamoto, Yoshike
(Sex)   female
Birth: Yamaguchi Ken, Yaji-Mura, Japan   Oct. [Nov.] 3, 1897
           (Place)   *(Date)*

Address: 765 Gridley Road, Norwalk, Calif.
Next of Kin: husband   Zenichi [James] Imamoto
           (Relationship) (Name)
           2311 Pennsylvania Ave., NW, Washington, D.C.
           (Address)

Apprehended: F.B.I.   Los Angeles, Calif.   3–13–42
           (Agency)   *(Place)*   *(Date)*

Received by INS: Los Angeles, Calif.   3–13–42
                  (Place)   *(Date)*

          Status   Location
Previous: Alien enemy parolee   Previous: Warrenton, Va.
Present: Released from parole   Present: same
Effective Date of Change: November 8, 1945
Remarks: Released from parole in accordance with order of the Attorney General of October 23, 1945, No. 146–13–2–12–2411.

November 8, 1945   [signed] Charles Frank
(Date of Report)   *(Officer in Charge)*

OUTGOING TELEGRAM

R. S. NEW, CHIEF ALIEN CONTROL DIVISION,
IMMIGRATION AND NATURALIZATION SERVICE
22 MARIETTA BLDG. ATLANTA 3, GA.

ZENICHI IMAMOTO, PAROLEE, ARN 5554616, DEPARTED MCGEHEE ARK. 9–14–45, TERMINAL LEAVE WASHINGTON D.C.

                    RAY D. JOHNSTON
                    PROJECT DIRECTOR WRA
                    ROHWER, ARK.

At the hostel father found a listing from a doctor and his wife, Dr. and Mrs. Kerr, who needed a couple to work for them. They lived near Pierce Mill. That's in Rock Creek Park on Tilden Street.

Dr. Kerr's first name was Harry. He was a surgeon. I think his wife's name was Dorothy. They had one son, who was an artist.

Were they nice people?

Very nice. And they respected my parents. They knew what the situation was. They knew what mother and father had been through.

[*Thinks.*] I could go to their home and stay with them during all my vacations from school. They were very nice to me. Lily and the kids were welcomed, too.

They also had a house in Nantucket—they lived there for the summer—and mother and father would go with them. The four of them. Marion and I went once. It was a beautiful house right in town. A lovely place. All these old antiques.

It sounds like they were friends.

Yes. The Kerrs were very kind to my parents.

[*Thinks.*] Mrs. Kerr came to see us on Mitscher Street [the house Ken and Alice purchased in 1956 and have lived in ever since] after Dr. Kerr died. She came just to visit.

How long did grandma and grandpa work for them?

Nine years.

Nine years? Why so long?

[*Softly.*] Paul, they had nowhere else to go.

Chapter Twenty-Two

What was it like to go back to school?

KEN

Well, I went back to the same dormitory where I was living when I first volunteered. Students' House? I ended up right back where I started. [*Laughs.*] This was in October of '45. The first semester had already started, so I couldn't get into school right away—the second semester didn't start until February of '46. But until then I could live in the dorm. I didn't have anything to live on—I no longer had my army pay—so I applied for a job down at the docks. There were a lot of navy ships coming in, and I got a job as what was called a checker. As cargo came in, I checked off what came in. [*Laughs.*] Sometimes there was nothing to check, so we'd bring crab bait and throw our lines in. I'd cook the crabs in the dormitory kitchen. One time somebody pulled an old sock out of the bottom of the pot. [*Laughs.*]

I'd been out of school for five years. From '41 to '46. That was a long time to be away. And to have been in such—how should I describe it? A lot of traumatic things had happened. You know, when you're in situations where you don't know if you're going to live or not, you're not going to be thinking about school. So to be in that kind of atmosphere and then to suddenly be back at school—

What I felt was a lot of uncertainty as to whether or not I could make it. Not being sure I would be able to adjust. So I gave myself one semester. If I didn't make good grades, I was going to quit. Just quit right there and go get a job. Do something else.

Tom Yamada [family friend] was my roommate. He served in the MIS. After the first midterm exams, I thought I had flunked one of the courses. I came back from the test and was sitting in the room. He and I talked. I told him I was going to the registrar's office and withdraw from the course because I had flunked the test. He told me not to do that—he said I should wait to see how I did. But by then it would be too late. Because once the midterms were over, your grade was determined, and I'd get an F.

He talked me out of it. A week after the exam, they passed out the tests. I was shocked. I had an A. By the end of the year, I had almost all As. If I hadn't done that well, I would have dropped out.

What would you have done?

I don't know. Gotten some kind of low-paying job. Unskilled.

Did you feel different from the other students?

Yes. The classes were a mixture of old veterans and young freshmen and sophomores. I was picking up as a sophomore—a twenty-six-year-old sophomore.

It turned out that the veterans were studying so hard we were making all the good grades. The freshmen and sophomores thought it was unfair. They thought they should be graded on a different system because they were getting all the lower grades. [*Laughs.*]

As it turned out, though, I didn't get my degree from Hawaii. I came up to the mainland.

Why?

I wanted to be in a big city. I liked Washington and thought it'd be a good place to go to school. A lot of veterans came to Washington for that reason. I knew some guys who were going to G. W. [George Washington University], and I ended up going there, too. My roommates were both G. W. students. Paul Asano and Hiroshi Sakai. Both served in the army. Sakai was in the MIS.

How did you pay for it?

The GI Bill.

How did that work?

[*Thinks.*] When I was still in Italy I was reading the army newspaper. *The Stars and Stripes.* There was a long article about how the government had passed a law stating that any veteran of World War II could go to school after discharge and the government would pay for it. You'd automatically get one year up front, and for every month you served, you'd get another month of education. So in other words, if you served two years, you'd get three years of education—one year up front and another two years for the two years you served. Three years of practically free education! You'd also get tuition and a monthly stipend—fifty dollars a month to go to school. You could go to barber shop school, any kind of school.

We were still in combat when I read that, and I thought that for all the suffering I was going through, I was going to get back as much as I could from the government. I was going to use every bit that was coming to me. That's when I decided to go back to school. I even wrote to my brother [Haruto] about it. I told him that if I ever made it through the war, I was going back to college on the GI Bill.

That, in my opinion, was the greatest piece of legislation ever passed by Congress. The nation got back many times over what it spent on educating the veterans, because many of them, like myself, got educated, got good jobs, and paid big taxes the rest of their lives. [*Laughs.*]

How much time did you receive?

I had two-and-a-half years of service, so that came to three-and-a-half years of free education under the GI Bill.

[*Firmly.*] And I used all of it. Every bit.

Chapter Twenty-Three

What did you do after you graduated from Oberlin?

ALICE

I went to Philadelphia to study with a famous [piano] teacher. Her name was Olga Samaroff Stokowski. She was married to Leopold Stokowski.

How did that come about?

I auditioned during my senior year to become one of her students. The audition was in her New York apartment. Beautiful apartment. Like a Park Avenue hotel. Very imposing. That was in '47.

She had a lot of famous students who concertized. That's what she primed you for—to play concerts. Natalie Hinderas was one. She went two years before I did. I heard her play at the Kennedy Center. She was a very fine pianist. People like Rosalyn Tureck—maybe you don't know these names. Eugene List. Kappell. William Kappell—he was probably the most well-known. He died in a plane crash.

What does it mean to study with someone?

At the beginning of the year she'd give you a whole list of stuff that you were to prepare. Then she'd give you a lesson on each one throughout the year. You'd have one lesson a month. So I was practicing like crazy.

One lesson a month? How long was the lesson?

[*Laughs.*] About an hour.

She lived in New York. She taught half of the time at Juilliard and came down to the Philadelphia Conservatory of Music to teach us.

When she agreed to take me, I considered studying with her at Juilliard instead of Philadelphia. I even got a room at the International House, which is across the street from Juilliard. But I got scared. I didn't want to go to New York.

[*Thinks.*] One time I played a Mozart concerto live on the radio with another student. Her name was Nancy Wilson—she played the concerto and I played the orchestral part. We did that at the Curtis Institute. That was about two blocks from the Philadelphia Conservatory of Music.

How long did you study with Olga Stokowski?

Just one year, because she died. I don't know why, but it was very sudden. Heart attack, possibly. We were her last students.

She was a beautiful lady. Very aristocratic. Yet she came from Texas and her real name was Hickenlooper. She decided she could never play concerts with a name like Hickenlooper, so she gave herself the name Samaroff. [*Smiles.*] Olga Samaroff. She concertized as a young woman, and that's how she met Stokowski. He conducted the orchestra while she played. [*Laughs.*]

This Hinderas? She was black, and her [real] name was Natalie Henderson. Samaroff changed her name to Hinderas.

Did she try to change your name?

No, but I wasn't at the point where I was ready to concertize.

How did you support yourself?

I worked for room and board as a domestic for a minister and his family. This was in Chestnut Hill, which was the elite section of Philadelphia, and they were Episcopalians. The elite of the elite were Episcopalians. Not Methodists or Presbyterians. They had a huge summer home in Maine. Like the Rockefellers? They had that kind of wealth. They were immature, spoiled people.

What did you do after Olga Samaroff died?

I came here [to Washington].

Why?

Because mother and father were here.

I got a temporary job at the Library of Congress in the information office. I answered the phones—I didn't know anything about the library. I did that for three months, and then I got a permanent job as a professional in the copyright office. I catalogued copyright music. It was boring as hell. [*Laughs.*]

What about music?

I joined the Friday Morning Music Club. At that time it was on 17th Street. I'm a charter member—I've been a member for fifty years. It's a wonderful organization. It provides music to the community, and in doing so gives its members a chance to perform.

Originally it was one of the elite social clubs. It's over 100 years old. I had to have two people sponsor me.

Did you give lessons?

Well, the Muratas [Jack and Betty, family friends] asked me to teach Steve [their son]. I wasn't planning to set up a shingle to teach—I was working full-time. But they asked me, and I said yes.

Did you ever stop to think, during those years, about how far you'd come?

Occasionally.

What would you think? What were your thoughts, looking back, on what had happened to you?

[*Long pause.*] If someone ever mentioned relocation, I would defend it. I would talk about the positive side. "Well, I never would have gone to Oberlin or Philadelphia or come to Washington. I never would have been able to do that. I never would have left California." That was my stock answer.

You defended it?

[*Softly.*] Yes. For fifty years. I never allowed myself to think it was immoral. Unjust. I never allowed myself to think that. I kept it out of my mind that an injustice had been done to me. I would not admit that for far too long.

Why?

It was a defense mechanism. Otherwise it would have crushed me.

What changed your thinking?

Well, after fifty years, I finally started to think about it. I started to read about it. This was only recently—within the past ten years or so. I started to read these books about relocation that I'd had throughout the years but never read. Friends of mine had given them to me, but I never read them.

Why not?

[*Shrugs.*] I guess I was busy with other things.

But finally I read them. And I thought, "Hey, this was not right. How could anybody do this? How could anybody go through this?" See, I was looking at it like it wasn't me. Like it was someone else. And I started to absorb everything.

What are your feelings now?

I feel some—oh, I get very upset because the same kind of thing is happening to Middle Easterners today. Maybe not on the same scale, but it's happening to them. How many people have been incarcerated? How many are innocent?

Are you bitter?

[*Adamant.*] No. What's the use? There's no reason for me to feel that way. I've had a good life. I've had a really good life.

When I think back on what was done to us—when I read things—it sometimes brings out anger. But you know, anger doesn't do anything. You can't keep dwelling on that.

Because there are a lot of people who *didn't* come out of it okay. There must be hundreds of people like that. Things didn't turn out for them. Dad [Ken] said that when he went to Chicago [after the war] there were all these *yogores*—drifters—just hanging out on the sidewalk.

Japanese Americans?

Yes. And you don't hear about them. There are a lot of single women who came to Washington after the war to work for the government and they never got married and now they live alone. They're still out there.

There's no feeling of community for them, and that's not right. It was taken away from them. See, we all came from these little communities. We were poor, but we never felt poor because we had that community support. We had that support. But it was taken away from us, and that's what's sad.

We were in the wrong place at the wrong time with the wrong faces.

Chapter Twenty-Four

Would you do it all over again?

KEN

Well, it's funny you ask that. In 1992 the 50th reunion of the Triple V was held in Honolulu, and I decided to go. A lot of guys were there, including Lefty, and he and I agreed to meet, just the two of us, before we parted ways. We met for breakfast on the last day. It was a Sunday morning. I went to his hotel, and we talked for a long time. One of the things I asked him was, "If you were faced with the same situation today that you faced in '42, would you volunteer for the Triple V? And knowing what you know now about war, all the terrors of war, all the hardships—the terrible hardships—and the fear, would you volunteer for the 442nd? Would you do it all over again?" He said yes. I asked him why. Because it's hard to answer a question like that. At that moment you don't have time to think. But he said, very simply, "I guess I'm just the volunteering type." [*Laughs.*]

Because if he had asked me the same question, I would have said no.

You would have said no?

[*Nods.*]

Why?

[*Long pause. Softly.*] I don't think there's any fear that can be equaled by the fear of being in combat. Having that day after day after day. You're thinking, "Today might be my last day." It's a terrible thing to go through. There's no stress equal to that. The fear. I was scared every day that I was at the front. And to go through that for three or four months—to see friends die, people get killed. To see dead bodies. To have some guy get killed just a few feet away from you. Thinking it could happen to you at any time—

and it almost did so many times. I had a machine gun firing right at me! Point-blank! And I didn't get hit. It's just luck. Just luck. It's only luck that kept me alive.

[*Thinks.*] Everybody's scared. On my first day I was thrown in with the 100th Infantry guys. They had already been through terrible combat. Cassino and all those terrible places. And they were scared! All scared. I'm sure their thinking was the same as mine: "I'm going to get killed today."

But during the dedication [of the National Japanese American Memorial in 2000] the thought came to me—for the first time I felt a great deal of pride in having fought with the 442nd. While I was sitting there, I thought for the first time about what the outcome had been of our service. All the benefits that came from it. Citizenship for our parents. Redress. [On August 10, 1988, House Resolution 442 was signed into law by President Reagan, providing individual payments of $20,000 to each surviving internee. *People Magazine,* in its December 3, 1990 issue, profiled Alice's mother; at ninety-three, she was among the few surviving Issei to receive reparations. "The past: I can see those things in my mind's eye," she said in the article. "But I try not to think of them very often."]

Because when we volunteered no one thought we would be making history. It never occurred to us. And it never occurred to me for a long time. All I wanted to do was forget the war. The impact from it was so tremendous, I couldn't get away from it for the longest time. I remember that first year in school. The nightmares I used to have. My roommate, Tom Yamada, once told me, "Gee, you must have had some bad dreams." I said, "Why?" He said, "You were moaning and groaning." When he said that, I remembered what I had been dreaming. That I had been shot in the stomach and my guts were hanging out. I was trying to crawl away. That's the kind of dream I used to have. I had them for the longest time.

Do you still have them?

Every so often. But they're all distorted now. All distorted. Very strange. I can't describe them.

When I was a boy, I remember you coming home from work early and sleeping in the afternoon.

I used to get headaches. I started getting them while I was still in the hospital in Italy. Excruciating pain. The nurse used to bring me a lot of aspirin. Didn't do a thing. It was so painful I'd keep my eyes closed all day long.

The guy next to me didn't realize I was pretty sick, and once he slapped my bed so hard I bounced. "Get up," he said. "Why do you sleep so much?" I got so angry.

There were times [in Washington] when I was on the streetcar going to school and my headaches were so bad I'd have to get off and take another one going back in the direction I just came from. I'd go home and go to bed.

I bought 1,000-pill bottles. Big bottles. I took ten a day, two every two hours. By the time I reached ten, it usually subsided. This went on for years. I took so much aspirin I eventually developed an ulcer. One night I got this tremendous pain in my stomach. By that point Ruth was born [in 1955], and mom and I were living in an apartment. I spent the whole night walking around. Mom asked me, "Is it like the pain you get when you're giving birth?" I said, "How would I know?" [*Laughs.*]

What made them go away?

I don't know. But all of a sudden they stopped. And once they stopped they never came back.

What caused them?

[*Shrugs.*] I asked the army doctors. They said, "Oh, you've got combat fatigue." That was the catchall phrase for anything they couldn't explain.

[*Pauses.*] Anyway, when I saw the memorial and heard all the speeches, I thought, "Well, this is all happening because we volunteered. This is a direct result of what we did." And that was the first time I felt that way. That we did the right thing.

Up until then you didn't?

No. Because all I could think about were the wasted lives. The guys who didn't come back. It's such a waste of lives. I thought it was a big mistake that I had volunteered.

[*Thinks.*] I was shocked by how many people were at the dedication. So many people came from so far away. California, Hawaii. I didn't expect so many people to be there. And you know what I found out? I found out that when you start a conversation with someone—anyone, a total stranger—you'll find people you know in common. That they know someone you know. Isn't that something?

How would you say the war affected your life?

[*Simply.*] The war was the most important thing that ever happened to me. I'm eighty years old now. I've had eight decades of life. All kinds of different experiences. And yet if you asked me what happened in, say, 1975, I wouldn't be able to tell you. But if you asked me about the war years, I could tell you in great detail about everything that happened. Volunteering. Being inducted. Going to basic training. Going overseas. Getting wounded. I can remember the smallest things.

Had I not joined the army, I wouldn't be here today. Before that, my universe was Hawaii, just the islands. It broadened my horizons. It opened my eyes to the world.

Do you think about things differently, having been through that?

There have always been moments when I think about the war. About my friends who died. Those thoughts have never left me. [*Voice thickens.*] I still think about them. I think about what they would have been today had they lived. Howard Urabe was in education, so he would have been a teacher. Gary Hisaoka and Hiromitsu Tomita were also in education, so they would have been teachers, too. Dan Betsui was in premed—he wanted to become a doctor. Jenhatsu Chinen was also in premed.

I think about the tragedy of being killed at age twenty. Twenty-one. Prime of life. I think about the bravery of the guys who went to war. I think about you. I think, gee, I'm so glad you never had to go in the army. Fight in a war.

I could never talk about the war. I couldn't talk about my experiences. My mother wanted to see where I was injured. She asked me several times to show her where I was wounded. And I wouldn't. She knew I was injured in my back, and one day she was sitting in a chair and as I was walking by she grabbed my shirt and lifted it up. She saw it.

She wanted to know how it felt when I was wounded, and I wouldn't say anything.

Minnie [his sister] recently told me in an e-mail that my mother prayed every day while I was away. [*Emotional.*] Every day. You know, she was Buddhist. She would put a bowl of rice before the—what do they call it?

Where they pray in the home? She would put a bowl of rice there and pray. Every day. I didn't know that.

What about you, mom?

ALICE

[*Long pause.*] Well, I guess I feel that we came out of it pretty good. All of us. My sisters. Relatively unscathed. But we had a lot of help. At least I did. All the people who were wonderful to me.

What are your feelings about this country?

KEN

There was a formal apology from the president of the United States when he signed the reparations bill. The Germans never apologized for what the Nazis did, killing six million Jews. Mass slaughter. They never apologized.

ALICE

The Japanese never apologized, either.

KEN

So this kind of thing, this kind of apology, could only happen in the United States. Correct the wrongs. Apologize for the wrongs.

ALICE

I feel that this is the best country to be in. Because I feel the U.S. will always try to correct its mistakes.

Are you proud to be Japanese American?

KEN

Oh, sure.

ALICE

Sure.

Have you always been proud?

KEN

Yes.

ALICE

No.

[To Alice.] You haven't?

ALICE

No. During those years anything Japanese wasn't good.

KEN

He said Japanese *American.* I'm proud of what we accomplished.

Yes, but then I asked if you've always been proud.

KEN

Well, initially, of course, before we did so much—
[*Firmly.*] I never was ashamed that I'm Japanese American.

[To Alice.] You're proud now?

ALICE

Oh, sure.
I think I'm proud of having survived it. Without any negative effects. I think you feel confident if you can come out of something like that. It gives you a feeling that you can cope with almost anything. Don't you think so, Dad?
I feel that I'm one of the lucky ones. That's how I feel. I feel lucky.

What about you, Dad? Do you feel lucky?
Yes. I'm lucky.
[*Thinks.*] Even when I was wounded. The shrapnel easily—less than an inch either way and I would have been paralyzed. So, yes. I've been lucky. I've been lucky throughout my life.

226

Epilogue

My parents met in 1948, when my father was working toward his bachelor's degree at George Washington University and my mother was working at the Library of Congress. They were married on January 28, 1951.

My father received three degrees from GWU—his bachelor's in 1948, his master's in 1950, and his doctorate in 1953.

"I wanted to do something in science," he said. "At one time I thought about medicine, but a lot of GIs were interested in becoming doctors and it was hard to get into medical school. There would be fifty applicants, say, for one slot. I also knew the social sciences weren't for me—I wasn't interested in psychology or sociology. But I'd taken a course in bacteriology and liked it."

The GI Bill paid for his bachelor's degree; his master's and doctorate were funded by a $200-per-month research fellowship from GWU. ("A big boost from the $50 a month I was getting under the GI Bill," he said.) He focused on virology, a young science at the time, specifically looking for inhibitors that would keep viruses from multiplying.

After receiving his PhD, he accepted a two-year postdoctoral fellowship from the National Institutes of Health, which in turn led to a full-time job—the only professional job he would ever have. He worked at the NIH for thirty-two years, researching viruses associated with human cancers. During that time he published 104 scientific papers and wrote chapters in nine books.

"You're doing something to further knowledge," he said. "You're doing original research, publishing papers, and others can build on that. So it's a continuing process."

When asked what gave him the greatest satisfaction, he spoke of the postdoctoral fellows who came to work with him just as he had once done after he got out of school. "These were all bright people, from the best universities," he said. "See, when you do science, it's not always being at the lab bench, doing experiments. The discussions are a big part of it, too. Frequently they're spontaneous—you bring up a subject and talk about it. The postdocs brought a lot to the lab in terms of that. They were all good people.

"It was fun to help them get started—to see them develop into capable scientists. That's what I liked the best. Many of them went on to have great careers."

He taught at the NIH graduate school and the University of Hawaii, and lectured at various universities and research labs, including Harvard, Yale, Johns Hopkins, and the Cold Spring Harbor Laboratory in New York. He received the U.S. Public Health Service Commendation Medal in 1970 and the Meritorious Service Medal—the Public Health Service's second-highest award—in 1975. He retired in 1984.

My mother never planned on becoming a music teacher, but from her first few students, taught in a series of small apartments ("In one of them, Ruth's crib was in the same room as the piano, so she'd be sleeping while I gave a lesson"), she gradually took on more, until as many as eighteen were receiving lessons on the concert grand piano that dominates the basement of their house.

"I wanted only beginners," she said. "That way, if they didn't turn out, it was my mistake. I didn't want to have to undo someone else's mistakes."

When asked what gave her the greatest satisfaction, she said, "Teaching kids the basics. Getting them to learn how to read [music]. Getting them to enjoy music."

She played her first major concert in 1961 with Mihran Kodjian, who went on to become the concertmaster of the National Symphony. "How he got my name I have not a clue, but we played two full concerts," she said. "I was so nervous I didn't sleep at all the night before each concert. I guess I did okay, because he wanted me to accompany him on a concert tour of colleges. But I said no. You kids were little—it wasn't something I wanted to do."

She played few concerts while her children were in school (when asked if she missed it, she replied, "I don't know. I never allowed myself to think about it"), a fourteen-year span that ended in 1975. Subsequently, she performed at the National Gallery of Art (three times), the Renwick Art Gallery (twice) and the Corcoran Gallery of Art, among other places. She gave numerous school concerts in the Washington area, and throughout her career played at the Friday Morning Music Club. She was also a member of the American University preparatory music department for seven years.

She retired from teaching in the late 1990s, after fifty years. "What I did was stop taking students, so as they graduated from high school, it tapered off, one by one," she said. "It was a good way to bring things to a close."

She gave her last formal concert at her 50th class reunion at Oberlin in 1997. "The reunion class gives a concert," she said. "This was in a small, beautiful concert hall, and the place was filled. There were about six of us performing. I played last. I played two pieces, one by Liszt, and one by Rachmaninoff, and when I was finished, they gave me a standing ovation. I told myself, 'That's it. That's my swan song.'"

Ken and Alice celebrated their fiftieth wedding anniversary on January 28, 2001.

They have three grandchildren: Ben, Molly, and Kara.

Index

LIBRARY OF CONGRESS
CATALOGING-IN-PUBLICATION DATA

Takemoto, Kenneth Kaname.
Nisei memories : my parents talk about the
war years / Paul Takemoto, [interviewer].
p. cm. — (The Scott and Laurie Oki series
in Asian American studies)
Transcript of interviews with Kenneth
and Alice Takemoto.
Includes index.
ISBN 0-295-98585-2 (pbk. : alk. paper)
1. Takemoto, Kenneth Kaname.
2. Takemoto, Alice.
3. Japanese Americans—Evacuation and
relocation, 1942–1945.
4. World War, 1939–1945—Personal
narratives—American.
5. Concentration camp inmates—
United States—Biography.
6. Japanese American soldiers—
Biography.
7. Oral history.
I. Takemoto, Paul.
II. Takemoto, Alice.
III. Title. IV. Series.
D769.8.A6T36 2005
940.53089'956073—dc22
2005026602

PAUL TAKEMOTO has a bachelor's degree from Ohio Wesleyan University and a master's degree in fine arts from the University of Iowa Writer's Workshop. He was a journalist for sixteen years and is now a spokesperson for the Federal Aviation Administration.